The Turnout Gap

In The *Turnout Gap*, Bernard L. Fraga offers the most comprehensive analysis to date of the causes and consequences of racial and ethnic disparities in voter turnout. Examining voting for Whites, African Americans, Latinos, and Asian Americans from the 1800s to the present, Fraga documents persistent gaps in turnout and shows that elections are increasingly unrepresentative of the wishes of all Americans. These gaps persist not because of socioeconomics or voter suppression, but because minority voters have limited influence in shaping election outcomes. As Fraga demonstrates, voters turn out at higher rates when their votes matter; despite demographic change, in most elections and most places, minorities are less electorally relevant than Whites. The *Turnout Gap* shows that when politicians engage the minority electorate, the power of the vote can win. However, demography is not destiny. It is up to politicians, parties, and citizens themselves to mobilize the potential of all Americans.

Bernard L. Fraga is Assistant Professor of Political Science at Indiana University. His research has been published in leading scholarly journals including the *American Journal of Political Science,* the *Journal of Politics,* and the *Stanford Law Review.* Fraga was also the recipient of the Midwest Political Science Association Lucius Barker Award and Latina/o Caucus Early Career Award. Findings from his work on race and elections have featured in various media outlets including the *New York Times* and the *Washington Post.*

The Turnout Gap

Race, Ethnicity, and Political Inequality in a Diversifying America

BERNARD L. FRAGA

Indiana University

CAMBRIDGE
UNIVERSITY PRESS

University Printing House, Cambridge CB2 8BS, United Kingdom

One Liberty Plaza, 20th Floor, New York, NY 10006, USA

477 Williamstown Road, Port Melbourne, VIC 3207, Australia

314–321, 3rd Floor, Plot 3, Splendor Forum, Jasola District Centre, New Delhi – 110025, India

79 Anson Road, #06–04/06, Singapore 079906

Cambridge University Press is part of the University of Cambridge.

It furthers the University's mission by disseminating knowledge in the pursuit of education, learning, and research at the highest international levels of excellence.

www.cambridge.org
Information on this title: www.cambridge.org/9781108475198
DOI: 10.1017/9781108566483

First published 2018
Reprinted 2019

Printed in the United Kingdom by TJ International Ltd. Padstow, Cornwall

A catalogue record for this publication is available from the British Library.

Library of Congress Cataloging-in-Publication Data
NAMES: Fraga, Bernard L., author.
TITLE: The turnout gap : race, ethnicity, and political inequality in a diversifying America / Bernard L. Fraga.
DESCRIPTION: Cambridge, United Kingdom ; New York, NY : Cambridge University Press, 2018. | Includes bibliographical references.
IDENTIFIERS: LCCN 2018020556 | ISBN 9781108475198 (hardback)
SUBJECTS: LCSH: Voter turnout – Social aspects – United States. | Political participation – Social aspects – United States. | Minorities – Political activity – United States. | Voting research – United States. | BISAC: POLITICAL SCIENCE / Government / General.
CLASSIFICATION: LCC JK1967 .F695 2018 | DDC 324.973–dc23
LC record available at https://lccn.loc.gov/2018020556

ISBN 978-1-108-47519-8 Hardback
ISBN 978-1-108-46592-2 Paperback

To maman Martine and papá Luis

Contents

Figures

Tables

Acknowledgements

I began compiling the chapters for this book in December 2015. By then the presidential campaigns were well underway, and most analysts, including the author, felt certain that 2016 would be an election that aligned with our well-developed understandings of American electoral politics. In retrospect, we should have known better. My initial interest in race and electoral politics was sparked by Barack Obama's victory in 2008, seeking to understand how future elections would continue to be shaped by the inclusion of long underrepresented voices in American politics. But, a year before Obama's election, few thought he could win either. I hope that this book faithfully reflects the knowledge I have so generously been given in the ten years since, but also provides a useful guide to the unexpected challenges to our assumptions that lie ahead.

So many individuals gave me the tools I needed to complete this project. First, I thank my dissertation committee: Stephen Ansolabehere, Claudine Gay, and Jennifer Hochschild. I am truly grateful for the opportunities they gave me. Many thanks to my other colleagues from graduate school who gave me invaluable advice on, and data for, my early work on race and voter turnout: Heidi Brockmann, Anthony Fowler, Kyla Noelle Haggerty, Max Palmer, Stephen Pettigrew, Evan Schnidman, Arthur Spirling, James Snyder, and Miya Woolfalk. The Inequality and Social Policy program at the Harvard Kennedy School gave crucial support to this research, including financial support from an NSF-IGERT grant.[1] I also thank the SSRC-Mellon Mays Graduate Initiatives Program and the

---

[1] "Multidisciplinary Program in Inequality and Social Policy" (No. 0333403).

Harvard University Center for American Politics, Department of Government, and Graduate School of Arts and Sciences for supporting my graduate studies.

After graduate school I was welcomed into a community of scholars whose knowledge has improved my research in countless ways. For providing valuable feedback on this book project, I am grateful to Allison Anoll, Matt Barreto, Lauren Davenport, Eric Juenke, Carl Klarner, Julie Merseth, Melissa Michelson, Kumar Ramanathan, Paru Shah, Brian Schaffner, Maya Sen, John Sides, Brad Spahn, and Sophia Wallace. I thank seminar participants at Rice, Vanderbilt, Columbia, Stanford, Duke, and Northwestern as well: their constructive criticism helped me sharpen my arguments and better explain the implications of my work beyond academia. Employees at Catalist, LLC gave crucial guidelines and, of course, data for this project; Yair Ghitza and Jonathan Robinson in particular. I am especially thankful for the advice and friendship of Eitan Hersh, who first introduced me to the Catalist data, and Ryan Enos, who helped guide me through the publication process.

My colleagues at Indiana University have also been instrumental in the completion of this project, and I am fortunate to have their support. Thanks to Ted Carmines, Christopher DeSante, Russ Hanson, Matthew Hayes, Margie Hershey, Dina Okamoto, Will Winecoff, Jerry Wright, and the many other graduate students and faculty at IU who contributed their thoughts and ideas. A special note of thanks goes to the Cox Research Scholars Program, and to the IU students who collected data for this book: Nina Wornhoff, Katherine Hitchcock, Lauren David, Kristine Marmureanu, Cleo Hernandez, Maya Wilson-Fernandez, and Donovan Watts. I also thank Laura Bucci for spending a summer aiding in the compilation of the CPS data I use in the first half of this book.

A discussion with Skip Lupia about what we were "missing" prior to the 2016 election eventually morphed into a book conference at the University of Michigan. I am grateful to Skip for organizing the conference and taking a chance on this work. I also thank Vince Hutchings for his faith that I would complete the book, and to the other participants in the conference for their in-depth feedback on the manuscript: Ted Brader, Chinbo Chong, Hakeem Jefferson, Jan Leighley, Rob Mickey, Steven Moore, Fabian Neuner, Vanessa Cruz Nichols, Mara Ostfeld, Stuart Soroka, and Nicole Yadon. I also thank the team at Cambridge University Press, especially Sara Doskow for her steadfast enthusiasm and patience for this project.

Finally, I would like to thank my friends and family for their constant support. Their willingness to celebrate even the small gains made as I completed this project gave me more confidence than they know. I am especially blessed in that I may draw on both the love and scholarly advice of my parents, Martine De Ridder and Luis Fraga, in my academic endeavors. I can only hope to follow in their footsteps.

In July 2013 I ended up "back home again, in Indiana" to start work at IU. Two weeks after the move a new colleague asked if I'd like to meet his only Hoosier friend – my future wife, Morgan. Without her advice, support, and most of all, love, I would not have had the strength to finish this book.

I

Introduction

*We have come too far. We have made too much progress and we're not
going back, we're going forward. That's why we all must go to the polls in
November and vote like we never, ever voted before.*
— Rep. John Lewis, July 26, 2016

On March 7, 1965, state and local police attacked 600 civil rights
marchers as they crossed the Edmund Pettus Bridge in Selma, Alabama.
The marchers' decades-long cause was well known in the American
South, and summed up by a simple phrase: "Give us the ballot."[1] The
increased national attention brought by "Bloody Sunday" forced President Johnson to take action, pushing for what would become the Voting
Rights Act of 1965 with the words "it is wrong – deadly wrong –
to deny any of your fellow Americans the right to vote."[2] In 1974,
Willie Velazquez founded the Southwest Voter Registration and Education Project, combating barriers to Latino political participation by
encouraging voter registration. Using the slogan *"su voto es su voz"*
(your vote is your voice), Velazquez mobilized tens of thousands of
Mexican Americans in Texas. When the Voting Rights Act came up for
renewal in 1975, Latinos gained federal voting rights protections thanks
in large part to advocacy by African American Representative Barbara
Jordan, who owed her career in federal politics to the Voting Rights Act.
The renewal also provided protections for Asian American voting rights,
with Japanese American Citizens League Executive Director David Ushio
stating "it was time now to look at the needs of all minorities. A citizen

[1] Title of address by Dr. Martin Luther King, Jr., May 17, 1957. Prayer Pilgrimage for
Freedom, Washington, DC.
[2] Transcript of speech by Lyndon Baines Johnson, March 15, 1965. Washington, DC.

must be able to vote."[3] Most Asian Americans would have been ineligible for citizenship, or voting, less than a generation before. The interconnected voting rights struggles of the mid-twentieth century shared a single goal: the promise of political equality in America. By the mid 1970s, it seemed as if this goal was in sight.

The expansion of African American, Latino, and Asian American voting rights is made all the more relevant when considering the dramatic demographic shift that coincides with increased access to the ballot: 90 percent of the adult population was White when the Voting Rights Act passed, but today, one in three American adults is non-White. Minority citizens now have the potential to shape national election outcomes in a profound manner. The growing minority population also looks quite different from how it did in 1965. While African Americans now make up 13 percent of the population, slightly up from 11 percent in 1965, Latinos[4] went from a small, mostly southwestern demographic composing roughly 4 percent of Americans in 1965 to over 18 percent today (Pew Research Center 2015). Only one-half of 1 percent of the United States was Asian American in the mid 1960s; today, the population is more than ten times as large.

Perhaps no manifestation of this potential was more obvious than the election of Barack Obama as President in 2008. The son of an African immigrant and a White Kansan, born in Hawaii and attending primary school in Indonesia, then-Senate candidate Obama remarked that "in no other country on Earth is my story even possible."[5] Four years later, with the backing of well over three-quarters of minority voters, the nation had its first Black president (National Election Pool 2008). A historic barrier had been overcome in an America more diverse than ever. Yet, Whites still made up more than 75 percent of the voting population, and analyses indicate that it was an increase in support from White voters that drove Obama's victory, not changes in national demographics (Trende 2013; Cohn 2016). Furthermore, with a similar level of support from minority voters and a more diverse voting eligible population, Hillary Clinton

---

[3] Quoted in *Pacific Citizen*, August 8, 1975 (Honda 1975).

[4] When referencing contemporary politics, I use the term "White" interchangeably with "non-Hispanic White," "African American" with "Black," and "Latino" with "Hispanic." The distinction between race and ethnicity, as understood by the U.S. Census Bureau, is kept in mind when constructing statistics for these societal groups (see Appendix A.1) but otherwise "race," "ethnicity," and "race/ethnicity" are used interchangeably as well.

[5] Transcript of speech by Barack Obama, July 27, 2004. Democratic National Convention, Boston, MA.

was unable to replicate Obama's success in 2016. America is increasingly Black, Latino, and Asian American, yet at the end of the day the preferences of White voters continue to drive political outcomes. How do we reconcile these competing perspectives of contemporary American politics?

In this book I suggest that these seemingly irreconcilable viewpoints are, in fact, tightly connected. Demographic change is indeed remaking American politics in a myriad of important ways; no one can dispute that non-Hispanic Whites are decreasing as a share of the population, such that year-over-year minority Americans gain greater potential to influence politics. Yet, it is impossible to ignore the political reality of today wherein election outcomes are driven in large part by the preferences of White electorates, even in places where minority citizens could be pivotal to election outcomes. The missing piece, I propose, is an understanding of the *causes and consequences of the persistent gap between minority and White voter turnout.* The epigraph from Representative John Lewis, one of the organizers of the Bloody Sunday march, suggests that the hard-fought victories in providing minority access to the ballot box are important, but not enough. Simply put, demographics are not destiny unless they manifest at the polls. It is the exercise of the vote that will lead to political equality, and as this book demonstrates, it is in the exercise of the vote that minority political power falls short.

As a result, I seek to explain why we witness racial/ethnic differences in who turns out to vote, and what this means for the future of American democracy. I find that African American, Latino, and Asian American turnout has almost always lagged behind non-Hispanic White turnout, even after the removal of *de jure* and *de facto* racial barriers to participation. I label the disparity between a minority group's rate of voter turnout and White voter turnout the *turnout gap*, leveraging decades of survey data along with new voter file-based analyses to determine when, where, and why the turnout gap persists. I show that socioeconomic disparities do not explain the turnout gap, nor differences in voter eligibility. I also confront an emerging narrative regarding election laws and their potential to suppress minority voting, finding that high minority turnout can and does occur even in the face of tremendous institutional barriers. Conventional explanations for racial/ethnic inequalities in voter turnout thus fall short, and cannot explain the variation we see historically or in recent elections.

Instead, I uncover a consistent pattern in who votes across all racial/ethnic groups, including Whites: *when a group is perceived to drive election outcomes, members of that group are more likely to turn out to vote*. The source of this pattern lies in familiar understandings of what produces political empowerment and mobilization: individuals are more likely to vote when they expect to be able to influence the political process, while candidates and political parties focus their mobilization efforts on minority groups when it is clearly advantageous for them to do so. Combining these notions, and given the size of the non-Hispanic White population in America, it should not come as a surprise that this group is more likely to vote than minorities in almost all situations. However, in places where the demographic composition has already shifted the electoral landscape in favor of African Americans, Latinos, and Asian Americans, racial/ethnic differences in participation have waned or even reversed.

A deep analysis of the turnout gap helps us understand not just past and present trends in voter turnout, but also why growing diversity could still be accompanied by limited minority political influence. Yet, the demographic changes the United States continues to experience have the *potential* to change this dynamic, closing the turnout gap and producing an America that better represents all of its people. The rest of the book documents these processes, but to further motivate the endeavor, let us begin by considering what impact disparities in participation have on contemporary politics.

POLITICAL INEQUALITY AND VOTER TURNOUT

We know a considerable amount about who votes and who does not. Nearly one hundred years ago, Merriam and Gosnell (1924) found that voter turnout in Chicago was lowest among African Americans, the foreign born, women, recent movers, and young people (27–29). Wolfinger and Rosenstone (1980) found similar patterns for the early 1970s, adding socioeconomic status to the list of correlates of non-voting (108).[6] In *Who Votes Now? Demographics, Issues, Inequality, and Turnout in the United States* (2013), Jan Leighley and Jonathan Nagler evaluate national survey data from 1972 to 2008 and find, once again, a racial, class, and age bias in who votes: minorities, the poor, and the young are less likely to turn out. These findings are consistent with a much broader literature on electoral politics in America (Downs 1957; Campbell et al. 1960;

---

[6] Women now vote more than men in presidential elections (File 2013). Merriam and Gosnell's (1924) finding regarding lower turnout for women might be attributable to the fact that women gained the right to vote in Illinois in 1913.

Browning, Marshall, and Tabb 1984; Rosenstone and Hansen 1993; Green and Gerber 2008), and extend to nearly all other democracies where voting is not compulsory (Powell 1986; Franklin 2004; Lijphart 2012).

These differences in who votes present a challenge to the operation of representative democracy. In his seminal work *The Semisovereign People*, Schattschneider (1960) contrasts the "60 million" voters with the "40 million" non-voters, indicating that the exclusion of 40 percent of Americans from political life is "the *sickness* of democracy" (102, emph. in original). He concludes that the legitimacy of the outcomes expressed by voters would be enhanced if everyone took part in politics. Verba, Schlozman, and Brady (1995) assert that it is the unrepresentativeness of the voting population itself that produces a failure of democracy: "The democratic ideal may be equal consideration for the needs and preferences of all, but the reality of participation is quite different" (2). Later work by these authors outlined a number of reasons why equal political voice may be desirable, and attempted to assuage qualms we may have about equal participation (Schlozman, Verba, and Brady 2012: ch. 4), while Lijphart (1997) goes further in arguing that compulsory voting should be considered in the United States as a "valuable partial solution" to reconciling the goals of popular participation and political equality. Buttressing these normative claims, empirical evidence suggests that representational outcomes are often skewed in favor of those who vote (Hill, Leighley, and Hinton-Andersson 1995; Griffin and Newman 2005). The fact that not all Americans take part in elections creates a dilemma wherein differences in who votes have, at very least, the potential to distort politics.

The above evidence notwithstanding, a skeptical reader may wonder whether the mobilization of non-voters would have a measurable impact on election outcomes. After all, individuals who are not voting are likely to be less politically engaged and less informed about politics; many Americans do vote, and their (more informed) views may look similar to the rest of the population. Wolfinger and Rosenstone (1980) find evidence to this point, as the partisanship of non-voters is skewed toward the Democratic Party but on a host of salient political issues, differences between voters and non-voters are slight (109–112). Highton and Wolfinger (2001) tell a similar story, and while Citrin, Schickler, and Sides (2003) also identify partisan differences, the dearth of competitive election outcomes makes the impact of non-voting minimal. Diverging preferences between voters and non-voters could mean who votes matters in specific elections (Osborn, McClurg, and Knoll 2010; Burch 2012), but do not confer an ever-consequential advantage to one of the two major parties (DeNardo 1980, but Tucker, Vedlitz, and DeNardo 1986). Hill (2017) goes even further, using data from Florida to assert that changes in turnout advantaged *Republicans* by a substantial margin in 2010, swamping the effect of converting consistent voters from the Democratic to Republican parties.

So does it matter who votes? The normative assertions here are compelling, but empirical evidence for non-voting influencing election outcomes is far more mixed. To get a sense of whether differences in who votes impact recent election outcomes, I turn to large-scale survey data. Previous studies relied on exit polls or small national samples, imputing preferences of non-voters and often assuming a similar relationship between demographic characteristics and vote choice across voters and non-voters (Highton and Wolfinger 2001; Citrin, Schickler, and Sides 2003). Here I leverage the Cooperative Congressional Election Study (CCES),[7] a large ($N > 35,000$/year), nationally representative survey of American adults where respondents are asked which candidate they would prefer *even if they did not turn out to vote* in elections from 2006 to 2016. The CCES is large enough that we can deduce voting preferences for elections to the Senate and House of Representatives, in addition to presidential contests. Aggregating these preferences to the House district, state, and national level, we can then see whether the overall distribution of partisan election preferences differs from the actual results we witnessed.

The CCES uses a matched random sample methodology to generate a nationally representative set of respondents from a large pool of online panelists. Demographic information from the American Community Survey, an annual survey conducted by the U.S. Census Bureau, is used to match and weight online panelists such that they have a demographic profile similar to the adult population in the state that they reside in. Because the sample is representative of American adults, and the survey asks preferences for presidential, senatorial, and individual House district contests, the method of aggregation and analysis is simple: sum expressed candidate preferences at the state or U.S. House district level,[8]

---

[7] http://cces.gov.harvard.edu

[8] U.S. House districts with fewer than 25 respondents expressing candidate preferences were not estimated, and instead the actual election result was imputed. This yields a conservative estimate of the impact of voter turnout on U.S. House election results.

TABLE 1.1 *Democratic Party electoral outcomes, actual results versus full turnout*

	U.S. House		U.S. Senate		President	
	Actual results (%)	*Full turnout* (%)	*Actual results*	*Full turnout*	*Actual results*	*Full turnout*
2006	53.6	56.9	51	49		
2008	59.1	59.3	59	56	365	390
2010	44.4	45.3	53	53		
2012	46.2	55.9	55	59	332	445
2014	43.2	43.0	46	52		
2016	44.6	49.0	48	53	232	354

Note: Actual results represents the percentage of seats won (U.S. House), number of seats held (U.S. Senate) or number of Electoral College votes won (President) by the Democratic Party after the November election in each year. Full turnout scenarios are counterfactual Democratic Party seats (U.S. House and U.S. Senate) or Electoral College votes awarded to the Democrat (President) based on candidate preferences expressed by CCES respondents in each year from 2006 to 2016.

then combine all of these jurisdiction-level estimates to determine what the counterfactual "full turnout" national distribution of partisan control would be.

Table 1.1 details counterfactual President, Senate, and U.S. House aggregate outcomes based on the preferences of all CCES respondents. Columns labeled "Actual results" indicate the Democratic Party's share of U.S. House seats, the number of U.S. Senate seats, or the number of Electoral College votes won by the Democratic nominee for President.[9] The "Full turnout" columns indicate counterfactual Democratic Party seat shares or Electoral College votes based on the expressed preferences of weighted CCES respondents.

The 2016 election produced a narrow victory for Republican Donald Trump in the Electoral College, despite losing the popular vote by nearly 3 million ballots. Three states, Wisconsin, Michigan, and Pennsylvania were narrow victories for Trump and the focus of many discussions regarding what went "wrong" for the Democratic campaign (Clinton 2017). However, a substantial number of Trump-supporting Whites also stayed home, in these states and elsewhere. In a counterfactual 2016 with

[9] During the period, three Senate seats were, for some duration, held by Independents. As each of these individuals caucused with the Democratic Party, they are considered to be Democrats for the purposes of this analysis.

full turnout, Clinton wins Wisconsin and Michigan, but narrowly loses and Pennsylvania. Instead, the Democrat would have secured an ample Electoral College victory through gains in the heavily minority Sunbelt states of Florida, Georgia, North Carolina, and Texas. Furthermore, Table 1.1 also shows that while Barack Obama won both the 2008 and 2012 elections by large margins, if all Americans voted, President Obama would have been elected with landslides not earned by a Democrat since Lyndon Johnson.

Senate outcomes tell a similar story, as indicated by comparison of the middle columns in Table 1.1. On average, only one-third of Senate seats are up for election in any given year, such that changes in election results in a single cycle will still impact the partisan composition of the Senate in a future cycle.[10] Evaluating the partisan preferences of all CCES respondents, we see that the Democratic Party may have narrowly missed out on gaining a Senate majority in 2006 if all Americans had voted and would have held three fewer seats after the 2008 election under a full turnout scenario. This echoes the analysis by Hill (2017), who found that Republicans can also be advantaged with higher voter turnout. However, the considerable gains made by Democrats in 2008 would have held to a much larger degree in the 2010 and 2012 elections than observed in reality, leading to a large boost in 2012 that would have sustained a Democratic majority in the Senate after the 2014 and 2016 elections.

The last decade has seen an unprecedented level of partisan gerrymandering of legislative districts (Royden and Li 2017). While "vanishing marginal" seats motivated research in congressional elections during the 1980s (Mayhew 1975; Jacobson 1987; Ansolabehere, Brady, and Fiorina 1992), U.S. House elections have become even less competitive since, with fewer than 7 percent of seats having a margin of victory of less than 10 percentage points in 2016. Simply put, most House seats are never in doubt, resistant even to dramatic changes brought by a wave election. Yet, in aggregating the expressed preferences of all adults through the CCES, Table 1.1 indicates that Democrats would have regained a majority of seats in 2012 if everyone voted, and in most other recent elections

---

[10] As there are partisan differences in which seats need to be defended in a given year, the result of differential turnout by Democrats and Republicans is more likely to be a product of electoral geography and candidate positions than in House races or presidential elections. See Citrin, Schickler, and Sides (2003) for a broader discussion of state-by-state variation in the impact of turnout differentials.

the Democrats would have increased their share of House seats substantially. As noted by Fowler and Hall (2017), a victory in one election increases the probability that the party will win the seat in subsequent elections, due to the incumbency effect and other factors. Thus, seats picked up by Democrats in the full turnout scenario may have been easier to defend in 2010 and subsequent elections with an incumbent Democrat, such that the projected percentage of House seats held by Democrats in a full turnout scenario is likely to be an underestimate. Furthermore, the above results are a function of the first-past-the-post system employed in nearly all U.S. elections. When looking at the national popular vote, results shift even more heavily toward the Democratic Party when everyone votes.

Between 2008 and 2016, the Democratic Party went from control of each branch of the federal government to complete exclusion. Defying the demographic-trends-based predictions outlined by pundits and academics alike (Judis and Teixeira 2002; Bowler and Segura 2012), demographic change has not *yet* resulted in a growing Democratic advantage at the federal level. Table 1.1 suggests that much of the recent decline in the fortunes of the Democratic Party may now be attributed to low voter turnout, as under a full turnout counterfactual, the Democratic Party would have held the presidency and Senate from 2008 through at least 2018. To emphasize, the above estimates are not the result of groups switching their vote, nor changing proportions of the population held by each group. By the time the surveys were fielded, candidates had chosen their platforms, campaigns had already run their course, and nearly all American adults had already decided who they would prefer to have as their representatives in the federal government. The only difference is that some individuals voted, and some did not.

As noted above, many scholars have examined the question of whether who votes matters. Indeed, the analysis performed here only serves as one demonstration of the potential relationship between significant disparities in voter turnout and inequitable representational outcomes. In many ways, this is an extremely strict test as well: as Leighley and Nagler (2013) note, examinations based on changing election outcomes do not address the very real *policy* consequences of distortions in who participates. Seminal theories of Congress by Fenno (1978) and Arnold (1992) see representatives as responsive, in one way or another, to their constituents' preferences. Gilens (2014: 173) indicates that elections force policy makers to take actions they would not otherwise take, including paying attention to issues of concern for low-income Americans. Perhaps

Table 1.1 does not reflect the electoral reality of a "full turnout" world, as parties would change mobilization strategies and platforms to cater to a new electorate. Yet, the possibility of such a change occurring once again demonstrates how important voter turnout is to both the current state of our democracy and the future of representative government.

DEMOGRAPHIC CHANGE AND THE TURNOUT GAP

In this volume I focus on one part of the political inequality of who votes: racial/ethnic differences in voter turnout. More than a half century has passed since implementation of the Voting Rights Act of 1965. Academics and journalists alike acknowledge tremendous progress in the decades since, and the results are difficult to dispute: according to self-reported voting participation in the American National Election Studies and Current Population Survey, Black voter turnout grew from 35 percent in the 1956 presidential election to 58 percent in 1968 and 67 percent in 2012. Southern Black turnout tripled between 1956 and 1968, and is now at parity, or even exceeds, Black participation in the North. Rates of Black voting have clearly improved since the days of Jim Crow. Amendments to the Voting Rights Act in 1975 attempted to remove barriers to Latino and Asian American voting, yet despite these gains, Latino and Asian American turnout continues to lag far behind the national average. After accounting for citizenship, Latinos and Asian Americans remain 15 to 20 percentage points less likely to vote than African Americans or Whites (File 2013, 2015). Even for African Americans, a group whose voting rates were roughly equal to Whites in the 2008 and 2012 elections, a notable decline in turnout occurred in 2016. Chapter 2 provides a more extended discussion of historical trends in voter turnout by race, but, for now, the key point is that voter turnout for non-White Americans overall has been and continues to be substantially lower than that for Whites.

Connecting this focus with the previous section, the partisan preferences of African American, Latino, and Asian American voters indicate that low turnout for these groups may exacerbate the representational consequences of non-voting. According to National Election Pool (NEP) Exit polls, less than one-tenth of African American voters backed Republican candidates for President from 2008 to 2016, along with less than one-third of Latinos and Asian Americans (National Election Pool 2008). While White voters display more variation in their partisan proclivities, Democrats have not won a majority of non-Hispanic Whites in a presidential election since Lyndon Johnson was elected in 1964. Previous work explored the consequences of low minority turnout for local elections, where the high concentration of minority citizens means turnout disparities are especially consequential (Hajnal and Trounstine 2005; Hajnal 2010). In our most recent national elections it appears that the Democratic Party would also often gain if everyone voted. If the effect of turnout is greater now than in the past, it may be due to the changing composition of the non-voting population: it is now more heavily minority, and thus more Democratic-leaning, than before. Growing differences in representational preferences between voters and non-voters are thus likely to be linked to racial/ethnic differences in voter turnout.

Persistent differences between minority and non-minority turnout are also more relevant given the growth of the non-White population over time. The left panel of Figure 1.1 indicates the change in the percent of the population that is non-White from 1960 to the present using information from the U.S. Census Bureau.[11] The panel quantifies the trend discussed earlier in the introduction: the United States has undergone a tremendous demographic transformation since the 1960s. In 1960, less than

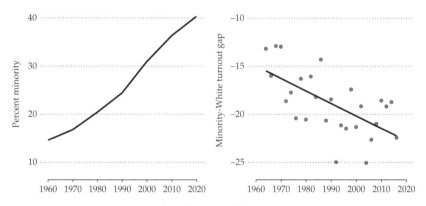

FIGURE 1.1 Demographic change and the turnout gap, 1960–2020
Note: "Minority" defined as individuals who are not non-Hispanic White. The "Minority–White Turnout Gap" is the difference in the rate of reported voter turnout for non-Hispanic White voting-age adults and the rate for minority adults, expressed in percentage points. Turnout rates calculated using data from the Current Population Survey November Supplements from 1964 to 2016. A small number of Latinos may be counted as non-Hispanic White from 1964 to 1970. See Chapter 2 for more details about how the turnout gap is calculated.

---

[11] Estimates for 2020 are projections generated by the Census Bureau in 2014, based on trends in immigration, birth rates, and mortality rates by racial/ethnic group.

15 percent of Americans were classified as coming from minority racial groups, nearly three-quarters of whom indentified as African American. Today, nearly 40 percent of Americans are from racial/ethnic minority groups, with two-thirds of non-Whites identifying as Latino or Asian American. These groups have substantially lower rates of voter turnout than Whites or African Americans, thus the growing minority population in the United States is disproportionately composed of Americans with low rates of voter turnout.

The rightmost panel of Figure 1.1 documents trends in minority and White voter turnout over roughly the same period of time, introducing one of the main metrics used in this book: the *turnout gap*. The panel uses data from the Current Population Survey Voting and Registration supplement to estimate rates of voter turnout for voting-age adults, which is the population corresponding most closely to the demographic shift found in the left panel.[12] Each point in the graph represents the difference in the rate of turnout witnessed for the White voting age population subtracted from the rate of turnout for the non-White voting age population, which constitutes a *gap* in voter turnout. For example, a value of −10 on the y-axis indicates that the minority turnout rate was 10 percentage points lower than the White turnout rate in an election: a Minority–White turnout gap of 10 percentage points. However, the gap between minority and non-minority turnout has never been this small: according to self-reports, the Minority–White turnout gap ranged from 13 percentage points in the mid 1960s to 25 percentage points in the 2004 election. That is, self-reported minority voter turnout was 25 percentage points lower than White turnout in 2004. At the same time as the U.S. population has become more diverse, the Minority–White turnout gap has widened. As discussed later in the book, trends in non-citizenship structure much of the difference we see in this panel, and Chapter 2 provides a more thorough explanation of the turnout gap and how it has changed over time for each non-White group. Yet when contrasted with the growth of the minority population over the same period, it becomes clear that the electoral impact of this demographic shift is far more muted than what is implied by looking at the composition of the population alone.

---

[12] The denominator in this calculation of voter turnout includes non-citizens and disenfranchised ex-felons, voting ineligible populations that have grown over time and are discussed in depth later in the book.

The growth of the Minority–White turnout gap has two clear consequences for American electoral politics. The first consequence stems from
the earlier discussion of political inequality and voter turnout, where evidence was presented that recent federal election results would shift if
everyone voted. Given that African Americans, Latinos, and Asian Americans are far more likely to support Democrats than Whites are, relatively
low minority turnout means that Democrats achieve less electoral success
than they "should" based on the preferences of the adult population.[13]
The second consequence has less to do with directly partisan outcomes,
but is perhaps all the more pernicious: as a result of the turnout gap, the
increased racial/ethnic diversity of the United States is not mirrored in the
electoral process. As Griffin and Newman (2008), Clifford (2012), and
others have noted, minority constituents are already less likely to have
their interests addressed by their elected officials, even above and beyond
what would be expected given their share of the population. The turnout
gap exacerbates this phenomenon. The voting population continues to be
more White than the adult population, and the expansion of the turnout
gap as indicated in Figure 1.1 suggests that White overrepresentation is
growing, not declining, over time. American democracy is becoming *less*,
not more, representative of the minority population, such that the political preferences of Whites continue to drive elections to a degree greater
than what would be dictated by demographics alone.

The preceding paragraphs indicate that who votes matters, and that
non-White Americans are less likely to vote than White Americans. Of
course, this book is not the first to indicate these trends, and indeed,
scholars have long understood that participatory distortions impact
who gets what in American politics (Verba et al. 1993; Lijphart 1997;
McCarty, Poole, and Rosenthal 2006; Schlozman, Verba, and Brady
2012), that there are racial/ethnic disparities in who votes (Verba and
Nie 1972; Wolfinger and Rosenstone 1980; Ramakrishnan 2005; Leighley and Nagler 2013), and that the intersection of these phenomena is a
particularly important challenge to democracy today (Hajnal 2010). The
goal of this book is to understand *why* we see turnout patterns that contribute to this growing political inequality in the United States. Why, fifty
years after passage of the Voting Rights Act, and one hundred more since
the 14th and 15th Amendments, do we continue to see racial/ethnic differences in who turns out to vote? Given the turnout gap, demographic

---

[13] I explore this phenomenon in Chapter 8.

change may be our destiny, but it is not at all clear that that destiny entails greater political equality.

EXPLAINING RACIAL/ETHNIC DISPARITIES IN VOTER TURNOUT

In the chapters that follow, I leverage past and present trends in voter turnout to explain why we see racial/ethnic differences in who turns out to vote. I demonstrate that *electoral influence*, operationalized as the relative size of a racial/ethnic group in a political jurisdiction, shapes the incentives for citizens to vote and politicians to seek that vote in turn. Thus when *any* racial/ethnic group is perceived to have greater electoral influence, they are more likely to get mobilized by elites and feel politically empowered in a manner leading to greater levels of participation in elections. Electoral influence can explain both the varied impact of historical and contemporary policies designed to hurt (or help) minority voting strength, and why in the *same* election today vastly different rates of turnout can be witnessed depending on the voter's race/ethnicity. Extending beyond past and present trends, I also show how an understanding of when minority groups do and do not have influence in election outcomes helps us chart the future trajectory of political participation, where I conclude that our country's elections can only reflect its ever-diversifying citizenry if the gap between minority and White turnout closes.

To conduct this analysis, I draw on decades of survey and observational data on White, African American, Latino, and Asian American voter turnout. In seeking to provide a complete history of race and voter turnout, I draw on the research of Walton, Puckett, and Deskins (2012a); Kousser (1999); Valelly (2004); Keyssar (2009), and others for pre-1940s information about voting rates by race/ethnicity. The quantitative analysis begins in the 1940s, using thousands of individual survey responses from the American National Election Study for information on turnout from 1948 to 1964. The much larger U.S. Census Bureau Current Population Survey, which began investigating voter turnout through a biennial Voting and Registration Supplement in 1964, extends self-reported accounts to the 2016 election. With over 3.1 million individual responses to these surveys, I am able to document national and regional racial/ethnic differences in participation for more than six decades.

When taking a deeper look at recent trends in turnout, I make use of 190 million individual-level voter registration records provided by Catalist, LLC, corresponding to elections from 2006–2016. Voter file data has transformed modern campaigns (Hersh 2015), and is increasingly common in political science research (Enos 2016; Fraga 2016a). However, the analyses in this volume are the first book-length application of this dataset to the study of race/ethnicity and voter turnout. As discussed in greater detail in Chapter 5, the Catalist data allows me to avoid issues of turnout misreporting that plague surveys while still measuring racial/ethnic trends through statistical modeling of individual race and ethnicity. The comprehensive data on individual turnout enables the comparison of rates of turnout for different racial/ethnic groups *in the same places* and *in the same elections* at small levels of geography, which is critical for demonstrating the validity of the theory of electoral influence. Such detailed data is particularly useful given that the period covers two of our most historic elections, 2008 and 2012, in which the first African American was elected president, and 2016, the most recent presidential election in which low minority turnout may have contributed to the Democrats' loss.

I begin the book by describing historical patterns of political participation across racial/ethnic groups, noting the failures of existing theories to explain a persistent gap in participation even after the removal of barriers to minority voting. I then take a closer look at contemporary disparities in voter turnout, demonstrating that the turnout gap closes when racial/ethnic minority groups have substantial electoral influence. I indicate that this pattern exists across groups, and even in the face of contemporary efforts to limit minority participation. At the end of the book I return to the themes discussed in this chapter, considering future trends in minority political participation and the implications of demographic change for political equality in the United States.

Chapter 2 presents historical trends in minority and White political participation, generating a common basis for comparison of non-Hispanic White, African American, Latino, and Asian American turnout rates over time. Qualitative evidence is presented regarding turnout in the 1800s and early 1900s, with an empirical analysis covering the period from 1948–2016. This chapter explains how I account for issues including differential citizenship rates over time, nonresponse in survey estimates, and differences in the turnout gap by region and state. Importantly, Chapter 2 evaluates minority turnout both before and after the passage and amendment of the Voting Rights Act, indicating that the turnout gap's change over time is not as tightly linked to this policy as previously thought. The chapter also shows how estimates from the American National Election Study, Current Population Survey, and Census Bureau should be combined to offer an accurate estimation of the turnout gap over time. As I demonstrate in the chapter, the gap between minority voter turnout and White voter turnout has varied, but persists today across minority groups.

Minority citizens are younger, have lower incomes, and lower levels of educational attainment on average than the White population, leading many to suggest that these sociodemographic characteristics produce the turnout gap. Examining racial/ethnic group-level trends in voter turnout by levels of income, educational attainment, and age, Chapter 3 demonstrates that commonly cited sociodemographic factors are not particularly helpful tools when seeking to understand the turnout gap. Drawing on approximately 3.1 million individual-level responses to the Current Population Survey, I show that the relationship between sociodemographic factors and participation is not linear even when looking at a single group over time, to say nothing of comparing across racial/ethnic groups. Today, the effects of income, age, and education are strikingly different for African Americans, Latinos, and Asian Americans than for Whites. Specifically, I show that young, low-income, and/or less educated Black, Latino, and Asian American citizens often turn out at *higher* rates than their White counterparts. The opposite is true for older, high-income, and/or highly educated minorities. As a result, the age and socioeconomic composition of the White, African American, Latino, or Asian American populations also fails to explain differences between minority and White turnout.

Given that policy and socioeconomic status do not explain the persistent turnout gap, what does? Chapter 4 lays out the specifics of my theory of electoral influence-driven voter turnout differences. I argue that turnout disparities are attributable to variation in the perceived influence each racial/ethnic group has in shaping election outcomes. In Chapter 4 I clarify that the theory I propose seeks to understand racial/ethnic differences in participation, rather than the raw rate of voter turnout witnessed across groups. However, it unites seemingly disparate theories of participation, including (1) the Downsian calculus of voting, which draws on economic understandings of voter behavior, (2) the empowerment hypothesis, which is largely specific to the racial and ethnic politics literature, and (3) mobilization-based theories of turnout, featured prominently in the literature on political campaigns. Operationalizing electoral influence as the relative size of a racial/ethnic group in a political jurisdiction, the major innovations of the theory of electoral influence are its applicability to *any* social group that could be perceived as a voting bloc and its ability to explain change (or lack thereof) in the turnout gap over time. I also address opposing theories that posit racial/ethnic differences manifest due to resource disparities, institutional barriers, or group-specific sociocultural forces.

Chapter 5 provides initial evidence of the explanatory power of electoral influence, examining geographic variation in the turnout gap in elections from 2006–2016. To do so, I introduce readers to voter file-based data provided by Catalist, LLC. The Catalist data contains records of every registered voter over the last ten years, including information about geolocation and voter turnout. However, the most important feature of the Catalist data is the availability of highly accurate estimates of individual race/ethnicity. Combining this resource with Census American Community Survey estimates of the citizen voting-age population by racial/ethnic group, I am able to map rates of voter turnout for Whites, African Americans, Latinos, and Asian Americans at the state and county levels. I show that the gap between minority and White turnout is smaller in states and counties where minority groups compose a larger share of potential voters, as predicted by the theory of electoral influence in Chapter 4. This also suggests a striking change from the patterns found in the pre-Voting Rights Act era in heavily African American areas of the Deep South, as the removal of institutional barriers was largely effective in ensuring minorities can have an impact on election outcomes in the very places where their vote is likely to matter the most. Nevertheless, I find that the gap between African Americans and Whites, assumed to be a product of the past, is considerable in most states and for most recent elections. Thus, aside from the few places where minority groups have substantial electoral influence, the turnout gap is even more severe than suggested by survey data.

A deeper empirical analysis of geographic patterns is presented in Chapter 6, focusing on how the racial/ethnic composition of congressional districts predicts turnout differences across groups. While the county-level patterns found in the previous chapter implied that minority groups are more likely to turn out when they have electoral influence, the district-level analysis in this chapter makes the link explicit. Taking a closer look at the period from 2006–2016, I demonstrate that turnout is higher for each racial/ethnic group when they make up a larger portion of the electorate within each congressional district. These patterns persist regardless of the race/ethnicity of candidates running for office, and the competitiveness of elections, challenging many current interpretations of what produces the turnout gap. I also demonstrate that this effect is causal and can be induced through the way congressional districts are drawn. Making use of Catalist-based panel data tracking over 5 million registration records from 2006 to 2016, I show that the Black–White turnout gap shrinks for those assigned to majority-Black districts, with White turnout decreasing and African American turnout increasing. The Latino–White turnout gap also decreases, and White turnout increases substantially for Whites who find themselves in a majority-White district for the first time. District composition is salient to voters, even in the first election cycle after redistricting, suggesting a key mechanism linking group size to perceived electoral influence and higher rates of voter turnout. Taking a closer look at elite behavior, I determine that when a group is not perceived to be relevant for election outcomes *despite their population size*, turnout does not increase. Taking a broader view, Chapter 6 demonstrates that much of the turnout gap can be attributed to the relatively low number of electoral districts where minority groups are perceived as critical to a candidate's electoral fortunes, a situation that could be remedied through modifying the electoral influence groups have in congressional elections.

Chapter 7 addresses contemporary election laws, considering whether modern policies that restrict access to the ballot have a large impact on minority voter turnout. Felon disenfranchisement is a prominent example of a policy disproportionately impacting minority voters, and is discussed in depth in this chapter. Since 2006, several states have also implemented policies mandating that photo identification be shown at the polls and/or limiting early voting. In the wake of the 2013 *Shelby County* v. *Holder* decision, such policies extended to areas that had a history of using election administration as a tool to limit African American and Latino political participation. Drawing on panel data tracking individual participation before and after voter identification laws were implemented, I determine the extent to which this policy in particular impacts the turnout gap. I find inconsistent and minimal effects of these and other barriers on turnout. However, in line with other work, it does appear restrictions are implemented in places where there is an electoral incentive to *exclude* minority citizens from the electoral process, exactly the kinds of places where minority turnout should be highest according to the theory of electoral influence advanced in this book. In this chapter I also discuss the ways in which election reforms could ameliorate the turnout gap, in particular, Voting Rights Act-mandated language assistance for Latinos and Asian Americans, and automatic voter registration which may facilitate the mobilization of historically low turnout groups.

The final chapter considers the implications of these findings for the future of American elections. Census population projections suggest that the minority share of the population will continue to grow, with most of the growth coming from Latinos and Asian Americans. Given that these groups are less likely to turn out to vote, their influence will be more muted than it would be in the absence of racial/ethnic differences in participation. Will this challenge the representativeness of our democratic system? Indeed, distortions in the voting population have become worse in recent decades. I demonstrate that Whites have a more disproportionate influence in the electoral process than they did prior to the Voting Rights Act, with the turnout gap having a sizable impact on recent election outcomes. The turnout gap thus forms one of the most consequential forms of political inequality today. Future trends in minority political participation are also discussed in this chapter, where I find that Whites will continue to dominate election outcomes nationwide and in nearly all states for at least a generation to come. Yet, as the electoral influence that minority groups hold will increase as they become an even larger share of the population, a tremendous opportunity exists if politicians and voters alike realize the potential for African American, Latino, and Asian American voters to shape the electoral process.

2

Race and Turnout in Historical Context

> *Sir, the ballot will finish the negro question; it will settle everything con-*
> *nected with this question ... The ballot will be his standing army. The*
> *ballot is the cheap and impregnable fortress of liberty ... Sir, the ballot is*
> *the freedman's Moses.*
> — Sen. Richard Yates, February 19, 1866

The 2008 and 2012 elections were historic moments in the saga of American race relations. With the election of Barack Obama, the nation turned
a page in its history and elected an African American to the presidency.
Fifty years after passage of the Voting Rights Act, and roughly 150 years
since the end of the Civil War, America seemed to be entering a period
where African Americans, if not all minority citizens, would have greater
political clout than ever before. Voter turnout in the 2008 election was
also higher than it had been since the 1960s, as more than 132 million
Americans went to the polls (McDonald 2017b). Yet, the *re*-election of
President Obama may have been all the more historic, at least from the
perspective of race and political participation. Comparing rates of voting
across groups, the Census Bureau and media reports proclaimed that in
2012 African American turnout exceeded White turnout for the first time
on record (File 2013; Wheaton 2013b). Thirty-five presidential contests
had come and gone since the franchise was extended to African Americans, but it was not until the 2000s that we recorded a reversal of one of
the most longstanding disparities in American elections. Why then, and
not before? What patterns do we see in race and voter turnout over time?

In this chapter, I begin the process of exploring racial and ethnic differences in voter turnout. I start by outlining the history of voting eligibility

and participation for minority groups in the 1800s and early 1900s, documenting substantial Black voting participation during Reconstruction that was almost completely eliminated in subsequent decades. Across minority groups, a common thread in this period is the importance of citizenship in defining the population that is eligible to vote and the power of *de jure* racial barriers to eliminate minority voting by the early twentieth century. I then explore racial/ethnic differences in voter turnout *after* the removal of *de jure* racial barriers, specifically the period from 1948 to 2016. Generating a common basis for the comparison of turnout rates across racial/ethnic groups, I document national and regional (South vs. non-South) trends in voting participation for Whites, African Americans, Latinos, and Asian Americans. The analysis clearly indicates that the gap between minority voter turnout and White voter turnout has waxed and waned, but persisted well after the removal of both *de jure* and *de facto* barriers to minority voting. Dramatic gains in Black voting participation in the 1950s and early 1960s, especially in the South, were followed by a persistent turnout gap with Whites that narrowed in the 2000s. However, Latino and Asian American turnout has not seen similar gains over time – if anything, the turnout gap between these groups and Whites has grown in recent decades.

RACE AND VOTING, 1789–1948

For most of U.S. history, the vast majority of Americans whom we would now define as non-White were denied access to the franchise. African American exclusion is the most widely known story, though even here the trajectory of voting rights prior to Reconstruction is notable. Five states allowed free African American men to vote in the first federal elections of 1788–1789: Delaware, Maryland, Massachusetts, New Hampshire, and Pennsylvania. While it is likely that some African Americans voted in the late 1700s and early 1800s, Walton, Puckett, and Deskins (2012a: 126) indicate that evidence to this effect is not readily available. Contemporaneous with expansion of the franchise to propertyless White males, they note that states did not similarly expand the franchise to free Black men such that by 1840 only seven of the twenty-six states (Georgia, Maine, Massachusetts, New Hampshire, New York,[1] Rhode Island, and Vermont) allowed African Americans to vote at all (Walton,

---

[1] Though a property requirement was in place for African Americans alone (Keyssar 2009: 320).

Puckett, and Deskins 2012a: 166,175). In Georgia, the only southern
state to allow free Blacks to vote between 1840 and 1864, there is,
again, no evidence that African Americans exercised the franchise (Walton, Puckett, and Deskins 2012a: 167). Thousands of Black men did vote
in the other states, in particular, New York and Massachusetts, influencing party politics in a non-trivial manner (Walton, Puckett, and Deskins
2012a: 127–128, 171). Yet, from the founding through the Civil War, the
dominant circumstance for African Americans, free and slave, North and
South, was *de jure* racial exclusion from the political process.

Native Americans[2] were also denied the franchise. Defining the population for apportionment as excluding "Indians not taxed" and the status
of American Indian tribes as "domestic dependent nations" paved the
way for an 1856 determination that Native Americans were "subjects"
of the United States instead of citizens (McCool, Olson, and Robinson
2007: 1–2). An attempt at naturalization by a Canadian national having
"half Indian blood" was denied in 1880[3] on the basis that he was not a
"white person" according to the law (Padilla 1980). In *Elk* v. *Wilkins*,[4]
where John Elk filed suit upon being barred from registering to vote,
the Supreme Court clarified that the 14th Amendment did not halt the
exclusion of Native Americans. The 1887 Dawes Act did allow for some
Native Americans to acquire citizenship, but only if they rejected their
culture, traditions, and residential patterns. It was not until the Indian
Citizenship Act of 1924 that all Native Americans were granted citizenship, though by that time two-thirds of American Indians had already
qualified under the Dawes Act's assimilatory mandate (McCool, Olson,
and Robinson 2007: 8).[5]

Latinos often had tenuous voting rights, though the Treaty of
Guadalupe Hidalgo granted the option of U.S. citizenship to all Mexican

---

[2] Here understood to include American Indians, the Alaska Native population, and Native Hawaiians.
[3] *In re Camille*, 6 Fed. 256 (1880).
[4] 112 U.S. 94 (1884).
[5] Due to difficulties in identifying American Indians in national surveys or voter file-based analyses, largely because of the small size of the Native American population in the twen-tieth century (0.4 percent in 1970, 0.9 percent in 2010), Native American voter turnout is not examined separately in this book. The exclusion of Native Americans from work on American political behavior is made all the worse by the fact that Native American voter turnout in federal and state elections is likely quite low, but may be higher in tribal elections (Wilkins 2002: 191). Future work must research these patterns more fully, but for more complete accounts of American Indian political behavior, see Wilkins (2002) and McCool, Olson, and Robinson (2007).

residents of territories acquired in the Mexican–American War. Similarly, all *Tejano* (Texas Mexican) residents at the time of Texas Independence (1836) were made citizens of Texas, and the first California constitution (1850) stipulated that "white male citizens of Mexico" who elected to become citizens of the United States were indeed citizens and could vote and seek office (Padilla 1980; Griswold del Castillo 1990: 69). *Tejanos* played an important role in the politics of the Republic of Texas (Montejano 1987), in particular, San Antonio (Brischetto et al. 1994), but 1850 estimates put the Mexican American population in former Mexican territories at only 80,302. Excluding residents of the New Mexico Territory, who were not eligible to vote for federal office, 9,178 Mexican Americans resided in California and 13,901 lived in Texas, or 10 percent and 6.5 percent of the Census enumerated population, respectively (Nostrand 1975). There is no record of California or Texas Mexican Americans electing to remain Mexican citizens (Griswold del Castillo 1990: 66). For this relatively small population, therefore, access to the franchise was *de jure* permitted. That said, Montejano (1987) describes the "fragile franchise" of Mexican Americans as subject to "protests and threats," particularly if their chosen candidate was not supported by the White population (39). Well-documented discrimination against the *Californio* and *Tejano* populations in the realm of property rights (Griswold del Castillo 1990) also indicates the decline in political power of Latino elites.

   The possibility of Asian Americans voting was dashed almost as soon as Chinese immigrants began arriving in the United States. Numbering 325 in 1849, 775 in 1850, 3,491 in 1851, and 23,517 in 1852, the first wave of Chinese immigrants were almost entirely male, settled mostly in California, and likely had little intent of staying in the United States. Yet, these immigrants appeared to be *welcomed* by California elites, with officials from Governor McDougal to San Francisco Mayor Geary praising the "China boys" as "equals," "worthy classes," and "newly adopted citizens" of California. The *Daily Alta California* went as far as to state that "the China boys will yet vote at the same polls, study at the same schools, and bow at the same altar as our own countrymen" (Takaki 1998: 79–80). Such openness to Chinese immigration did not last, as European-origin migrants to California balked at Asian and other non-White Californians, pressuring politicians to curb Chinese immigration and social incorporation. In *People* v. *Hall*,[6] the California Supreme Court vacated the murder conviction of a White settler on the grounds

---

[6] 4 Cal. 399 (1854).

that testimony from a Chinese witness was inadmissible, as the California Constitution did not intend for non-Whites to have "all the equal rights of citizenship" lest "we might soon see them at the polls" (Foner and Rosenberg 1993: 18). With this perspective, and the Naturalization Act of 1790s prohibition on non-White acquisition of citizenship, it appears that the voting rights of Asian Americans were nonexistent in the mid 1800s.

Reconstruction

The first significant expansion of the franchise to non-Whites was implemented in the wake of the Civil War. More complete histories of the Reconstruction era are provided elsewhere (Du Bois 1971 [1935]; Foner 1988; Frymer 1999; Valelly 2004), but there are two points worth noting as it pertains to African American enfranchisement during this period.

First, Black voting was substantial in southern states for the 1868 presidential election. The Reconstruction Acts of 1867 and 1868 mandated that former slaves be given the right to vote, and charged (Northern) military commanders with the process of voter registration (Walton, Puckett, and Deskins 2012a: 233). The result was dramatic: more than 700,000 African American men were registered to vote by December 1867, outnumbering White registrants by a large margin in Louisiana, South Carolina, Alabama, Florida, and Mississippi (Walton, Puckett, and Deskins 2012a: 247). Given the concentration of former slaves in the South, the percent of Black men that were voting eligible nationwide increased from less than half of a percentage point to 80.5 percent by the end of 1867 (Valelly 2004: 3). Davidson (1992) estimates that two-thirds of eligible Black men voted in presidential and gubernatorial contests in the South during the high point of Reconstruction (10).[7] Thus, it is quite possible that African-American voters handed the presidency to Grant and ensured Radical Republican control of the South by 1868 (Walton, Puckett, and Deskins 2012a: 263–264). The 14th (1868) and 15th (1870) Amendments solidified the ability of African American men to vote and achieve political representation, extended Black voting rights to the non-South, and through the Enforcement Act of 1870, allowed the federal government to ensure state officials did not interfere with Black suffrage.

---

7 Valelly (2004) puts the number even higher for a few states, citing estimates generated by Roland F. King (2000) which put Black turnout at 78 percent or more in South Carolina (78).

The sincere hope of some Northern Republicans was that through these efforts "[t]he ballot will finish the negro question" (Foner 1988: 278), obviating the need for continued northern intervention in the South.

Second, Whites in the South resisted Black enfranchisement throughout Reconstruction. While some Democrats publicly stated that they would support universal suffrage, in reality the Democratic Party and the "Redeemer" movement saw elimination of Republican rule and Black suffrage as a proximate goal (Foner 1988: 424; Keyssar 2009: 85). Initially, this took the form of violence and intimidation of African Americans and White Republicans. Violence committed against potential Black voters was common in the postbellum South, but in the Reconstruction era Black political power persisted. Kousser (1999) notes that violence was "relatively politically ineffective" at reducing Black voting (23–24), and Foner (1988) indicates that efforts at curbing the Ku Klux Klan using federal power were largely successful by late 1871 (458). Legal efforts to disenfranchise Black voters were perhaps more important. In the *Slaughter-House* cases,[8] the Supreme Court severely limited the scope of the Fourteenth Amendment making prosecution of civil rights violations difficult. Subsequent rulings in *U.S. v. Cruikshank*[9] and *U.S. v. Reese*[10] set perhaps the greater precedent, as they opened the door to states restricting voting rights through local discretion in interpreting facially race-neutral franchise restrictions, thus invalidating key portions of the Enforcement Act of 1870 (Keyssar 2009: 85; Goldman 2001: 105). That said, *de jure* allowance for Black voting rights meant that significant numbers of African American men voted, despite extreme hostility from Whites acting in both a private and governmental capacity.

The Reconstruction Amendments were not interpreted to extend citizenship to other minority groups, however. Native Americans continued to be restricted from citizenship until the Dawes Act, but this precedent was also cited as a reason for local officials to prohibit Mexican immigrants with indigenous ancestry from the franchise in Texas (De León 1979). The Naturalization Act of 1870, which extended the right to naturalize to "aliens of African nativity and to persons of African descent," extended the language of the Naturalization Act of 1790 to include both African Americans and Whites, but simultaneously barred other non-Whites from naturalizing (Haney López 2006: 37) and strengthened

---

[8] 83 U.S. 36 (1873).
[9] 92 U.S. 542 (1875).
[10] 92 U.S. 214 (1876).

provisions that restricted voting to verified citizens or naturalization applicants. The decision to continue the exclusion of non-Whites and many White non-citizens was intentional, and reflected northern fears of the effect of an expanded franchise in their backyard (Foner 1988: 447). Despite the advances in voting rights for African Americans during the Reconstruction Era, other minority groups were left out of the electoral process.

End of Reconstruction through World War II

The Compromise of 1877 led to the removal of the last remaining federal troops in the South and signaled the end of the Reconstruction era. A decline in Black voting rights ensued, though the decline in Black political participation was not as rapid as some assert (e.g. Davidson 1992; Keyssar 2009). If the estimate of the apex of Black voter turnout during Reconstruction is accurate (Davidson 1992 put this figure at roughly 66 percent), by 1880 Black turnout in Southern states was still high, at 61 percent on average (Redding and James 2001: 148). White turnout was only slightly higher, at 67 percent. Yet, Northern Republicans who supported Black suffrage only as an alternative to military occupation would soon become disillusioned with gains by Southern Democrats (Foner 1988: 278), which was compounded by opposition to Reconstruction in the North. Ironically, stricter enforcement of the 14th and 15th Amendments likely would have obviated the need for Republicans to end Reconstruction, as alluded to in this chapter's epigraph by Illinois Senator Richard Yates. Yet after 1876 Republican interest in Black rights in the South waned (Foner 1988: 582). The failure of the Lodge Force Bill in 1890, largely due to Republican opposition in the Senate, made it clear that the federal government would not step in to protect Black voting rights in the South (Kousser 1999: 39).[11] Between 1880 and 1892, Black turnout dropped from 84 percent in Florida to 14 percent, 70 percent in Tennessee to 31 percent, and 45 percent in Mississippi to 1 percent or less. States that had not yet implemented legal disenfranchisement also saw drops in turnout, most notably, South Carolina (77 percent to 17 percent). However, declines in Black voting were, on average, larger in states with disenfranchisement in their constitutions (Valelly 2004: 52). Furthermore, White turnout changes did not appear to be associated

---

[11] For a more detailed exploration of the Lodge Bill and national party politics that enabled disenfranchisement, see Walton, Puckett, and Deskins (2012a: ch. 18).

with Black turnout changes during the late 1800s and early 1900s (Redding and James 2001: 154), indicating that disenfranchising efforts were specifically designed to reduce African American voting strength.

Given the 15th Amendment, what techniques were used to block African American voting after Reconstruction? While fraud was a common feature of the pre- and post-Reconstruction era, in several Southern states African Americans continued to cast ballots and have them counted as intended in the 1880s (Valelly 2004: 55). Perman (2001) distinguishes between an era of "voter manipulation" (commencing in 1880) and "voter elimination" (commencing in the early 1890s) where the goal was elimination of any African-American political participation (6). During the "voter elimination" era, Southern states rewrote their constitutions with the specific aim of disenfranchising African Americans (Davidson 1992: 10–11; Walton, Puckett, and Deskins 2012a: 368). Drawing on techniques already used in the North to disenfranchise immigrants (Keyssar 2009), Southern states implemented systems of voter registration and literacy tests (Kousser 1974: ch. 2).[12] The poll tax was also in place throughout the South by 1904 (Kousser 1974: ch. 3). While these measures did not have *explicit* racial language,[13] exceptions were granted to Whites through grandfather clauses (Goldman 2001: 138). Northern states also used some of the above measures to target White immigrants, instead of singling out the small Black population. Yet the explicit restriction of primary voting to Whites, termed the White Primary, was the "ultimate guarantee" of Democratic Party unity and supremacy in the South (Perman 2001: 303, 313). With any remaining Black voters *de jure* barred from participating in the only meaningful election (the Democratic Primary) politicians no longer had the *opportunity*, much less the need, to cater to African American interests. African Americans no longer had any hope to form meaningful political alliances with Whites (Kousser 1999: 38).

The result of these barriers was a much more dramatic decrease in Black voter turnout. Black turnout declined from 61 percent in the eleven former states of the Confederacy in 1880 to 17 percent by 1900 and 2 percent by 1912. White turnout also dropped, but only to 55 percent

[12] The Australian ("secret") ballot was a *de facto* literacy test with pernicious effects on Black (but not White) voter turnout (Kousser 1974: 55–56).

[13] Though in discussing these measures politicians openly stated that they were designed to reduce Black voting. Disenfranchisement was not always instigated by Democrats in heavily Black areas of the South, but Whites in these areas played a pivotal role in passage and generally supported a transition from "manipulation" to "elimination" of Black voters (Perman 2001: 324–326).

in 1900 and 40 percent in 1912 (Redding and James 2001: 154). Clearly the *de jure* racial restrictions on voting were effective at decreasing the political participation of Southern Black voters, producing what Valelly called "mammoth effects," swamping a nontrivial effect of *de facto* barriers through intimidation and violence (2004: 129; Kousser 1974: 5, 1999: 23–24, Acharya, Blackwell, and Sen 2018: ch. 6).[14] Indeed, Kousser (1999) further separates Perman's (2001) second era into "disenfranchisement" and "lily-white" stages (23), with the lily-white era precluding any Black participation whatsoever. Correspondingly, Black turnout remained low until the elimination of the White Primary in the 1940s (Davidson 1992: 11–12), discussed in greater detail in the next section.

The end of Reconstruction also coincided with an increase in the size of the Asian American population in the United States. The Chinese population alone reached over 100,000 in 1880, and Chinese immigrants made up a large portion of the population in many Western states (Takaki 1998: 87, 111). As the plausibility of large numbers of Asian Americans seeking citizenship solidified, the courts sought to clarify that Asians would not be eligible for citizenship. The 1878 *In re Ah Yup*[15] case determined that "a native of China" could not be considered White, and Asians were meant to be prohibited from naturalization even when not listed as a distinct group in legislation (Haney López 2006: 39). Similar cases established that Hawaiians and Japanese were also barred,[16] along with those of mixed White-Asian ancestry.[17] Even the few Asian American citizens who found a way to naturalize could have their citizenship revoked (Haney López 2006: 42).[18] The Chinese Exclusion Act of 1882 barred Chinese immigration entirely, and was extended subsequently to all Asians (aside from Filipinos) in 1924 (Gyory 1998: 254). But what of the *descendants* of Asian immigrants to the United States? Here, the 14th Amendment took on a greater role in minority voting rights by granting citizenship to native-born Asians, even if their ancestors were not citizens. In *United States* v. *Wong Kim Ark*,[19] the court found that Wong, the San Francisco-born son of two Chinese immigrants who were not themselves

---

[14] Though in heavily Black counties *de facto* barriers likely played a larger role (Bertocchi and Dimico 2017).

[15] 1 F. Cas. 223 (1878).

[16] *In re Kanaka Nian* 21 Pac. 993 (1899); *In re Saito* 62 Fed. 126 (1894).

[17] *In re Knight*, 171 F. 299, 300 (1909).

[18] *In re Gee Hop*, 71 F. 274 (1895).

[19] 169 U.S. 649 (1898).

eligible for citizenship, was nevertheless a citizen of the United States. Combined with the Chinese Exclusion Act and later immigration restrictions, however, the number of Asian Americans eligible to vote remained small until World War II.[20]

Latinos also came to be excluded from voting, though not as fully as other groups. With the citizenship rights of original Spanish/Mexican inhabitants and their descendants assured, initial efforts at disenfranchising Latinos centered on the ability of Mexican immigrants to naturalize. It was not until the *In re Rodríguez*[21] case that the right of Mexicans to naturalize as individuals was clearly established (De León 1979). Yet it would be incorrect to interpret the case as extending "whiteness" to Mexicans. Presiding Judge Thomas Maxey delineated between the applicant's eligibility from the "standpoint of the ethnologist" and "the spirit and intent of our laws upon naturalization" (De León 1979: 12). As Mexican nationals had been granted citizenship through treaties in the past, they would be allowed to become citizens in the future, racial status notwithstanding (Padilla 1980). In areas of South Texas, White *patrones* controlled the vote of the Mexican-origin population, organizing political machines that entailed substantial Latino voting but little political voice for even the long-time Mexican American residents of South Texas (Montejano 1987: 40). Such techniques were opposed by new Anglo migrants to Texas, who stated that Mexican Americans were a "political menace," "unfit to have the vote," and "foreigners who claim American citizenship but who are as ignorant of things American as the mule" (Montejano 1987: 130–131). Statehood for New Mexico was delayed until 1912 by both territorial politicians and Congress until the White population could grow enough to counterbalance the *Nuevomexicanos* (Holtby 2012: 34). Thus, even for Mexican American citizens non-Whiteness continued to be a means of exclusion. At the same time as *In re Rodríguez* allowed for Mexican naturalization, several Texas counties began using variations of the White Primary to bar Mexican Americans from voting in the only election where candidate selection took place (Brischetto et al. 1994). The size of the Mexican American population in the border counties was so great that successful politicians in the early 1900s were forced to use patronage tactics instead of appealing to Whites. By the mid 1910s and

---

[20] At the time of the *Wong Kim Ark* decision, fewer than 10,000 U.S.-born Asian Americans resided in the United States. This number grew to roughly 168,000 by 1940 (Gibson and Jung 2006).

[21] 81 Fed. 337 (1896).

1920s, though, machine politics was severely reduced in South Texas (Anders 1982: 141–168, 282–283).

VOTER TURNOUT BY RACE/ETHNICITY, 1948–2016

An important takeaway from the previous section is that *de jure* racial barriers to voting played a fundamental role in limiting minority participation. While standing in contrast with Key's (1949) understanding of post-Reconstruction disenfranchisement as *fait accompli* prior to legislative actions, the above discussion confirms that many African Americans were able to overcome the *de facto* barriers that were present both during and after Reconstruction. Furthermore, Latinos were able to vote and had some measure of political influence in Texas in the early 1900s, until the end of machine politics and the advance of *de jure* restriction from participation in the White Primary.

De jure racial restrictions for citizens were dismantled in the 1940s. The White Primary, while not initially viewed as relevant to Black disenfranchisement (Kousser 1974: 82), is now seen by scholars as critical in removing even the chance of meaningful Black political participation (Kousser 1999: 37). Keyssar (2009) goes so far as to say that the White Primary was "probably the most efficacious method of denying the vote to African Americans" by the 1930s (199). The importance of the White Primary increased further as Black partisanship shifted toward the Democratic Party during the Roosevelt administration[22] and other explicitly racial measures such as the grandfather clause (outlawed in 1915) were eliminated. Yet in 1944, the Supreme Court ruled that the White Primary system of Texas was unconstitutional. Despite attempts at several workarounds by southern Democratic parties, the South could no longer rely on this *de jure* racial barrier and by 1948 southern states were forced to accept the *possibility* of non-White influence in the Democratic Party (Weeks 1948; Klarman 2001; Mickey 2015: ch. 3).[23] As Mickey (2015) notes, the dismantling of the White Primary precipitated a shift in the politics of the South, as a Black electorate could plausibly gain political

---

[22] See Frymer (1999) and Walton, Puckett, and Deskins (2012a) for extended discussions.

[23] The *Elmore* v. *Rice* decision in 1947 ended the possibility of deregulating political parties to maintain racial bans on primary participation, and while racial restrictions on pre-primary candidate selection continued until 1953, *de jure* racial restrictions on the franchise had already been eliminated. See Klarman (2001) for a more complete discussion of the White Primary cases.

power within the ruling party (62). The reinforcement of *de facto* barriers in the South was a response to this opening, diminishing the potential effect of the end of the White Primary in this region. As detailed in Parker (2009), Black WWII veterans returning to the South resisted these *de facto* restrictions, advocating for voting rights and registering Black voters despite the constant threat of violent reprisals. Yet, opportunities for African American political participation opened in the North as well. Black voting in the North increased in the 1930s and 1940s, with much of the increase attributable to growth in the Black population stemming from the First Great Migration (Walton, Puckett, and Deskins 2012a: ch. 19). African American empowerment in urban centers was key to Black politics in the North pre-WWII (Walton, Puckett, and Deskins 2012a: 408). However, Valelly (2004) also indicates that Black turnout increased an average of 37 percent in Chicago, Cleveland, Detroit, and New York, where most of the Black population in the North lived (154).

The late 1940s and early 1950s also saw the removal of bans on naturalization for Asian Americans, culminating in the 1952 McCarran-Walter Act (Takaki 1998: 412–414). While the act continued several restrictions on immigration, it opened the door to naturalization (and thus voting rights) for any person legally residing within the United States. The key barrier to the franchise for non-Black minority groups, citizenship, had fallen. Mexican Americans had already been granted the right to naturalize in *In re Rodríguez* in 1897, and the Jones–Shafroth Act of 1917 granted U.S. citizenship to all Puerto Ricans born after the U.S. takeover of the island.[24] McCarran-Walter also ensured that other Latinos immigrating to the United States could gain citizenship. Thus, explicit racial/ethnic restrictions on access to the franchise were gone by 1952.

As a result, the systematic comparison of White voter turnout to African American, Latino, and Asian American turnout should begin in the elections after the elimination of the White Primary and racial restrictions on citizenship acquisition. Survey data from the late 1940s and early 1950s will allow us to measure trends in turnout during this period, but before continuing, it is necessary to discuss the landmark legislation that continues to dominate discussions of race and voting: the Voting Rights Act of 1965.

---

[24] Puerto Ricans residing in the United States have the right to vote in federal elections. Puerto Ricans residing in Puerto Rico, along with other residents of United States insular areas, are not included in the statistics found in this book.

The Voting Rights Act of 1965

Studies of minority political participation rightly note the important role played by the Voting Rights Act of 1965 (VRA). President Lyndon Johnson gave Acting Attorney General Nicholas Katzenbach a mandate to produce "the goddamndest, toughest voting rights act that you can devise" the very same day he signed the Civil Rights Act in 1964 (May 2013: 48). Student Nonviolent Coordinating Committee (SNCC) leader and Mississippi Freedom Democratic Party founder Fannie Lou Hamer's powerful testimony at the 1964 Democratic National Convention also brought the continuing discrimination against southern Black voters to the forefront of national attention (Walton, Puckett, and Deskins 2012a: 607). Nonetheless, it is generally recognized that the violent response to the Selma to Montgomery march in early 1965 forced President Johnson to take stronger action, pushing Congress to pass the Voting Rights Act in a nationally televised address (Davidson 1992: 16).

The Voting Rights Act targeted the *de facto* barriers to Black voting that persisted in the South despite *de jure* equality after elimination of the grandfather clause and White Primary. A combination of poll taxes, literacy tests, residency requirements, and burdensome registration procedures served to diminish Black voting opportunities (Valelly 2004: 201). Racially discriminatory implementation by local registrars further ensured a disparate impact of these measures, targeting African Americans throughout the South along with Mexican Americans in Texas (Keyssar 2009: 89). The Voting Rights Act suspended the "tests and devices" outlined above in southern states and counties with low voter turnout, but perhaps more importantly, shifted the burden of proof from minority registrants alleging discrimination to jurisdictions who had to prove that any voting procedures would *not* have a discriminatory impact *before* implementing said measures (Davidson 1992: 19). These *preclearance* provisions of the Voting Rights Act, ensconced in section 5 of the act, severely limited state and county officials' ability to implement new *de facto* barriers to voting without scrutiny from federal officials. The act also forced counties with low turnout and a history of discrimination to allow federal registrars to register voters, further limiting local discretion.[25]

The Voting Rights Act was later extended in a series of renewals, and most notably for purposes of analyzing the turnout gap, gained

---

[25] For more details regarding the provisions of the Voting Rights Act, see Davidson (1992) and Davidson and Grofman (1994).

provisions to protect "language minority groups" (Latinos, Asian Americans, and Native Americans) in 1975. The formula for gaining the strictest forms of voting rights protections added "English-only" elections as a test or device impeding minority participation (de la Garza and DeSipio 1993). This added the entire states of Texas, Arizona, and Alaska, boroughs in New York City, and a smattering of other counties across the country. The expanded VRA was the product of advocacy by Rep. Barbara Jordan, an African American member of Congress representing the Houston area. Testimony from Vilma Martinez of the Mexican American Legal Defense and Education Fund (MALDEF) called discrimination in Texas "strikingly reminiscent of the Deep South in the early 1960s" (de la Garza and DeSipio 1993: 1482). The amended VRA also calls for the provision of multilingual election materials if certain population thresholds are met, and today, a sizable share of the limited English-proficient Latino, Asian American, and Native American citizen population can vote in their heritage language.[26]

The Voting Rights Act ensured minority voting rights would not be entirely contingent on local desires to restrict the franchise, desires that defined the politics of many parts of the South (Key 1949; Mickey 2015). Alt (1994) presents clear evidence that in the most heavily African American counties of the Deep South, the Voting Rights Act's provision of federal registrars led to a significant increase in Black voter registration immediately after implementation of the Act. Yet, outside of these areas, Black voter turnout had already increased over the course of the 1950s and early 1960s; a finding that is often not emphasized in favor of a more triumphant tone regarding the success of the VRA (e.g. Davidson and Grofman 1994: 380; Bositis 2006: 113–114). Lawson (1976) and McClain et al. (2006) document the building of mobilizing institutions after the elimination of the White Primary, culminating in a critical period between 1960 and 1964 where substantial Black mobilization occurred even without the VRA's protections. Fannie Lou Hamer's testimony points to the importance of local mobilization efforts even in the face of violent reprisals against African Americans who managed to register to vote. As documented in detail by May (2013), efforts during this era focused on attempting to register Black voters in the most blatantly discriminatory areas of the Deep South in an effort to draw national attention and achieve exactly the sort of legislation gained with

---

[26] A discussion of the specific impact of VRA-mandated language assistance may be found in Chapter 7.

the VRA; tactics that manifested in the Selma to Montgomery march and Bloody Sunday. Clearly, therefore, the *post*-VRA mobilization of African Americans is owed in great part to the *pre*-VRA mobilization activities.

What impact did the VRA have on the turnout gap? Matthews and Prothro (1963, 1966) analyze trends in Black and White voting pre-VRA, finding that southern Black voter registration increased a large amount from the 1940s to the early 1960s, but that disparities between Black and White voting had not narrowed as they had in the North (Matthews and Prothro 1966: 44–45). Lawson (1976) suggests that the link between Black registration and the VRA was facilitated by both the presence of VRA-mandated federal registrars and community organizations who pre-dated the Act itself (330–342). Again, Alt (1994) provides a statistical analysis of county-level voter registration data to indicate that the VRA was able to break through resistance for counties most heavily invested in Black disenfranchisement: counties where Black voters, if mobilized, would drive election outcomes. However, Walton, Puckett, and Deskins (2012a: ch. 25) take a broader view and find that Black registration increases post-VRA were higher in counties that did not have federal registrars by the early 1970s, suggesting that the long-term effect of the act was realized through voluntary compliance with the provisions (630). Furthermore, and in some ways confirmed by Alt (1994), the researchers indicate that White registration increased significantly in counties with Black majorities (Walton, Puckett, and Deskins 2012a: 640), such that the impact of the VRA on the turnout gap may be more muted than suggested by previous work. Studies probing the causal effect of the VRA on African American voter turnout also find a significant, positive impact of VRA implementation on both Black and White turnout (Fresh 2018). White resistance to Black voting rights thus turned to spurring white mobilization, and later, the dilution of African American electoral power through districting and other measures designed to limit Black officeholding (Mickey 2015: 273).

Empirical evidence regarding the impact of the extension of the VRA on Latinos and Asian American turnout is even less forthcoming. In Texas, where the Chicano-led Raza Unida Party won victories in local elections by mobilizing Mexican Americans during the late 1960s and early 1970s (Gutiérrez 1999; Navarro 2000), participation rates still lagged behind Whites by a large margin (Berman 2015b). Efforts by Whites to further reduce Mexican American voting motivated the extension of the act to Latinos in 1975. That said, the limited empirical evidence offered by de la Garza and DeSipio (1993) indicates that Latino voter registration and voter turnout did not increase appreciably after extension of the VRA. The national- and regional-level analyses in this chapter will allow us to evaluate trends in African American, Latino, and Asian American voter turnout before and after these groups gained federal voting rights protections.

Survey Data

I draw on two sets of national surveys to quantify rates of voter turnout over time. The first dataset is drawn from the American National Elections Studies (ANES).[27] The ANES has been a critical source of information about voting behavior since the 1950s (Campbell et al. 1960). Administered via in-person interviews, the ANES was originally designed and implemented by the Survey Research Center at the University of Michigan. While there have been changes to the types of questions asked in ANES surveys, the primary advantage of the ANES is the fact that some form of the study has been fielded in every presidential election since 1948.

The ANES surveyed approximately 1,100–2,200 American citizens each election from 1952 to 2008.[28] As a result, it can be difficult to gain information about demographic subgroups using ANES data (Wolfinger and Rosenstone 1980: 4–5). For the purposes of this chapter, the relatively small sample size of the ANES means that one must be cautious in interpreting information about the voting behavior of minority citizens, especially earlier in the period. While race has been queried since the beginning of the ANES, including information about Hispanic ethnicity from 1966 onward, fewer than one hundred Latino respondents were polled in each year prior to 1984. The number of Asian American respondents has never exceeded one hundred, even in the much larger 2012 study. Thus, the ANES is only used to gauge White and Black turnout and only in the absence of other data.[29]

---

[27] http://electionstudies.org

[28] A sample of 662 was used for the 1948 study, and a much larger survey of over 5,000 respondents was fielded in 2012.

[29] Though the small sample size used by the ANES also makes it difficult to be certain of African American turnout rates, such information is likely a reasonable approximation of trends in Black voting and certainly the best national data available on pre-1960s behavior. For instance, in the 1952 ANES, African Americans were 9 percent of respondents, with 68 percent living in the Census-defined South. This compares favorably

The second source of information about race and voter turnout is the Current Population Survey (CPS). The CPS is a national survey of U.S. households conducted by the Census Bureau for the Bureau of Labor Statistics. With origins in the late 1930s and early 1940s, the primary purpose of the Current Population Survey is to track levels of labor force participation and unemployment on a monthly basis.[30] Since 1964, however, the survey has also measured voter registration and turnout in the November coinciding with each federal election.[31] The Current Population Survey Voting and Registration Supplement (CPS) queries voter registration and turnout through a series of questions appearing at the end of the otherwise standard monthly questionnaire and has a sample size of over 60,000 households and 130,000 individuals in recent years. Polling roughly twenty times as many individuals as the ANES, the CPS is generally considered to provide superior estimates of voter turnout when inspecting small demographic groups or geographic levels (Wolfinger and Rosenstone 1980; Jang 2009; Rocha et al. 2010).

The CPS thus provides vital data on voting in the United States, and has proven highly valuable to researchers studying political participation, the characteristics of voters, and the voting patterns of racial/ethnic groups (e.g., Wolfinger and Rosenstone 1980; Nagler 1991; Leighley 2001; McCarty, Poole, and Rosenthal 2006; Leighley and Nagler 2013). Survey researchers often use the CPS figures to calibrate and weight small sample surveys of the American electorate, understanding the CPS to be widely respected both within and outside of the academic community (Hur and Achen 2013). Indeed, in oral arguments associated with *Shelby County v. Holder*,[32] Chief Justice Roberts cited CPS figures on registration and voting when questioning the government's lawyers.[33]

While the large sample size of the CPS allows for the best available subgroup estimates of voter turnout over time, it is still susceptible to the misreporting and nonresponse issues affecting other surveys (Traugott and Katosh 1979; Cassel 2004), including the ANES (Jackman and

---

to the 1950 U.S. Census, where 10 percent of the population was African American and 68 percent of African Americans lived in the Census-defined South. Furthermore, a substantial portion of the 1952 ANES Black sample lived in rural areas of the former Confederacy (22 percent), only moderately less than what we would expect based on Census demographics (Heinicke 1994: 187).

[30] www.census.gov/prod/2002pubs/tp63rv.pdf

[31] www.census.gov/hhes/www/socdemo/voting

[32] 570 U.S. 2 (2013).

[33] www.oyez.org/cases/2010-2019/2012/2012_12_96

Spahn 2016). Recently, several academics have noted irregularities in the turnout projections of the CPS overall. In 2009, Michael McDonald noted that the turnout estimates from the CPS showed a decrease in voting from 2004 to 2008, even though the actual percent of persons voting increased.[34] He attributed this problem to nonresponse to the vote question and other items within the survey used as screening questions for the voting and registration supplement. Peer-reviewed work later confirmed this phenomenon (Hur and Achen 2013). Here I remove nonrespondents from the denominator, which is consistent with recommendations made by these researchers and broader practices in survey analysis.[35]

Defining Voter Turnout

Before examining the survey data, a discussion of how I define voter turnout is in order. Media reports and press releases often describe voter turnout in terms of the number of individuals who voted in an election (File 2013). However, academic analyses generally define turnout in terms of the *rate* of voting, with the number of voters as the numerator and a figure corresponding to the potential electorate as the denominator. In early work, the voting-age population (VAP) was seen as a viable measure of the eligible electorate (Andrews 1966). While some continue to levy only an age restriction when computing turnout rates (Teixeira 1992: 9–10), a transition has been made away from using the VAP as the denominator to a more nuanced version that takes into account eligibility. Building on work by Burnham (1965) and Andrews (1966), McDonald and Popkin (2001) offered a complete inventory of the many factors that should be accounted for when trying to determine who *could* vote. In their article, they focus on removing non-citizens and disenfranchised felons from the VAP, and then adding overseas military and civilian personnel who are not included in the Census or most surveys of the electorate. The authors note that other modifications

---

[34] This observation was made on Professor McDonald's blog in June 2009, and has been updated with data for subsequent elections: www.electproject.org/home/voter-turnout/cps-methodology

[35] As a result, the estimates I provide here differ from official reports from the Census Bureau (e.g. File 2013). These differences are especially acute for rates of Latino and Asian American turnout in the 1970s, 1980s, and 1990s, as CPS nonrespondents were considered to be eligible non-voters despite the fact that many, if not most, of these individuals were non-citizens. See Appendix A.2 for additional details as to why and how nonrespondents are removed when analyzing the CPS.

are desirable, such as removing those ineligible due to state residency requirements, mental incompetence, or Census undercounts, but consistent, over-time information about these populations at the national level is scarce (McDonald and Popkin 2001: 965).

McDonald and Popkin (2001), and continuing work by McDonald (2017b), seek to measure the rate of voter turnout at the state and national levels. To aggregate voter turnout rates by racial/ethnic group, though, additional tradeoffs must be made. First among these is the fact that most states do not provide information about the race/ethnicity of voters. In Chapter 5, I note that campaigns and academics have found a variety of solutions for overcoming this data issue. The most common method of confronting this problem is to rely on survey data with self-reported race/ethnicity, the approach taken in the rest of this chapter (Ramakrishnan 2005; Wong et al. 2011; Leighley and Nagler 2013; McDonald 2017c). A second issue concerns the population defined as being eligible to vote; surveys do not provide information about past felony convictions of respondents and are not meant to capture either the institutionalized or overseas citizen populations. However, McDonald and Popkin (2001) find that citizenship is by far the largest factor that delineates the voting-*eligible* population (VEP) from the voting-*age* population (VAP) over at least the last five decades. Combining citizenship status with information about age, we can thus approximate the VEP and construct a denominator similar to what has been used in previous studies of voter turnout at the social group level (Wolfinger and Rosenstone 1980; Leighley and Nagler 2013): the citizen voting-age population (CVAP).[36]

Debates about citizenship access may persist when discussing modern rates of political participation, but restricting the denominator to citizens only is absolutely critical when considering the historical record. As noted earlier in the chapter, the primary means of limiting minority access to the franchise was to restrict citizenship.[37] Furthermore, no academic

---

[36] Felon disenfranchisement disproportionately impacts African Americans, and in particular, African American men (Manza and Uggen 2008). This has a substantial impact on relative rates of voter turnout in recent elections (Wheaton 2013a). Chapters 5 and 7 discuss felon disenfranchisement in more detail, but as there is limited over-time data on felon disenfranchisement rates by race, this form of disenfranchisement is not addressed in this chapter.

[37] A careful reader will note that there was no blanket prohibition on non-citizen voting until the 1920s (Keyssar 2009). Until the 1920s, immigrants eligible for citizenship who filed their "first papers" (essentially documenting their decision to remain in the United States permanently) were able to vote in many states (Keyssar 2009: 337–338). Since all

study includes those ineligible due to age when calculating voter turnout rates, despite changes in the age requirement in the 1960s and 1970s. As discussed in depth in Chapter 3, the age structure of the African American and Latino population differs from that of Whites and Asian Americans, so it is critical to account for these differences when constructing the denominator. The estimates I produce rely on self-reported age and citizenship status to exclude those who are ineligible to vote on these two dimensions.

National

I first provide estimates of the rate of voter turnout in presidential elections. Figure 2.1 indicates the proportion of citizens who voted in each presidential election from 1948 to 2016, with one line for each of the four racial/ethnic groups I examine in this book. The ANES is used to report voter turnout from 1948 to 1972, and results using the CPS are provided for the period from 1964 to 2016. Overlap is shown between

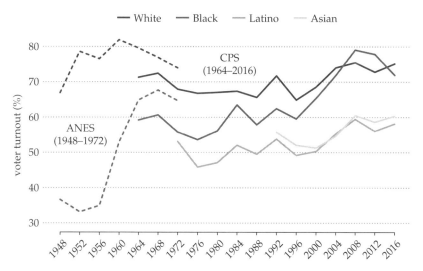

FIGURE 2.1 Voter turnout in presidential elections, 1948–2016
Note: Denominator is the CVAP for each racial/ethnic group. Missing data have been removed from the denominator when calculating turnout. ANES data indicated with a dashed line, CPS data with a solid line.

Asian immigrants and many Native Americans were ineligible for citizenship, they were also not eligible to vote as non-citizens. Today, a small number of communities allow non-citizens to vote in local elections. For a broader discussion of non-citizen voting, see Renshon (2009) and Hayduk (2006).

the ANES and CPS estimates for the 1964, 1968, and 1972 elections to give a clear picture of the comparability of trends in voter turnout; as found in previous work, the ANES estimates of turnout are somewhat higher than the CPS.

Looking at non-Hispanic Whites[38] first, we see that voter turnout has declined somewhat since the 1950s and 1960s, with White turnout reaching a high point of 82 percent in 1960 according to the ANES. From 1972 to 2000, White voter turnout stabilized at a rate between 65 percent and 69 percent of the eligible electorate with the exception of the particularly high turnout in the 1992 election. The three most recent elections, though, featured substantially higher White turnout, with 75 percent of Whites voting in 2008 according to the CPS.[39]

Turnout rates for African Americans are sharply lower for much of the period. Consistent with continuing *de facto* disenfranchisement of African Americans in the South, Black turnout was dramatically lower in the 1940s and 1950s, where only 33 percent of African Americans voted in the 1952 presidential election. By the early 1960s, however, Black turnout was markedly higher, as in the 1964 election where 59 percent of Black voting-age adults turned out to vote. Thus, prior to the VRA, African Americans had already made appreciable gains in participation at a national level. A slight increase in the first presidential election after the VRA was not sustained in the 1970s, and as with Whites, Black voter turnout fell with only 54 percent of African Americans voting in the 1976 election. Black turnout was higher in 1984 (63 percent), but similar to Whites, a dramatic increase in voter turnout was witnessed in the 2000s. As noted in the introduction to this chapter, the CPS indicates that Black turnout exceeded White turnout in the 2012 election; after removing non-respondents, Black turnout reached 79 percent in 2008 and 78 percent in 2012 before declining in 2016 to 72 percent.

Early versions of the CPS did not provide information about Latino or Asian American voters.[40] In Figure 2.1, Latino turnout is indicated

---

[38] The ANES estimates of White turnout from 1948 to 1966 and CPS estimates from 1964 to 1972 may include some Hispanic respondents. That said, efforts were made to identify and remove Hispanic respondents from estimates of White turnout by using place of birth and parents' place of birth.

[39] As noted previously, non-response rates have increased across all groups during this period. It is plausible that the increase in turnout in the 2000s is an artifact of missing data on non-voters. See Appendix A.2 for a discussion of why it is imperative to remove non-respondents when studying racial/ethnic differences in voter turnout over time.

[40] De la Garza and DeSipio (1993) indicate that Latino voting in Los Angeles and large cities in Texas in the 1960s was substantial, though only occasionally matching non-Latinos.

for the period from 1972 to 2016, and Asian American turnout is shown from 1990 to 2016. For both groups, we see that turnout was far lower than for Whites or African Americans. In the 1976 election, the first election after the VRA was extended to Latinos, just 46 percent of Latino citizens turned out to vote. The rate of turnout thus *did not* increase substantially with nominal inclusion in an amended VRA. Despite the growing size of the Latino population nationally, Latino turnout only hit 55 percent in the 2000s. Leighley and Nagler (2013) noticed this persistently low Latino turnout as well (35), and though Latino turnout increased in the 2000s as with other groups, it still lags behind Whites and African Americans by a large margin. Asian American turnout rates mirror that of Latinos, though here data is only available from the 1992 election onward. At 60 percent for the 2016 election, Asian American political participation has only increased slightly from the 56 percent figure recorded in 1992.

Voter turnout in midterm elections is considerably lower than in presidential years. Figure 2.2 indicates that large racial/ethnic differences in who votes also manifest in midterms. As the ANES time series only started quantifying midterm voting in 1958, we do not have the same ability to examine dramatic differences between Black and White participation prior to that time. That said, for the period in which we do

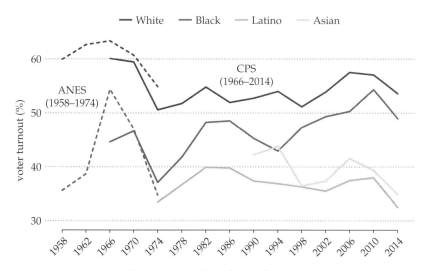

FIGURE 2.2 Voter turnout in midterm elections, 1958–2014
Note: Denominator is the CVAP for each racial/ethnic group. Missing data have been removed from the denominator when calculating turnout. ANES data indicated with a dashed line, CPS data with a solid line.

have data we see a pattern similar to presidential elections. White voter turnout was higher in the 1960s than today, reaching 60 percent or more in 1966. A sharp decline appears in the CPS and ANES data from 1970 to 1974, corresponding with the implementation of the 26th Amendment and extension of the franchise to all 18-year-olds (Wolfinger and Rosenstone 1980; McDonald and Popkin 2001). Turnout in midterms stabilized at 50 to 55 percent of eligible Whites by the 1970s, increasing in 2006 and 2010 before falling back to 54 percent in 2014. African American turnout shows a trend analogous to that of Whites, though with higher turnout in the 1966 election (according to ANES data) that may reflect a short-term effect of the VRA. Yet a much clearer increase in Black voter turnout is visible in the 2000s. In 2010, Black turnout came close to equaling White turnout, with 54 percent of African Americans and 57 percent of Whites stating that they voted. Throughout the period, though, White turnout was higher than Black turnout. Latino and Asian American turnout also lags Black and White turnout in midterms, but to an even greater degree than in presidential elections. Even after accounting for non-citizenship, in no midterm election have more than 45 percent of Asian Americans or 40 percent of Latinos voted. If anything, the trends here suggest that Latino and Asian American turnout may be *declining*: 2014 featured the lowest rates of Latino (33 percent) and Asian American (35 percent) voter turnout ever recorded in the CPS.

Regional

Are there regional differences in rates of voter turnout by race/ethnicity? Given the discussions in preceding sections of this chapter, it stands to reason that Black voter turnout was likely far lower in the South than in the non-South before the 1960s. Figure 2.3 breaks down the ANES and CPS data into southern[41] and non-southern states from 1952 to 2016. The first trend to note is that turnout is lower in the South, across groups. While rates of turnout have largely equalized between regions in recent

[41] In this chapter, the South is defined as the eleven states that composed the former Confederacy. However, the CPS did not provide information about state of residence until 1978, and instead used the Census definition of the South which includes the eleven states plus Oklahoma, Kentucky, West Virginia, Maryland, Delaware, and the District of Columbia. These states are a relatively small share of the total southern population, and for many analysts, these "border states" have at least some cultural and political similarity to neighboring southern states. Thus, while covering a different geographic area for 1964 to 1976, total rates of turnout by race/ethnicity are likely quite similar across the two definitions.

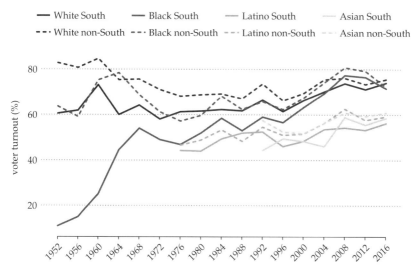

FIGURE 2.3 Voter turnout in presidential elections by region, 1952–2016
Note: Denominator is the CVAP for each racial/ethnic group. Missing data have been removed from the denominator when calculating turnout. ANES data used prior to 1964, CPS for turnout statistics from 1964 onwards.

years, turnout is still slightly higher in the non-South for Whites, African Americans, Latinos, and Asian Americans.

While White voter turnout in the non-South declined between 1952 and 1980, it remained 10 to 15 points higher than White turnout in the South. Since then, turnout rates between the regions have tracked together, with Southern Whites voting at a rate ever closer to their non-Southern counterparts. The situation for African Americans is somewhat different, but context is necessary in order to understand the relevance of regional differences for Black turnout. In the 1940s, 1.4 million African Americans left the South, more than doubling the number that left the South in the "First Great Migration" from 1910 to 1930. By 1950, the Black population in the non-South equaled that of the South. Another 1.1 million left during the 1950s, and by 1970, more than 30 percent of African American adults born in the South were living in the non-South (Gregory 2009). Thus, despite the small number of African Americans in the North historically, by the period addressed in Figure 2.3 African American involvement in the politics of the North (especially in cities) was a reality. Black voter turnout in the non-South was far higher than Black turnout in the South until the late 1960s, and given changes in the distribution of the population across regions, southern Black turnout was a bigger driver of overall Black turnout (Figure 2.1) earlier in the period. In 1952, only 11 percent of southern African Americans reported voting, versus 60 percent of Black adults in the non-South. Black participation for those remaining in the South grew substantially year over year, until falling into a pattern with regional differences similar to Whites. Black turnout in the non-South was far higher. In fact, the CPS reports 78 percent of African Americans in the non-South voted in 1964, versus 75 percent of Whites.[42] While it is possible that Black migrants to the North were already more likely to vote (Gregory 2009, but Acharya, Blackwell, and Sen 2018), the *de facto* disenfranchisement of African Americans likely had a more profound effect on reducing Black turnout in the South.

Using regional data, we can delve deeper into the impact of the Voting Rights Act of 1965 on African American turnout in the region targeted by the act. Black turnout did indeed increase in the 1968 election, the first presidential contest after VRA implementation. However, turnout was already on the rise for more than a decade before the VRA, suggesting the removal of *de facto* barriers may not be the sole factor explaining Black political empowerment *even in the South*. Many African Americans were able to overcome *de facto* racial restrictions on participation prior to the VRA, suggesting that the enduring legacy of the VRA is not found in its broader impact overall, but rather in its effectiveness against the most entrenched areas of electorally motivated anti-Black voter suppression. As these areas were exclusively in the South, Black turnout overall in the region would rise. Yet, VRA implementation cannot explain the sharp increase in both Northern and Southern Black voting after the 1990s.

Prior to the 1970s, disparities between regions were quite apparent for both Whites and African Americans. Evaluating Latino and Asian American turnout, which were only recorded by the CPS starting in the 1970s and 1990s respectively, we see more limited regional differences. Latino turnout in the South (almost exclusively Texas, and later, Florida) was slightly lower than turnout in the non-South. Regional differences in Asian American turnout show more variability, though the small size of the Asian American population in the South makes comparison somewhat difficult. By the late 1990s, regional variation in voting rates was minimal when comparing within any racial/ethnic group, and paled in comparison with the persistent between-group differences in turnout.

---

[42] The ANES also puts Black turnout as higher than White turnout in the non-South, at 85 percent and 83 percent, respectively.

Even when disaggregating by region, turnout now appears to be clustered into two pools, with Whites and African Americans at the top, and Latinos and Asian Americans at the bottom. Racial differences in turnout appear to have nationalized.

DEFINING AND VISUALIZING THE TURNOUT GAP

The evidence presented so far points to considerable racial/ethnic differences in who votes. These differences have changed over time for some groups, especially in response to the presence or absence of *de jure* racial barriers to voting. By the middle of the twentieth century, *de jure* barriers were removed, yet even after accounting for variation in age and citizenship across racial/ethnic groups, disparities in political participation persist today. It is these disparities that are the focus of this book, and what I label the *turnout gap*.

The turnout gap, as defined in this volume, is a relative measure of political participation that quantifies racial/ethnic differences in voter turnout. For instance, we may calculate the Black–White turnout gap as the difference between the turnout rate for African Americans and the turnout rate for non-Hispanic Whites.[43] The Latino–White turnout gap can be calculated in a similar fashion: the Latino turnout rate minus the White turnout rate. The turnout gap is calculated for a specific moment in time, or a specific election: as implied by the figures earlier in the chapter, the turnout gap between African Americans and Whites appears to have decreased in recent presidential election years. As it is a simple subtraction of rates of years turnout, the turnout gap may be generalized to differences between any two sets of politically relevant groups, or combinations of different groups (e.g., the Minority–White turnout gap discussed in Chapter 1).[44]

While a simple transformation of the turnout data presented earlier in the chapter, measuring racial/ethnic differences in participation through the turnout gap has a number of advantages. First, the turnout gap accounts for trends in turnout that are universal to all groups. For instance, voter turnout may have been higher nationwide prior to the

---

[43] Conceptualizing of the gap in this way may be contrasted with approaches that "control" for socioeconomic differences across groups (Leighley and Vedlitz 1999). But, as Sen and Wasow (2016) point out, such differences are post-treatment. See Chapter 3 in this text for a broader discussion of the role of socioeconomic differences in producing the turnout gap.

[44] For a formalization of the turnout gap, see Chapter 4.

1970s.[45] Comparing rates of voter turnout across racial/ethnic groups, we can determine the degree to which growing disparities between White and non-White turnout account for this pattern as well. Midterm turnout is also lower for all groups; a measure that examines relative rates of voter turnout allows us to remove the non-racial component of this variation. Second, the use of a relative rate of voting allows us to study differences in voter turnout when drawing on different sources of data. If, for instance, features of a survey cause all respondents to "over-report" their level of participation (Hur and Achen 2013; Jackman and Spahn 2016), then when comparing across different data sources we would want to use relative rates of voter turnout instead of the raw rates across surveys.[46] Finally, and most succinctly, to understand racial/ethnic differences in voter turnout we must scrutinize *the difference* in rates of turnout. When noting rates of participation for different groups, the discussion of historical trends and the explanations of Figures 2.1–2.3 contrasted turnout rates for different groups to each other. The placement of race and voting in historical context therefore necessitates the *comparison* of rates of voter turnout for each racial/ethnic group at the same moment in time.

An analysis of the causes and consequences of the turnout gap may be found in subsequent chapters. First, however, we can rescale the data presented in Figures 2.1–2.3 to construct the turnout gap for each non-White racial/ethnic group. Figure 2.4 uses the same data as in Figures 2.1 and 2.2, but presents African American, Latino, and Asian American voter turnout as the gap between each group and non-Hispanic Whites. The rate of turnout for non-Hispanic Whites is held constant, while Black, Latino, and Asian American turnout varies in comparison to that baseline rate. Thus, a value of zero in the figure indicates parity with White voter turnout for the year indicated on the *x*-axis. As the turnout rate is election-year specific, variation in turnout that is experienced by all groups is removed and the turnout gap for midterms can be displayed along with the gap for presidential elections.

In Figure 2.4, we see that the Black–White turnout gap has decreased over time, reaching a rough parity in recent elections. Prior to 1964,

---

[45] Though changes in the size of the non-citizen population could account for much of this difference (McDonald and Popkin 2001).

[46] There is mixed evidence of differential rates of over-reporting by racial/ethnic groups (Ansolabehere and Hersh 2012; McKee, Hood, and Hill 2012). See Chapter 5 for a discussion of turnout over-reporting.

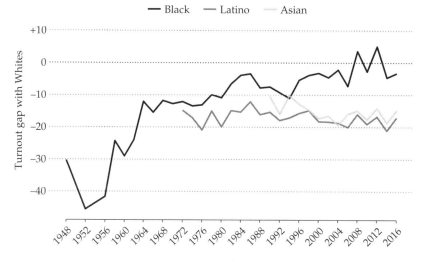

FIGURE 2.4 Turnout gap with Whites, 1948–2016
Note: Denominator is the CVAP for each racial/ethnic group. Missing data have been removed from the denominator when calculating turnout. ANES data used prior to 1964, CPS for turnout statistics from 1964 onwards. Turnout gap displayed as the difference between [non-Hispanic] White turnout and turnout for the racial/ethnic groups indicated in percentage points.

the disparity between Black and White turnout was over 20 percentage points, with the 1952 presidential election featuring a Black–White turnout gap of 45.5 percentage points according to the ANES.[47] Using the relevant rates of turnout as our metric, the VRA does not have a clear impact on the national level Black–White turnout gap, as it remained relatively stable at approximately 12 percentage points from the 1964 election through the 1970s before decreasing further to near parity with Whites in the 1984 presidential and 1986 midterm elections. After growth in the disparity between White and Black turnout in the 1988 through 1994 elections, largely due to a marked decline in Black turnout, the turnout gap again shrank in the 1990s before switching back and forth between a slight turnout advantage for Whites and a slight advantage for African Americans in the 2000s. While the diminution of the Black–White turnout gap does not follow a perfectly linear trend, it

---

[47] The Black–White turnout gap was smaller in 1948 mainly due to low White turnout, not high Black turnout.

does appear that the disparities found before the 1980s are a relic of the past.

The Latino–White and Asian–White turnout gaps have not decreased substantially since survey data was first available for these groups. According to the CPS, Latino turnout lagged 15 points or more behind White turnout in every election since 1990, exceeding the Black–White turnout gap in any year after passage of the VRA in 1965. In 2016, the Latino–White turnout gap was 17 percentage points, larger than the 15 percentage point gap in 1972. The trend in Asian American turnout, when rescaled relative to Whites, looks even worse. While the Asian–White turnout gap was only 10 percentage points in the 1990 and 1994 midterm elections, similar to the Black–White turnout gap, in 2004 the gap reached its maximum at 19 percentage points. Recall that turnout rates are calculated with non-citizens excluded from the denominator; the persistent and perhaps growing Latino–White and Asian–White turnout gaps appear after accounting for citizenship.

Figure 2.5 uses the data featured in Figure 2.3 to show regional trends in the turnout gap. Once again, here we clearly see a large separation between Black and White turnout rates in the South before the 1960s,

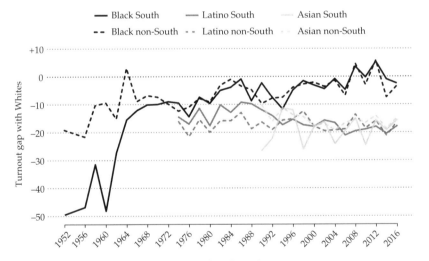

FIGURE 2.5 Turnout gap with Whites by region, 1952–2016
Note: Denominator is the CVAP for each racial/ethnic group. Missing data have been removed from the denominator when calculating turnout. ANES data used prior to 1964, CPS for turnout statistics from 1964 onwards. Turnout gap displayed as the difference between [non-Hispanic] White turnout and turnout for the racial/ethnic groups indicated in percentage points.

reaching 50 percentage points in the 1952 election. The Black–White turnout gap in the South largely caught up with the Black–White gap in the non-South by the mid 1960s, although the CPS reports that Black turnout was slightly higher than White turnout in the 1964 election outside of the Census-defined Southern states. Since then the Black–White turnout gaps in both regions have largely tracked together, again indicating that turnout differences between Whites and African Americans nationalized after passage of the VRA. Note, however, that gains in southern Black turnout relative to Whites *before 1965* dwarf gains *after* the VRA. The Latino–White turnout gap and Asian–White turnout gap do not present the same pattern. Relative to Whites, Latino turnout in the South outpaced Latino turnout in the non-South until the 2000s. Asian American voter turnout in the South shows more variation, perhaps a result of the small number of Asian Americans in the South. Yet, on the whole, regional differences cannot account for persistently low Latino and Asian American turnout relative to the non-Hispanic White or African American populations.

TURNOUT OF REGISTRANTS, CITIZENS, OR ADULTS?

The preceding analysis examined voter turnout as a share of the citizen voting-age population (CVAP), finding a persistent turnout gap between Whites and minority voters. However, this ignores an unusual feature of American elections: voter registration. Researchers seeking to compare turnout rates in the United States with other nations have struggled to account for voter registration, which is the responsibility of the government in most other countries (Lijphart 1997; Teixeira 1992). Nearly universal in the United States by 1940 (Keyssar 2009: 184), today North Dakota is the only state without a voter registration list. Evidence suggests that the introduction of voter registration depressed turnout a moderate amount (Ansolabehere and Konisky 2006). That said, even a brief glance at the history of voter registration indicates that it may not be a neutral measure. Systems of voter registration were developed in the 1800s as a tool to suppress voting by minority groups and immigrants (Keyssar 2009: 122–128). Furthermore, voter registration was implemented strategically in the South to remove voters prior to important elections, such as referenda on disenfranchising constitutions (Kousser 1974: 49). During the 1960s, the struggle for African American voting rights often centered on ensuring Black citizens could register to vote, with a strong emphasis on removing laws that reduced Black voter registration (Alt 1994). Voter registration must sometimes serve as a proxy for political participation, especially given that federal monitoring related to the VRA often focused on improving rates of voter registration (Davidson 1992; Walton, Puckett, and Deskins 2012a). But after the removal of *de jure* restrictions on voting, voter registration *purges* were often implemented to remove Black registrants immediately prior to an election (Walton, Puckett, and Deskins 2012b: ch. 23). Thus, the number of African Americans who voted *given that they were registered* could be quite high in the pre-VRA era despite *de facto* disenfranchisement. Given that barriers to registration were implemented with the clear purpose of limiting minority voting participation, this chapter's focus on historical trends in voting may help us to understand the intended effect of discriminatory laws more clearly than a focus on registration rates alone.

Even today, voter registration is not as uniform a process as it appears to be. Well into the 1990s, there was substantial variation in the procedures states used to register voters (Keyssar 2009: 253). Reforms such as the National Voter Registration Act of 1993 helped to standardize systems across states, but states continue to differ in the availability of online voter registration and "automatic" voter registration, where state governments register eligible voters through drivers' license records. Some states allow same-day or election-day registration, effectively removing voter registration as a barrier to participation (GAO 2016).[48] States also vary in the rate at which they maintain or "clean" their voter registration databases (Ansolabehere and Hersh 2014). State-by-state differences in voter registration systems make it particularly difficult to compare rates of registration across groups, but perhaps more importantly, individuals may not accurately understand whether they are registered to vote at any given point in time. Self-reported data on voter registration status, therefore, is likely even less reliable than self-reported voting.

At the other end of the spectrum, the analysis restricts the denominator to exclude non-citizens. What are the implications of this decision? As mentioned above, Teixeira (1992) and others argue that citizenship is a minimal factor in explaining changes in voter turnout over time, and thus it is not necessary to remove non-citizens (but McDonald and Popkin 2001). Yet, there may be other reasons to include non-citizens when studying turnout. For instance, non-citizens may have distinct political preferences from the rest of the electorate, such that the removal of non-citizens understates the degree of political inequality we see in

---

[48] Chapter 7 addresses the potential effect of such measures on the turnout gap.

contemporary American elections (McCarty, Poole, and Rosenthal 2006: ch. 4). Chapter 1 of this book indeed shows that the Minority–White turnout gap has grown at a much faster rate when including non-citizen adults in the denominator. Hayduk (2006) goes even further in suggesting that representational equality can only be achieved if non-citizens are granted the franchise. Such a perspective is important to acknowledge when calculating Latino and Asian American turnout; many Latinos and about half of Asian Americans are non-citizens. The subject of this analysis, and broader book, is thus the political inequality that *remains* after "removing" inequality due to non-citizenship. The consequences of, and potential solutions for the turnout gap as conceptualized here may not address the more thorny political issue of non-citizen voting (Renshon 2009), but may be seen as a first step toward addressing the broader set of inequities present in contemporary American elections.

FROM BARRIERS TO BALLOTS

Examining the trajectory of minority political participation, the initial tendency may be to focus on the history of limited non-White voting due to both *de jure* and *de facto* barriers. Yet, *de jure* access to the franchise seems to be the more critical element to understanding African American and other groups' political empowerment. During Reconstruction, the newly enfranchised Freedmen and Southern Whites turned out to vote at a similar rate, despite intimidation and *de facto* barriers. Continued *de facto* disenfranchisement was not enough to stop these gains, but the return of *de jure* limitations in the late 1800s was, such that Black turnout was minimal through the 1940s. Attempts to exclude Latinos and Asian Americans centered on qualifications for citizenship, leading to only partial involvement for Latinos through political machines and the nearly wholesale exclusion of Asians from the eligible electorate. Again, *de jure* barriers were key. Survey data on voter turnout from the 1940s to today indicate appreciable gains in Black voter turnout in the 1950s and early 1960s even before the VRA, though the act was instrumental in ensuring Black participation in the South. According to survey data, African American turnout and White turnout reached near parity in the 2000s. Latino and Asian American turnout, however, continues to demonstrate a substantial gap with non-Hispanic Whites.

The goal of this book is to understand why there are racial/ethnic differences in voter turnout. With this focus, the preceding chapter clarified the source of and evidence for these disparities, challenging understandings that prioritize legal restrictions on participation in two key ways. First, African Americans were able to overcome significant impediments to voting in contexts where *de jure* Black voting rights were secure but *de facto* barriers were far more severe than they are today. Second, despite the removal of most, if not all, barriers to minority voting by the mid 1970s through the VRA and other measures, the Latino–White and Asian–White turnout gap remains large and the Black–White turnout gap has closed only recently. What explains the turnout gap if not the presence or absence of institutional impediments to voting? In the next chapter I turn to another commonly cited explanation for the turnout gap: sociodemographic differences between minority citizens and the White population.

3

Are Sociodemographic Factors the Answer?

Disparities in who votes are just one of many longstanding racial/ethnic inequalities in the United States. According to the 2010 Current Population Survey (CPS), 14.8 percent of citizen voting-age Whites had a household income of $20,000 or less, versus 31 percent of African Americans and 22.7 percent of Latinos. At the upper end of the income spectrum, 34.7 percent of Whites had a family income over $90,000, compared with 20.2 percent of citizen Latinos and only 16.5 percent of African Americans. Gaps in educational attainment are also striking, with 31.5 percent of Whites over 25 years old holding a college degree in 2010, versus 18 percent of African Americans and 15.9 percent of Latinos. While there were notable gains in African American income and education attainment between the 1940s and 1960s, even relative to Whites, the reduction of Black–White gaps in socioeconomic status slowed by the mid 1970s (Waters and Eschbach 1995; Klinkner and Smith 1999: 320–321), and along with growing disparities between Latinos and Whites, overall Minority–White disparities in income and education are now wider than they were forty years ago (Pew Research Center 2016). Furthermore, the African American and Latino citizen population is significantly younger than the White population, with 73.3 percent of voting eligible Whites being older than 35, versus 65.3 percent of African Americans and 58.6 percent of Latinos.

In the previous chapter, I found that the removal of *de facto* barriers to minority political participation did not eliminate the Minority–White turnout gap. The rest of the book focuses on voter turnout in a world where *de facto* disenfranchisement is largely absent, but the turnout gap remains. Might these socioeconomic and age differences explain persistent racial/ethnic disparities in voter turnout?

In this chapter, I evaluate the extent to which the turnout gap is attributable to three sociodemographic factors: *income, education,* and *age*. We have good reason to believe that these resources are associated with voter turnout, as in the words of Ramakrishnan (2005), "[t]he likelihood of voting increases among those who are older, wealthier and more educated. These findings have constituted the bedrock of studies of voting participation since the 1960s" (41). Leighley and Nagler (2013) corroborate this viewpoint, stating "[i]t would be impossible to find a study of voter turnout in presidential elections where demographic characteristics are not central to the enterprise" (54). Verba et al. (1993) go so far as to claim that the "source of differences in political activity among Latinos, African-Americans, and Anglo-Whites [is] disparities in their politically relevant resources" (494).[1]

That said, traditional socioeconomic characteristics have a mixed track record in predicting African American, Latino, and Asian American turnout at the individual level (Verba and Nie 1972; Leighley 1995; Leighley and Vedlitz 1999; Leighley and Nagler 2013). Authors also note that socioeconomic differences do not seem to predict persistently low turnout for Asians relative to Whites (Conover 1984; Lien 1994; Shaw, de la Garza, and Lee 2000; Jang 2009; Anoll 2015). Asian American citizens have higher incomes (43.8 percent with incomes exceeding $90,000), higher levels of educational attainment (47.6 percent holding a college degree), and have an age profile *even among citizens* that is similar to Whites (71.7 percent of adult citizens are over 35 years old) as of 2010. Given the prominence of socioeconomic models in understanding voter turnout, it is worth reexamining the evidence regarding sociodemographics and voter turnout disparities.

The chapter begins by describing group-level trends in voter turnout by levels of income, educational attainment, and age over time. As in Chapter 2, I rely on the CPS Voting and Registration Supplement to measure rates of voter turnout for each racial/ethnic group. The analyses in this chapter demonstrate that the relationship between these sociodemographic factors and participation is not linear *even when examining a single group over time*, to say nothing of comparing across groups. I then produce adjusted turnout rates for the period from 1976 to 2016, seeking to understand whether differences in the demographic composition of the

---

[1] Though it is important to note that religion, civic involvement, and language ability are included in the analysis that allows Verba et al. (1993) to reach this conclusion. See Jones-Correa and Leal (2001) for a discussion of the relationship between religion, civic involvement, and racial/ethnic differences in voter turnout.

White, African American, Latino, or Asian American populations can explain dynamics of the turnout gap. While there is indeed some evidence that the turnout gap would be smaller if the income, education, or age structure of minority populations was similar to that of Whites, the aforementioned nonlinearities indicate that the majority of the turnout gap and changes in the turnout gap over time cannot be explained by sociodemographic factors.

INCOME AND TURNOUT

Income has long been viewed as a key component of socioeconomic status-driven models of participation (Verba and Nie 1972; Wolfinger and Rosenstone 1980; Verba, Schlozman, and Brady 1995). Leighley and Nagler (2013) go even further, stating that "income is the most meaningful available measure of socioeconomic status to use in studies of turnout" (24). Figure 3.1 visualizes the relationship between income and voter turnout for non-Hispanic Whites, African Americans, Latinos, and Asian Americans.[2] Household income has been binned into four categories, using constant 2016 dollars: less than $20,000, $20,000–$55,000, $55,000 – $90,000, and a category for individuals in households with an income over $90,000.[3] Note that the median household income in the United States was approximately $55,000 in 2016; the first two bins indicate income below the median while the second set are above the median. Leveraging the large sample size of the CPS, the datapoints used to construct each line are the mean level of voter turnout witnessed in each presidential election for individuals in the indicated racial/ethnic group, excluding non-citizens and those under 18.

Each panel of Figure 3.1 suggests that individuals with higher incomes are more likely to vote, regardless of race/ethnicity. This is true across years, though there are notable shifts in the income–turnout relationship for some racial/ethnic groups.[4] For Whites, who form the base of most analyses of voter turnout, the relationship between income and participation has not shifted a large amount from the 1970s to today. A 30-point turnout disparity persists between those in the lowest income

---

[2] In this chapter, Black and Asian respondents who also identify as Hispanic are only included in totals for Latinos. This differs from CPS practice (and thus the figures presented in Chapter 2), but ensures that racial/ethnic categories are clearly delineated. See Appendix A.1 for more information.

[3] Individuals who left the income question blank are excluded from this portion of the analysis.

[4] Note that for ease of presentation, Figure 3.1 and subsequent figures documenting raw turnout rates exclude midterm elections.

FIGURE 3.1 Turnout in presidential elections, by race/ethnicity and household income
Note: Data from the CPS Voting and Registration Supplement. Individuals in households that did not take the Voting and Registration supplement have been removed from the denominator when calculating turnout, along with noncitizens and individuals under 18. Income adjusted to constant 2016 dollars.

category and those in the highest income category. A similar gap was present for African Americans in the 1976 election. However, as Black turnout rose in the 2000s, we see that gains were disproportionately among African Americans with lower household incomes. In 2008, for instance, the difference between the lowest income Black citizens and highest income Black citizens was less than 20 percentage points. A similar narrowing has taken place for Latinos, though turnout overall is lower for this group. For instance, in 2012 turnout for Latino citizens in households making over $90,000 was roughly equivalent to African Americans making less than $20,000. Asian Americans, while

only indicated in the CPS from 1992 onward, show a less strong relationship between income and turnout as compared to any other racial/ethnic
group, driven by equal rates of voting for Asians in the lowest two income
brackets.

Figure 3.2 depends on the same statistics as Figure 3.1, but rescales the
data for African Americans, Latinos, and Asian Americans to indicate the
turnout gap between Whites and each of these groups at every level of
income. Such a visualization facilitates our interpretation of how each
ethnic group's turnout compares to similarly resourced Whites over time.
The first panel of Figure 3.2 demonstrates that the turnout gap between
African Americans and Whites has closed for all income groups. In fact,
in the 2000 election there was essentially no difference between Black
and White turnout at each level of income. Since that time low income
African Americans have made substantial gains over low-income Whites
in rates of participation, while on average the highest-income African
Americans and Whites continue to show roughly equal turnout rates.
The second panel of Figure 3.2, displaying the Latino turnout gap by
levels of income, tells a different story: Latino turnout has decreased
relative to White turnout since the 1980s for every income category,
except those with incomes under $20,000. While the gap between Latino
turnout and White turnout for lower-middle to high-income Latinos was
roughly 15 percentage points in 2016, the gap in the lowest-income category was only 6 percentage points. A similar, though more dramatic story
appears for Asian Americans. While low-income Asian American turnout
is significantly worse than that of Whites in midterm elections, in recent
presidential elections Asian Americans making less than $20,000 have
much more comparable rates of turnout with Whites. For Asian Americans with higher incomes, the turnout gap with Whites has expanded
since the early 1990s.

EDUCATION AND TURNOUT

Education is also understood to be a crucial socioeconomic determinant
of participation, with Wolfinger and Rosenstone (1980) noting that the
independent effect of education is generally stronger than income. Figure
3.3 visualizes the relationship between educational attainment and voter
turnout for Whites, African Americans, Latinos, and Asian Americans.
Educational attainment has also been binned into four non-overlapping
categories, based on the highest level completed by each individual: did
not complete high school, high school diploma (or equivalent), some

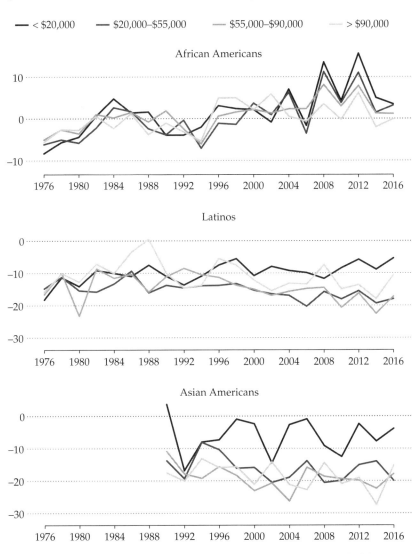

FIGURE 3.2 Turnout gap with Whites, by race/ethnicity and household income
Note: Data from the CPS Voting and Registration Supplement. Individuals in households that did not take the Voting and Registration supplement have been removed from the denominator when calculating turnout, along with noncitizens and individuals under 18. Y-axis indicates the difference between [non-Hispanic] White turnout and turnout for the group indicated in percentage points. Income adjusted to constant 2016 dollars.

college attendance (including those currently enrolled in college) or an associate degree, and a category for individuals who graduated college with a bachelor's degree or similar accreditation.[5] Again the data used to construct each line consists of the mean level of voter turnout witnessed in each presidential election for individuals in the indicated racial/ethnic group, excluding non-citizens and those under 18.[6]

Figure 3.3 again suggests that those with more resources turn out at higher rates across racial/ethnic groups and over time. Yet the turnout–education relationship has changed for Whites, where there has been a considerable decline in turnout for those without a high school education. In fact, a 50 percentage point disparity has opened up between Whites with a college degree and those who did not finish high school. As with income, the gap between African Americans with fewer years of formal education and those with a college degree narrowed in the early 2000s, driven by increases in participation for those with lower levels of education. One interesting trend to note is that those who have finished high school, but do not have a four-year college degree once showed rates of turnout similar to co-ethnics who did not finish high school. Their rates of participation have become more similar to college-educated African Americans over time, though the 2016 election saw a larger decline in turnout for African Americans with low levels of educational attainment. A wide split in participation by educational attainment persists for Latinos, but again, rates of turnout for the highest attainment category still lag 10 percentage points behind White and Black college graduates. Asian Americans again show a somewhat less consistent relationship between resources and turnout than Whites, African Americans, and Latinos, though a decline in turnout for less educated Asian Americans in the 2016 election produces patterns of turnout by education mirroring other groups. Turnout for college-educated Asian Americans lags 10 points behind Latino citizens and 20 percentage points behind African Americans and Whites.

---

[5] Note that this method of grouping differs from Leighley and Nagler (2013) in that it does not measure educational attainment as a relative category as compared to others in a given election year. Instead, the actual level of education completed serves as the grouping. Individuals who left the educational attainment question blank are excluded from this portion of the analysis.

[6] Many analyses of education and turnout exclude individuals under 25, on the assumption that they may not have completed their schooling before that time. For consistency with the other analyses, I do not remove these individuals.

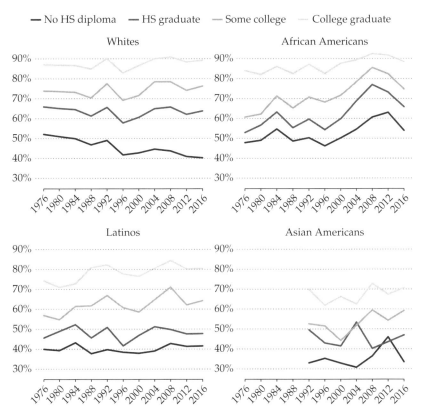

FIGURE 3.3 Turnout in presidential elections, by race/ethnicity and educational attainment
Note: Data from the CPS Voting and Registration Supplement. Individuals in households that did not take the Voting and Registration supplement have been removed from the denominator when calculating turnout, along with noncitizens and individuals under 18.

By the 2010s, turnout by African Americans, Latinos, or Asian Americans without a high school diploma equaled or exceeded that of Whites. Figure 3.4 documents that, over time, African American turnout at nearly every level of education has come to exceed that of Whites, with initial diminution of the gap for the least educated African Americans later met with increases by the middle categories. However, the Black–White difference in turnout for those completing college is minimal and does not manifest on a consistent basis after the early 1980s. Latino turnout trends appear similar to African Americans, but shifted downward 10–15 percentage points. Again, low education Latinos "outperform,"

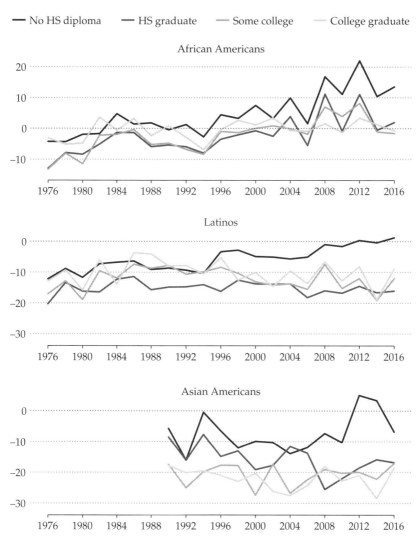

FIGURE 3.4 Turnout gap with Whites, by race/ethnicity and educational attainment

Note: Data from the CPS Voting and Registration Supplement. Individuals in households that did not take the Voting and Registration supplement have been removed from the denominator when calculating turnout, along with noncitizens and individuals under 18. Y-axis indicates the difference between [non-Hispanic] White turnout and turnout for the group indicated in percentage points.

with participation rates far closer to Whites with the same level of attainment than Latinos with higher levels of education. Strikingly, Asian American turnout also displays the same tendency in the last panel of Figure 3.4.

AGE AND TURNOUT

Age joins income and education as a common variable used to predict individual voter turnout, as younger citizens are less likely to vote even after accounting for income and education (Wolfinger and Rosenstone 1980; Rosenstone and Hansen 1993; Leighley and Nagler 2013). Figure 3.5 indicates patterns of participation by age for each racial/ethnic group in the study. Like the socioeconomic characteristics, age is binned into four groups: 18–24, 25–34, 35–54, and 55–80.[7] When binning age in this manner clear differences emerge between the age categories, despite the fact that the first two bins cover only sixteen years.

Figure 3.5 again demonstrates a robust relationship between age and voter turnout for Whites, African Americans, Latinos, and Asian Americans. However, most of the variation manifests when comparing individuals who are in their mid thirties or older to those in their teens or twenties. Older Whites have become slightly more likely to turn out over time, but otherwise a similar relationship exists between age and voter turnout as was witnessed in the 1970s. African Americans, on the other hand, show across-the-board increases in turnout, with the largest gains among younger African Americans from 2000 onward. Similar to Whites, older Black citizens are not considerably more likely to vote than the middle aged. Latino turnout does not show as much variation over time, with the important exception of 18–24-year-old Latinos who increased their turnout by approximately 16 percentage points over the course of the 2000s. Asian American turnout shows a more compressed arrangement of participation by age, where younger Asian Americans have gained ground on their older co-ethnics.

When rescaling turnout as the gap with Whites, as in Figure 3.6, we see that the inclusion of midterm elections produces more obvious variation in the turnout gap, especially for Latinos. Yet the overall pattern

---

[7] All individuals in the CPS indicate their age. Individuals 81 years of age or older have been removed from the analysis in this chapter, for two reasons: First, the over-80 population is skewed heavily White due to the historical racial/ethnic distribution in the United States and differential life expectancy. Second, a drop off in turnout occurs for individuals in their eighties and beyond, presumably due to disability. Thus to ensure that the 55 and older population is roughly comparable across groups, I limit the analysis to those between the ages of 18 and 80.

FIGURE 3.5 Turnout in presidential elections, by race/ethnicity and age
Note: Data from the CPS Voting and Registration Supplement. Individuals in households that did not take the Voting and Registration supplement have been removed from the denominator when calculating turnout, along with noncitizens and individuals under 18.

suggests that the turnout gap is smaller for young African Americans, Latinos, and Asian Americans than for older minority citizens, especially in recent elections. Note that neither Figure 3.5 nor 3.6 provides compelling evidence that certain cohorts are more likely to vote than others, as changes in turnout have either been relatively consistent across most age groups over time (African Americans), or not present at all (Whites and Latinos).

ADJUSTING TURNOUT FOR DEMOGRAPHIC DIFFERENCES

Many authors have suggested that racial/ethnic differences in socioeconomic status or age could explain a significant portion of the

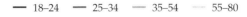

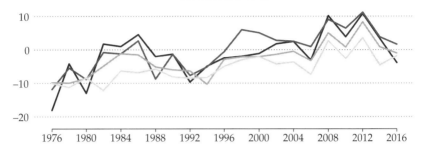

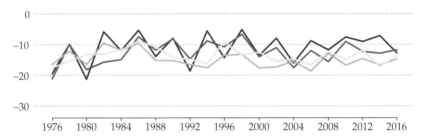

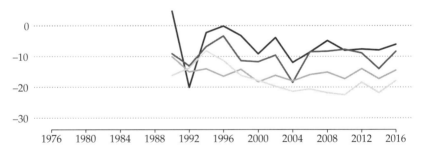

FIGURE 3.6 Turnout gap with Whites, by race/ethnicity and age
Note: Data from the CPS Voting and Registration Supplement. Individuals in households that did not take the Voting and Registration supplement have been removed from the denominator when calculating turnout, along with noncitizens and individuals under 18. Y-axis indicates the difference between [non-Hispanic] White turnout and turnout for the group indicated in percentage points.

Minority–White turnout gap (Matthews and Prothro 1963; Teixeira 1992; Verba et al. 1993; Leighley and Nagler 2013). As noted at the start of this chapter, there continue to be substantial differences in income, education, and age structure across racial/ethnic groups. Latinos and African Americans are, on average, lower income, lower education, and younger than Whites and Asian Americans. Thus, despite rising (inflation-adjusted) incomes, educational attainment, and median age among citizens of all racial/ethnic groups since 1980, these sociode-mographic differences continue to be linked to race and therefore may depress turnout for Black and Latino citizens.

However, Figures 3.1 through 3.6 showed that the relationship between sociodemographic traits and voter turnout is not linear and has shifted over time. These phenomena are most apparent for non-Whites, especially in recent elections. Lower-income, lower-education, and younger minorities significantly "outperform" their higher income, higher education, and older co-ethnic counterparts as compared to Whites. As a result, a standard linear regression model predicting voter turnout with racial/ethnic control variables would misstate the impact of these factors on racial/ethnic differences in participation, as it would assume the relationship between income, education, or age and voter turnout for minority groups is the same as it is for Whites. A fully inter-active model would deal with the possibility of differential impacts of socioeconomic status on minority groups (Anoll 2015), yet even if we examine a single group in isolation we see nonlinearities in the effect of income, education, or age. Such deviations will not be fully accounted for with common parametric techniques.

The alternative approach I pursue does not rely on assumptions about the functional form of the sociodemographics–turnout relationship for different groups. Instead of using regression modeling, I rely on the large number of respondents to the CPS survey in any given year and reweight the sample such that the proportion in each income, education, or age grouping is equivalent to the non-Hispanic White population.[8] Note that the rate of turnout within each income, education, or age group is not changed in any way; only the number of people in said groups. Putting aside for the moment the fact that income and education are, at least in part, determined by one's racial/ethnic background (Sen and Wasow 2016), these adjusted turnout rates serve as a counterfactual

---

[8] Such a procedure is similar to the nonparametric adjustments to Hispanic voter registration conducted by Morrison (2014).

where we ask what minority turnout would look like if we equalized these sociodemographic variables with Whites.[9]

Figure 3.7 displays the unadjusted turnout gap between Black, Latino, and Asian citizens with Whites, and the adjusted turnout gap after reweighting the Black, Latino, or Asian population within each year to have the same income, education, or age structure as Whites. Leighley and Nagler (2013) note that "Blacks vote less than whites, but the multivariate analysis shows that all of this difference can be accounted for by the other demographic characteristics of blacks as compared to whites" (80). The upper panel of Figure 3.7 does indeed confirm that, in most of the years studied by Leighley and Nagler (2013), Black turnout is approximately equal to Whites after accounting for the income or education distribution differences noted above. Yet this ignores the fact that low-income and low educational attainment African Americans significantly outperform demographically similar Whites. There are considerable Black–White disparities in resources, and a clear correlation between said resources and rates of participation for Black citizens. Yet, Chapter 3 indicated the Black–White turnout gap has largely closed since the 1990s, an improvement that does not coincide with stagnation in socioeconomic disparities between African Americans and Whites. The diminution, and according to the CPS, reversal of the Black–White turnout gap cannot be explained by changes in the demographics of the Black or White populations.

Income, education, and age have been found to be important correlates of Latino turnout (Uhlaner, Cain, and Kiewiet 1989; Logan, Oh, and Darrah 2009), and though the effects of socioeconomic status on turnout may be relegated to U.S.-born Latinos (Garcia-Rios and Barreto 2016; Leighley and Nagler 2016), age seems to be a critical factor

---

[9] Note that in each case, I do not present the intersection of the categories for each group, for two reasons. First, and as Verba and Nie (1972: 133) indicate, there is likely to be an intervening variable producing the relationship between political participation and income, education, and age. It is beyond the scope of this chapter to sort the causal mechanisms producing the turnout–sociodemographics relationship, though the theory advanced in Chapter 4 and the rest of the book suggest mobilization and empowerment to be key factors. Second, despite the large number of observations the frequencies in some cells for some groups are in the single digits. For example, few respondents are simultaneously young, have low levels of education, and have high incomes, rendering the adjusted turnout rates less reliable than when varying each trait in isolation. For each group, adjusting the turnout gap with the intersection of all variables does not produce a diminution of the turnout gap with Whites greater than the maximum reduction indicated in Figure 3.7.

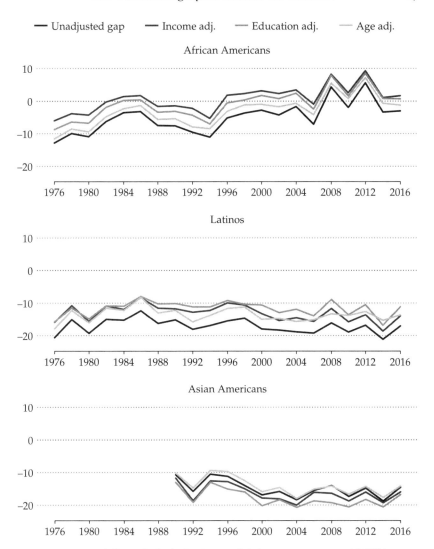

FIGURE 3.7 Adjusted Black, Latino, and Asian turnout gap with Whites
Note: Data from the CPS Voting and Registration Supplement. Individuals in households that did not take the Voting and Registration supplement have been removed from the denominator when calculating turnout, along with non-citizens and individuals under 18. Y-axis indicates the difference between [non-Hispanic] White turnout and turnout for African Americans, Latinos, and Asian Americans in percentage points when not equalizing for any demographic characteristics, or when equalizing income, education, and age.

driving lower Latino political participation (Arvizu and Garcia 1996; Morrison 2014). Adjusting Latino turnout to compensate for income, educational attainment, and age demonstrates the impact of these variables on the Latino–White turnout gap over time. In the second panel of Figure 3.7, we see evidence that about one-third to one-half of the disparity between Latino and White turnout across elections can be attributed to education or, more recently, differences in the age structure of the Latino population. But, a clear Latino–White turnout gap remains even if sociodemographic characteristics of Latinos and Whites were equalized.

While sociodemographic resources may correlate with participation for Asian Americans at the individual level (Wong et al. 2011: 27), lower Asian American voting participation *in the aggregate* is generally understood to be explained by factors outside of these demographic traits (Uhlaner, Cain, and Kiewiet 1989; Aoki and Nakanishi 2001). The third panel of Figure 3.7 examines Asian American turnout. Unlike for other minority groups, adjusting for demographic traits does not produce a diminution of the turnout gap. In fact, the Asian–White turnout gap would widen when reweighting the Asian American population to have income and education levels similar to non-Hispanic Whites. As others have noted, Asian Americans underperform in voting rates given their resource levels. In 2008, the gap between White turnout and Asian American turnout would have been five percentage points *greater* if not for Asian Americans' relatively high levels of education. Interestingly, adjusting for age does not produce the same turnout gap exacerbating effect. Keep in mind that Asian American citizens are, on average, older than Whites, and that older Asian Americans turn out more than younger Asian Americans, as with other groups. However, the fact that older Asian Americans lag so far behind older Whites in participation means that when reducing the share of the Asian American population that is 55 to 80 years old turnout increases overall.

BEYOND SOCIODEMOGRAPHICS

The goal of this chapter was to determine whether sociodemographic factors can account for the gaps we see in turnout between Whites, African Americans, Latinos, and Asian Americans. To summarize, income, education, and age do not explain the entirety of persistent gaps in voter turnout between Whites and minority groups, either in contemporary elections or the historical change in the gap over time. Despite substantial socioeconomic and age differences between minorities and Whites, and a clear correlation between these factors and voter turnout across groups, sociodemographics do not explain the turnout gap mainly because the relationship between these traits and turnout is weaker for minority groups than it is for Whites. Dissimilarities in the relationship between sociodemographics and turnout by race/ethnicity have become especially pronounced in the post-2000 period. While younger, lower-income, and less-educated Whites turn out *less* than they did prior to 2000, low-SES minority citizens have become *more* likely to turn out than they were previously. In addition, older, wealthier, and highly educated Latinos, Asian Americans, and even African Americans do not turn out more than their White counterparts. Given that the distribution of these sociodemographic factors by race has not changed significantly over the past forty years, it is clear that income, education, and age are not especially useful for understanding the dynamics of the turnout gap over time.

Two caveats should be acknowledged before accepting this conclusion: first, and as noted above, socioeconomic status may be seen as a *post-treatment* characteristic of individuals, in that income and education are, at least in part, a product of the life circumstances an individual finds herself in *as a result of her race* (Sen and Wasow 2016). Therefore, rebalancing the distribution of these socioeconomic variables within a racial/ethnic group is not equivalent to "controlling for" racial differences. Previous scholarship seeking to understand the applicability of socioeconomic status-based models of participation for minority groups has also recognized this reality (Anoll 2015). Yet extending the argument further, one could also assert that the differential *effects* of each of these variables by race are post-treatment, perhaps even including age.[10] For instance, young Latinos may have a smaller turnout gap with young Whites that would not exist if not for the fact that young Latinos make up such a large portion of the Latino population. Efforts to equalize on the basis of this variable (even keeping rates of turnout constant within each group) are not representative of a counterfactual where the population distribution was different. Such a claim would only further the idea that we should not attribute the turnout gap to demographic variables, and may buttress a more fundamental critique of demographics-based explanations of persistent disparities in participation (Walton 1985: 11–12).

---

[10] Age is not a post-treatment characteristic when considering differences across racial/ethnic groups, as it is also "assigned" at birth. However, the differential effect of this variable could be something that exists only because of an individual's race/ethnicity.

Second, if we examine a single election in isolation, it would be correct to say that demographic differences across racial/ethnic groups predict disparities in voter turnout. Nearly half of the Latino-White turnout gap in 2008 disappears when equalizing differences in educational attainment, and changes in the age structure for Latinos does explain much of the recent decline in Latino turnout relative to Whites.[11] In other words, if we believe the expansive literature suggesting SES is associated with turnout, and we acknowledge SES to be differentially distributed by race/ethnicity, it *must* be true that the relationships between race and turnout would be different if we varied the distribution of these sociodemographic factors. Keep in mind, though, that African American turnout would be even higher than Whites if not for their socioeconomic status, and Asian American turnout has declined relative to Whites despite any changes in the demographic composition of the population. In fact, if not for their relatively high levels of education and income, Asian turnout would have lagged even further behind Whites in recent elections according to the SES-focused model. Gains in turnout for low income, younger, and less-educated Asian Americans have been offset by (raw) stability and (relative) declines in turnout among older, higher-income, and more educated Asian citizens.

More generally, the fact that we witness relatively high turnout for some groups with lower socioeconomic status, but low turnout for other groups with high socioeconomic status, may indicate that our understanding of the resource–participation relationship is incomplete. While traits such as income, education, and age may allow individuals to more easily bear the "costs" of voting, these traits may not modify the desire to bear such costs. All else equal, we indeed witness a broad pattern where older, wealthier, and better-educated individuals from each group are more likely to vote. However, the substantial cross-group variation in the net effect of a given level of resources on turnout suggests either a differential willingness to take on such costs, or the presence of intervening factors outside of the domain of sociodemographic traits.

Some of the earliest analyses of political behavior asserted that higher socioeconomic status is correlated with increased rates of voter turnout, both in the United States and abroad (Connelly and Field 1944; Gosnell 1948; Lane 1959: 47; Lipset 1960: 184). Such a relationship does exist,

---

[11] Though the relationship between age, generational status, and growth of U.S.-born population over time should give pause to those asserting that the distinctiveness of the age structure for Latinos is not fundamental to the Latino political experience in America.

but sociodemographics-driven turnout differences are perhaps less useful for understanding disparities in minority turnout than assumed by even the most careful researchers. Combined with findings from Chapter 2, we are left with the conclusion that neither the removal of institutional barriers nor a simple story about limited sociodemographic resources can explain the turnout gap. Instead, we must reevaluate our existing understandings of why we vote, seeking a new framework that can account for the variation in turnout that we witness.

4

Electoral Influence and the Turnout Gap

If a discipline can be understood by the publications that stem from it, then the study of voter turnout clearly occupies a special place in American political science. Works now forming the canon of American political behavior addressed the question of "who votes," including Downs (1957), Campbell et al. (1960), Wolfinger and Rosenstone (1980), and Verba, Schlozman, and Brady (1995). The earliest birth pangs of behavioralism also focused on who chooses to participate, as in *Non-Voting: Causes and Methods of Control* (1924), where Charles Merriam and Harold Gosnell open their inquiry by stating that they seek to "ascertain the situations under which the franchise is not exercised by those who possess it" (1). Yet, the study of race and voting participation has an even earlier heritage. The first issue of the *American Political Science Review* featured five articles, two of which evaluated African American access to the ballot in the wake of *de jure* disenfranchisement in the South (Rose 1906; Stephenson 1906).[1] The institutional sources and consequences of racial restrictions on political access continued to feature prominently in discussions of southern politics (Lewinson 1932; Key 1949), and though race has not always been the central part of the broader discipline's understanding of politics (Walton, Miller, and McCormick II 1995; Hutchings and Valentino 2004; McClerking and Block Jr. 2016), the historical study of American voter participation requires careful attention to racial disparities in who votes (Keyssar 2009).

While sharing a critical place in the earliest works of political science, more careful scrutiny of the above literatures reveals a disconnect with implications for understanding voter turnout in an increasingly diverse

---

[1] *Political Science Quarterly*, an even older journal, published "The History of Negro Suffrage in the South" by Stephen B. Weeks in 1894.

United States. The individual decision to vote is fundamental to the non-race-focused work on political behavior, while the focus on institutional and socioeconomic barriers in studies of race and elections yields a very different starting point for determining why racial and ethnic minority groups participate in politics. Do minority citizens not experience individual-level psychological processes in the turnout decision? Can frameworks drawn from the study of minority turnout be applied to Whites? Our understanding of the turnout gap is, at the very least, hampered by the gap between these literatures. An integrated approach may offer new insights.

In this chapter I attempt to reconcile the important understandings derived from these literatures, producing a single framework that tells us why we would expect racial/ethnic differences in who votes to manifest and be sustained over time. Keeping the findings from Chapters 2 and 3 in mind, I begin by reviewing the explanations provided for low minority turnout, focusing on the theoretical justifications and mechanisms through which others have accounted for the turnout gap. Isolating the common factors that underlie each explanation, I bridge these perspectives with a theoretical construct centered on the idea of *electoral influence*. Electoral influence, as defined here, is indicated by the relative size of ethnic groups within a jurisdiction, and predicts racial/ethnic disparities in voter turnout as groups perceived to have lower levels of electoral influence are less likely to vote than groups with higher levels of electoral influence. After outlining the theory, I address the role of electoral institutions and partisanship, then conclude by noting the implications of the framework for the empirical tests featured in subsequent chapters.

EXPLAINING MINORITY TURNOUT

Chapter 2 outlined the persistence of racial/ethnic disparities in voter turnout, as rates of participation for African Americans, Latinos, and Asian Americans lagged behind that of Whites for most of American history. African American participation has increased dramatically since the 1950s, sometimes reaching parity with Whites according to self-reported survey data, but Latino and Asian American turnout is as much as twenty percentage points lower than White and Black turnout in the CPS. I indicated that the removal of *de jure* impediments to political participation provided a key opening for the diminution of the Black–White turnout gap in the South, and that despite tremendous *de facto* barriers African American voter turnout rates were already on the rise prior to implementation of the Voting Rights Act. Further indicating that the Minority–White turnout gap cannot be reduced to institutional barriers, Latino and Asian American turnout did not increase after the 1975 Voting Rights Act Amendments that provided protections for language minority citizens. Thus, despite the fact that *de jure* barriers to minority participation are now well in the past, and that most *de facto* barriers were eliminated by the 1970s, the turnout gap continues to be a feature of American electoral politics.

So why is non-White turnout lower than White turnout? Distinct conclusions have been reached for each group when studied in isolation. For African Americans, low socioeconomic status was once seen as the main cause of low turnout (Matthews and Prothro 1966; Verba and Nie 1972), though this could be overcome through a combination of high group consciousness, the presence of organizing institutions such as churches, and elected representation by African Americans (Walton 1985; Bobo and Gilliam 1990; Dawson, Brown, and Allen 1990; Verba et al. 1993; Tate 1994; Harris 1999). Low Latino turnout was attributed to languages barriers or cultural differences with Whites, and especially in work prior to the 1990s, lack of interest in politics (Wolfinger and Rosenstone 1980; Verba et al. 1993). More recent work suggests that this last dynamic can be shifted through targeted mobilization or Latino candidates (de la Garza and DeSipio 1993, 1997; Shaw, de la Garza, and Lee 2000; Pantoja, Ramirez, and Segura 2001; Barreto, Segura, and Woods 2004; Barreto 2007, 2010). Asian American turnout is far less studied, but again acculturation features prominently (Lien 1994; Cho 1999; Lien 2004; Ramakrishnan 2005; Wong, Lien, and Conway 2005; Wong et al. 2011). As indicated in Chapter 3, the low turnout of Asian Americans despite relatively high socioeconomic status and high turnout of African Americans in recent elections appears contrary to socioeconomic explanations for low non-White turnout.

Leighley and Vedlitz (1999) were two of the first researchers to lament the lack of a single set of forces explaining turnout across racial/ethnic groups. In their pioneering study of voter turnout by Whites, African Americans, Mexican Americans, and Asian Americans in Texas, they examine voter turnout for each racial/ethnic group in separate regression-based analyses. Leighley and Vedlitz (1999) find some common features across groups, such as the importance of socioeconomic indicators and political engagement/interest in predicting raw rates of voter turnout, but less evidence for the importance of group identity or group threat. Leighley (2001) greatly expands on this approach, adding an analysis of the role of county-level racial/ethnic diversity, minority officeholding, and relational goods as conceptualized by Uhlaner (1989a) to understandings of when minority groups are mobilized and when they are more likely to vote. Again, however, there is inconsistency across racial/ethnic groups in both the determinants of mobilization and political participation itself (Leighley 2001: 169, 171).

The failure to account for racial/ethnic differences in turnout in some ways reflects a disconnect between the focus on individual-level determinants of behavior and the phenomena of interest, namely, persistent group-level gaps in who votes. While Leighley and Vedlitz (1999) and Leighley (2001) broke new ground in comparing predictors of voter turnout across groups within the same analysis, they still attempted to explain *relative* rates of voter turnout between groups with a theoretical construct built on voter turnout for each group as rooted in phenomena measured separately. A hypothesis developed for raw rates of voter turnout may clarify intra-group variation, but be less relevant when investigating differences across groups. Furthermore, we may be ignoring important forces driving racial/ethnic variation in turnout when contrasting correlations present for each group in isolation. If a regression coefficient is statistically significant for Whites, but not Latinos, is the variable producing the Latino–White turnout gap, or not? Finally, one potential reason for the inability to find a unified theory of turnout applicable to multiple racial/ethnic groups is the lack of a unified theory of *White* voter turnout. Several competing explanations exist in helping us to understand why *anyone* votes; attempting to elucidate racial disparities in participation in the course of describing the entire set of reasons why any American participates is likely a fool's errand.

Below I construct an integrated theoretical framework that seeks to explain racial/ethnic differences in voter turnout. To do so, I draw on three perspectives of the individual-level voter turnout decision: the Downsian calculus of voting, empowerment theory, and elite mobilization. Translating these understandings into inferences relevant to the variation in voter turnout we witness across racial/ethnic groups, I demonstrate that each perspective, while having separate starting points, could be applied to the turnout gap and suggests mechanisms that can produce group-level differences in voter turnout. Again, the interest here is in clarifying why we see *differences* in turnout, not the entire set of determinants for who votes and who stays home.

Downsian Calculus of Voting

While not the first theory of voter turnout (e.g. Merriam and Gosnell 1924), the Downsian calculus of voting has become the most common starting point for scholars seeking to understand what motivates electoral participation. Outlined by Downs (1957), and elaborated upon by Riker and Ordeshook (1968), the decision to vote may be viewed as a cost–benefit analysis made by individuals who participate only if the (usually small) benefits outweigh the (usually smaller) costs of participation. Expressed in formal terms: $R = PB - C + D$, with R representing the probability of voting, P the probability of an individual's vote being decisive, B indicating the benefit accrued to the individual depending on the winner, C indicating direct or indirect costs of voting, and D indicating non-electoral benefits such as the fulfillment of a "duty" to vote. As understood by scholars for decades, this model predicts a much lower level of voter turnout than observed in actual elections, at least if relying on purely electoral benefits (B) and costs (C) as determinative of turnout (Fiorina 1976; Leighley 1995; Leighley 2001: 16). Non-electoral, or at least *indirectly* electoral benefits (D) must play a key role. For instance, Aldrich (1993) suggests strategic politicians may impact the voting calculus, primarily by inducing long-term benefits and shaping the expressive value of voting for electoral advantage (Aldrich 1993). One could argue, though, that an understanding of the voting calculus built solely on manipulation of the D term no longer resembles a mathematical, *rational* decision-making process.

Is there a way to solve the "paradox" produced by such models of participation? On its face, the Downsian framework would seem to preclude social dynamics related to individual social identity, at least outside of the D-term. However, Uhlaner (1989a, 1989b) and Morton (1991) incorporate social and political group dynamics into a rational choice approach. Specifically, Uhlaner (1989a) demonstrates that collective benefits may be incorporated into the calculus of voting, such that the individual cost–benefit calculation could shift toward participation when there is an opportunity for the individual's group to be determinative of election outcomes and thus deserving of (policy) benefits from politicians they support (391–392). Given the salience of racial and ethnic identities in American politics, it stands to reason that African Americans, Latinos, and Asian Americans could be pushed to mobilize when their group is perceived to influence election outcomes. Extending this logic further, Morton (1991) states that group-based rational voting is contingent on size of the group in question being large enough to impact outcomes, and the total number of perceived groups in the electorate (761). Thus, the reified construct of racial and ethnic groups in the United States makes them obvious candidate social identities for an explanation of voter turnout rooted in group-level processes (Fraga 2016a).

Seeking a group-benefits-based account of the turnout gap, we can imagine that group-based voting behavior and the boost in turnout contingent on this phenomenon are more likely to occur under a generalizable set of circumstances. First, as it pertains to social identities like race/ethnicity, when a group is perceived to have a larger impact on candidate fortunes it is more likely that group members will perceive politics *as a group* and be motivated to vote for instrumental reasons (*B*). Second, while the political visibility of minority groups in many contexts would seem to suggest that they are ripe for identification *as groups* (see Uhlaner 1989a: 392), we must keep in mind that the largest racial/ethnic group in almost all electoral contexts is non-Hispanic Whites. Thus, the persistent Minority–White turnout gap may be the result of the heightened relevance of Whites to politicians influencing perceptions in the electorate and boosting the perceived relevance of participation to White citizens.

Empowerment

Empowerment theory, as outlined by Bobo and Gilliam (1990) and drawing on the notion of political incorporation advanced by Browning, Marshall, and Tabb (1984, 1986), argues that individual African American voters will react to the political context they find themselves in and are more likely to turn out to vote when living in contexts of Black political empowerment. Bobo and Gilliam (1990: 378–379) describe their theory as follows:

> By political empowerment...we mean the extent to which a group has achieved significant representation and influence in political decision making...[S]uch empowerment should influence mass sociopolitical participation.

The primary mechanism by which empowerment is thought to operate is an internal, psychological process dependent on the racial/ethnic context surrounding the voter. In contexts of empowerment, voters perceive that their participation is likely to have an impact on politics and thus are encouraged to participate (Bobo and Gilliam 1990; Gay 2001; Barreto,

Segura, and Woods 2004; Barreto 2007). The way such contexts were operationalized in Bobo and Gilliam (1990) and most subsequent studies was African American officeholding or candidacy (Brace et al. 1995; Gay 2001; Griffin and Keane 2006; Keele et al. 2014; Lublin 1997; Tate 2003). A smaller set of studies instead focused on empowerment as it manifests through the relative size of the Black population in a jurisdiction, which is predictive of Black officeholding (e.g. Browning, Marshall, and Tabb 1984; Lublin 1997) but at least results in greater opportunities to shape the electoral process. In such contexts, Black turnout is indeed higher (Spence and McClerking 2010; Fraga 2016a).

Empowerment theory was later extended to Latinos (Barreto, Segura, and Woods 2004; Barreto 2007, 2010). Operationalized as Latino candidacy, the notion of *potential* Latino officeholders as agents stimulating Latino turnout is a crucial component in the framework outlined in Barreto (2010). The causal impact of Latino candidates has come into question (Henderson, Sekhon, and Titiunik 2016). Yet, as with African Americans, other work has demonstrated that conceptualizing of "representation and influence in political decisionmaking" as the relative size of the Latino population reveals a more clear turnout relationship (Fraga 2016a), at least at a correlational level (Fraga 2016b). To date, Asian American turnout has not been demonstrated to be influenced by empowerment-like mechanisms, and indeed, some evidence suggests that a sense of linked fate with other Asian Americans may be *negatively* associated with voting participation (Wong, Lien, and Conway 2005).

Again, we would expect the relative rate of turnout to vary with the level of empowerment experienced by each racial/ethnic group. With the same set of candidates, and in the same election, voter turnout should be relatively higher for the empowered group. If we extend empowerment theory to Whites, we can deduce that a *lack* of empowerment may be one of the reasons why minority turnout lags White turnout in most years. White voters almost always live in contexts of White "empowerment"; as noted by Barreto (2007: 438), the rare instances where Whites are not in an empowering context may lead to a reduction in White turnout relative to other groups. Of course, nearly all elections in the United States feature at least one White candidate (Branton 2009; Fraga 2014) and fewer than 10 percent of Whites live in Congressional districts where they compose less than a majority of the adult population (Fraga 2016a). Thus, an understanding of voter turnout as contingent on group empowerment, including empowerment for White voters, may help to explain the turnout gap.

Elite Mobilization

The perspectives addressed so far consist of individual-level responses to political context. However, both the group-based rational choice framework and empowerment theory suggest that political context structures rates of voter turnout: the individual decision to vote is conditional on the politics that surrounds it. With Mayhew (1975) noting that politicians will do what it takes to win office, it is evident that politicians will attempt to shape who turns out to vote. Scholars have long asserted that partisan mobilization influences voter turnout (Berelson, Lazarsfeld, and McPhee 1954; Caldeira, Clausen, and Patterson 1990) and campaign activity is associated with higher rates of voter turnout overall (Enos and Fowler 2017). Rosenstone and Hansen (1993) provide a comprehensive model of political mobilization, and indicate that politicians and interest groups will seek to "get the most effective number of people involved with the least amount of effort" (30). Such strategic mobilization has implications for who is most likely to be mobilized by elites, and as continues to be confirmed in recent scholarship, this includes citizens who are likely to be political allies (Panagopoulos 2016), those central in social networks (Rolfe 2012), and adults who are already most likely to vote (Enos, Fowler, and Vavreck 2014; but cf. Berelson, Lazarsfeld, and McPhee 1954: 176).

Leighley (2001) connects theories of elite mobilization to racial differences in who votes. While building on the work of both Rosenstone and Hansen (1993) and Uhlaner (1989a), Leighley uses elite interviews and analyses of survey data to provide direct evidence of both the racial/ethnic dimension of mobilization efforts by elites and how these efforts manifest in turnout for White, Black, and Latino voters. Addressing mobilization, party targeting, and voter turnout in turn, Leighley determines that the behavior of politicians is a crucial stimulus and that individuals will vote when asked to do so (Leighley 2001: 173). Relative group size is an important component of her argument, as "where minorities make up a large, or significant, portion of the electorate, they will be more likely to be targeted" (Leighley 2001: 26). Though later work indicated that party contact may also matter for Asian American voter turnout (Wong, Lien, and Conway 2005), in Leighley (2001), the link between mobilization and turnout varies somewhat across groups and is contingent on the broader racial/ethnic context (142–144). This may be due to a disconnect between self-reported measures of campaign contact and actual mobilization by campaigns. Leighley (2001: 40–42,

93–95) does indicate that Black and Latino citizens in heavily Black or Latino areas are more likely to get mobilized according to reports by party officials. Mobilization was also particularly important in the immediate post-VRA South, as even in rural areas the presence of elites courting African American votes in heavily Black areas predicted higher Black turnout far better than socioeconomic status (Morrison 1987: 175). Contemporary Democratic campaigns continue to focus on mobilizing Black voters in heavily Black districts (Glaser 1996: 176–178), and Ramakrishnan (2005) indicates that Black, Latino, and Asian immigrant-origin citizens are more likely to vote in states where their racial/ethnic group is a large share of population (99–102). Finally, the theoretical link between group size and voter turnout via mobilization also coincides with findings that congressional district composition is associated with higher rates of voter turnout (Fraga 2016a).

When it comes to elite mobilization, it is easy to imagine how this perspective translates into the turnout gap. Campaigns have finite resources, and thus are forced to choose which groups to mobilize. Since minority voters rarely compose a majority of electoral jurisdictions, and Whites almost always do, the turnout gap may be a function of differential incentives for politicians to cater to each group. A smaller literature demonstrates that individuals are more likely to be mobilized to vote when concentrated into a geographic area with individuals sharing politically salient identities (Oberholzer-Gee and Waldfogel 2005). Tailored approaches may be more effective at stimulating turnout for minority groups (García Bedolla and Michelson 2012, but cf. Abrajano 2010: 91), such that if the incentive structure for politicians were changed Black, Latino, and Asian American voters *could* be stimulated to vote. Minority voters may be at an additional disadvantage, however. Minority citizens are less likely to be contacted by mobilizers (Ramírez, Solano, and Wilcox-Archuleta 2018), even after accounting for partisanship and vote propensity (Stevens and Bishin 2011). Minority voters may also be taken for granted by political parties, leading to fewer efforts to mobilize (Frymer 1999). Mobilization by itself may not explain the entirety of the turnout gap, but could coincide with variation in the severity of the gap across jurisdictions.

A THEORY OF ELECTORAL INFLUENCE

The three perspectives outlined above are often presented as competing mechanisms by which individuals decide to vote. Yet, when generalized across groups, and transformed into relative rates of participation, we see more commonality in these understandings than previously assumed. The Downsian framework, as expressed in the work of Uhlaner (1989a) and Morton (1991), depends on an interaction between groups and candidates which then modifies the individual voting calculus such that members of groups with greater relevance in political outcomes are more likely to turn out than members of "smaller" groups.[2] The empowerment hypothesis, as outlined in Bobo and Gilliam (1990), sees political participation as more likely in situations where individuals perceive that they have "representation and influence in political decisionmaking," again pointing to variation in group-level electoral relevance as key. Finally, in bringing elite mobilization to the study of race and voter turnout, Leighley (2001) also indicates that politicians are more likely to stimulate turnout for groups who are a sizable portion of the electorate. It is with this common element, the *electoral influence* of the group, that I seek to explain the turnout gap.

The theory outlined in this chapter is built on the notion that the political behavior of both citizens and elites is a product of the electoral context they find themselves in. As each of the above three perspectives suggests, the individual decision to vote does not take place in a vacuum; potential voters respond to the context that surrounds them and decide to vote based on their perception of whether or not it is worth the effort to cast a ballot. Political elites adopt strategies that take into account the pool of potential voters, considering whether or not it is worth mobilizing a particular voter. Get-out-the-Vote efforts encourage participation by indicating to voters that their vote is important or that a politician will represent their interests, drawing again on the well-known understandings of turnout discussed above.[3] As demonstrated in previous work, the mechanisms distinguishing the effect of empowerment from the effect of mobilization are difficult to adjudicate (Fraga 2016a, 2016b). Figure 4.1 indicates that group relevance (through the group-based Downsian framework), empowerment theory, and elite mobilization *all* reinforce one another and contribute to the turnout decision. In other words, these forces are endogenous and will necessarily be challenging to "identify" in both an observational and causal sense.

---

[2] Alternatively, the expanded rational choice framework as understood by Aldrich (1993) places emphasis on the incentives of strategic politicians to modify the calculus, which resembles the elite mobilization framework.

[3] The social pressure models of turnout in Green and Gerber (2010) also enhance the perceived relevance of voting to the voter, and while this may be due to a different psychological process than the three frameworks I draw on, the result is the same.

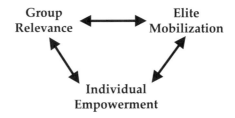

FIGURE 4.1 Relationship between mechanisms influencing voter turnout

When analyzing the turnout gap, however, the need to adjudicate between these individual mechanisms is less important than establishing the conditions under which such mechanisms are likely to manifest differentially across ethnic groups. To do so, we must keep in mind two points. First, one must consider the average value of these variables within racial/ethnic groups. While there will be variation in levels of individual empowerment within a racial/ethnic group, unevenness in the extent to which someone is mobilized, and likely differing perceptions about the relevance of the group on election outcomes, the search is for circumstances where *on average* these turnout-inducing mechanisms appear at higher or lower rates. Importantly, the averaging should take place at the level of the group; leveraging minority citizens whose experiences are closer to that of Whites than others from their racial/ethnic group is not a valid method of determining the impact of race in politics (Sen and Wasow 2016). Second, if each of these mechanisms contributes to voter turnout and is associated with one another, yet we still witness differential rates of voter turnout across racial/ethnic groups, it is likely that a common factor activating these mechanisms but varying across groups accounts for at least some of the turnout gap.

Fortunately, the theoretical perspectives already provide a variable that is a central predictor of each mechanism and varies substantially across groups: group size. *It is the relative size of a racial/ethnic group that is the key measure of group-level electoral influence, which in turn leads to greater voter turnout relative to other groups.* In jurisdictions where a racial/ethnic group composes a larger share of the population, incentives for elites to mobilize the racial/ethnic group should increase, group members should feel more empowered, and the group should be perceived as more relevant for political outcomes. In other words, the racial/ethnic group should have greater influence in the election. Compared to places where the racial/ethnic group is a smaller share of the population, we should thus on average see a diminution, or even a reversal, of disparities in participation with other groups. Stated formally, for two groups (B and W)[4] in two electoral jurisdictions (1 and 2), if $(Size_{B1} - Size_{W1}) > (Size_{B2} - Size_{W2})$, then $(Turnout_{B1} - Turnout_{W1}) > (Turnout_{B2} - Turnout_{W2})$.

Based on the theories above, *at least* one of the following two postulations must be true in order for this effect to manifest. First, we could assume that elites will focus efforts on mobilizing groups who are especially relevant to election outcomes. As a result, when a group is larger group members will be more likely to be mobilized by politicians or interest groups. Some conceptualizations of elite mobilization state that co-ethnic mobilization is necessary to see a boost in minority turnout (Uhlaner 1989a; Barreto 2010). As Leighley (2001: 17–18) indicates, same-race candidates may be especially effective at mobilization based on the Uhlaner (1989b) "relational goods" framework. However, as co-ethnic politicians become more likely to emerge from jurisdictions where the group in question makes up a larger share of the electorate, the need for co-ethnic candidates can also be satisfied with this first assumption. Second, we could assume that voters have some knowledge of the racial/ethnic composition of the electoral districts they are part of or the race/ethnicity of their elected representative, such that they would know if they are in a place traditionally associated with their group's empowerment. In this instance, elite mobilization would be doing less of the work and instead individual-level psychological processes would be dominant. Both of these assumptions, if true, are mutually reinforcing as they pertain to voter turnout, but only one must hold to see a relationship between relative group size and relative rates of voter turnout. Further implications of the theory are discussed at the end of this chapter.

Bridging the (Theoretical) Gap

The theory of electoral influence is not designed to *replace* understandings of minority turnout, but rather to synthesize an existing body of research and identify the shared factor that may explain racial/ethnic differences in who turns out to vote. As noted above, the common element I identify is the relative size of racial/ethnic groups. Similar to

---

[4] Here the contrast is most natural when considering voter turnout of a single minority group as compared to non-Hispanic Whites, as the White population is larger than the minority population in nearly every electoral jurisdiction nationwide. However, this is not a necessary condition in the model, and in expectation the turnout gap with any other group will be smaller (or reverse) as the size of the group of interest increases.

the "racial/ethnic context" variable identified by Leighley (2001: 7–8), I establish that said context can impact both the behavior of elites and the behavior of citizens: it is likely that differences in the voting calculus, individual empowerment, and elite mobilization were *all* at work in producing disparities in participation we witness today. Unlike Leighley's framework, I examine a single part of the racial/ethnic context and suggest that the same forces are at work across groups. Yet, the theory is designed to clarify reasons for group-level variation in who votes, not voter turnout writ large. This distinction is particularly important when considering the many theories ensconced in our understanding of voting behavior. For instance, much evidence suggests that wealthy and more highly educated individuals vote at higher rates (Verba et al. 1993). Except as they produce and perpetuate the turnout gap, such forces are not the primary interest of this volume.[5] Similarly, competition may influence voter turnout in myriad ways (Franklin 2004). But the goal in this book is to try to isolate these contextual forces influencing every citizen in a similar way from the forces with a distinctly racial/ethnic impact. Finally, a growing literature focuses on the specific mobilization techniques that may be most effective in inducing turnout (Green and Gerber 2010), including which techniques would be most effective at stimulating minority turnout (García Bedolla and Michelson 2012). While it is critical to understand methods that *could* impact who votes, such perspectives will be used only insofar as they can help us account for the persistent turnout gap.

In so doing, I seek to shift individual-level understandings of who votes into the arena of contextually contingent behaviors. As noted in Walton (1994: 8), the focus on individual-level factors governing African American political participation ignores the importance of group, organizational, institutional, and elite forces shaping the Black political experience. The same may be said of Latinos, Asian Americans, and perhaps even Whites as our understanding of the fundamentally social nature of voting participation has expanded (Green and Gerber 2010; Rolfe 2012). When it is made clear that a group "counts," group members will turn out to vote. Thus, a key innovation of the theory of electoral influence is its applicability to *any* social group that could

---

[5] See Chapter 3 for an analysis of the impact of socioeconomic disparities on the turnout gap.

be perceived as a voting bloc.[6] As it pertains to the relative size of racial/ethnic groups, it may seem odd to think of Whites as a politically salient grouping. However, when considering each of the three theories above, it is easy to see why Whites have the highest rates of voter turnout in most contemporary elections. Whites are almost always the largest racial/ethnic group in the electorate, and even when looking within each political party in recent presidential elections, Whites compose a majority of voting Democrats (Cillizza and Cohen 2012). Thus, and as citizens and elites intuit, almost all racial/ethnic contexts feature non-Hispanic Whites as the political group determinative of outcomes and the group catered to in election campaigns (Frymer 1999).

Finally, the theory of electoral influence can also be used to understand the historical phenomena witnessed in the pre-VRA South. Chapter 2 pointed to literatures providing a fuller discussion of Black and White turnout patterns in the pre-VRA South, but even during this era we see that the electoral influence of African Americans was of paramount concern to politicians. As found by authors from Key (1949) to Acharya, Blackwell, and Sen (2018), Black disenfranchisement was most intense in heavily Black counties in the South in the late 1800s and early 1900s. The standard hypothesis is that this was due to the potential political threat caused by African Americans. In the early 1900s, efforts to disenfranchise African Americans were focused on the possibility that, without *de jure* barriers, they could be numerous enough to leverage splits among White Democrats (Kousser 1999: 37). Disenfranchisers often explicitly stated that their goal was to reduce the size of the Black electorate (Kousser 1999: 34). Recent research also suggests that, above and beyond *de jure* factors, lower Black voter registration was witnessed in heavily Black counties in 1890s Mississippi due to *de facto* disenfranchisement through intense violence and intimidation (Bertocchi and Dimico 2017). In a pre-WWII South where African American political influence was almost nonexistent, there was still a recognition by White elites that the greatest political threat was in the heavily Black areas of

---

[6] For example, McConnaughy (2013) and Harvey (1996) indicate women's suffrage extension and mobilization, respectively, were in part driven by partisan incentives to build or sustain electoral coalitions via women's votes. While it is beyond the scope of this book to examine how particular social identities become electorally relevant, group size does appear to be a key factor (Uhlaner 1989a). See McConnaughy (2013) for a discussion of women's enfranchisement and partisan mobilization, and Jusko (2017) for a discussion of how the geographic concentration of voters by socioeconomic class status informs the partisan mobilization of low-income voters.

each state, and that this potential political influence of African Americans had to be limited as much as possible. Black electoral influence, and thus, Black political participation, would have been much higher even in the face of *de facto* restrictions were it not for these redoubled efforts.

Perceived Influence or Actual Influence?

Above I propose a relationship between the electoral influence a racial/ethnic group holds in an election and relative levels of voter turnout: where a racial/ethnic group has greater electoral influence, I expect to find a diminution or reversal of the turnout gap with other groups versus places where a racial/ethnic group has less electoral influence. Still, the three perspectives I draw on emphasize the individual decision to participate, despite being driven by contextual forces. Elite mobilization, individual empowerment, and the group-centric cost–benefit calculation rely on citizens and elites *perceiving* particular racial/ethnic groups to be relevant to outcomes. Thus, it is the individual's *perception* of her group's electoral influence that is most clearly indicated by the theory I put forth here. These perceptions of influence could be contrasted with *actual* electoral influence, in other words, a circumstance where a group *does* influence election outcomes. Such influence can only be known after an election has taken place and thus after the decision to vote has been made.[7] A post-election measure, such as share of the voting population or co-ethnic officeholding is, at least in part, an *outcome* of individual turnout decisions and thus individual perceptions of influence pre-election.

The desire to find a consistent operationalization of perceived electoral influence drives the decision to focus on groups' relative size in the potential electorate. It is simple to understand that, at extremes, size is determinative of a group's electoral relevance. If a group's size is zero, they have no influence.[8] If group members are 100 percent of the electorate in a jurisdiction, they have complete power over the voting outcome. In Chapters 5 and 6, I operationalize relative group size as the group's percentage of the eligible electorate using Census data, allowing

---

[7] Given the manner by which empowerment theory has been operationalized, it stands to reason that influence in politics *beyond* a specific election (through representation) is an important determinant of participation. However, the maintenance of such representation in a democracy is contingent on election outcomes.

[8] Of course, in this circumstance the group also has no potential voters.

for complete geographic coverage, consistency over time, and independence from election results. An instructive contrast may be made with the notion of pivotality. Some assert that racial/ethnic minority groups, in particular, Latinos, will be catered to when they are perceived as pivotal to election contests (Barreto, Collingwood, and Manzano 2010). However, the largest group is by definition always most likely to be pivotal, and at the other extreme any group could be pivotal as a candidate's margin of victory approaches zero. Since all groups have the potential to influence election outcomes with this understanding, we again return to a group's size relative to other groups as a distinguishing criterion.

Are citizens capable of perceiving the relative size of their group in a jurisdiction? The innumeracy of the public regarding the racial composition of large geographic areas is well known (Nadeau, Niemi, and Levine 1993; Sigelman and Niemi 2001), and while Fenno (1978) asserts that members of Congress have a firm grasp of their district's traits, ongoing research challenges this assumption (Broockman and Skovron 2017). On the other hand, more recent research suggests that citizens have a level of awareness of their racial/ethnic context that aligns with government-produced statistics (Velez and Wong 2017), and that innumeracy related to racial composition is similar to other challenging quantification tasks for citizens (Landy, Marghetis, and Guay 2017). Chapter 6 provides more direct evidence of citizen knowledge of their congressional district, where I find that even in the first election after a redistricting cycle citizens who are redistricted have knowledge of the racial/ethnic makeup of their new jurisdiction. Such a finding further reinforces the validity of relative group size as an indicator of perceived influence.

Of course, these perceptions can be shaped by contextual forces beyond relative group size. Perhaps most especially, partisanship and party coalition formation processes may allow for certain groups to perceive that they have an outsized influence over candidate selection. The presumed reality perceived by the voter will be correlated with relative group size, but is a translation of size into a perception of influence. I address the role of partisanship in the theory of electoral influence below, but the fact that this translated influence is what is relevant to racial/ethnic differences in turnout may allow us to understand why at equivalent levels of electoral influence (that is, when two groups are of equal size) we may still see unequal rates of voting. Campaigns will seek to mobilize supporters, but as Stevens and Bishin (2011) note, even with the same propensity to support a given candidate minority voters may be less likely to get mobilized. As Figure 4.1 indicated, mobilization, empowerment, and group relevance are endogenous, reinforcing, and cyclical; at very least empowerment and group relevance are built on voter psychology and perceptions rather than a strict numerical formula. Even when a group's size changes, there may be path dependence in the perceived impact a given group has on electoral outcomes. The success of non-partisan actors in mobilizing groups, particularly groups that have had low turnout historically, may counteract this tendency (García Bedolla and Michelson 2012; May 2013). Perceptions of group size are thus correlated with actual group size, but we should not necessarily expect each group to react in an equal manner when holding equivalent levels of electoral influence. Instead, I simply argue that differences in turnout between two groups should vary as a function of the relative size of each group.

The Role of Electoral Institutions

Chapter 2 challenged the notion that the removal of *de facto* racial impediments was the necessary ingredient for increased turnout by African Americans. African American participation rose despite the presence of significant barriers to participation, and the Black–White turnout gap in the South in 1964 was already half of what it was in the 1950s. Latino and Asian American turnout has not increased relative to Whites since the 1970s and 1990s, respectively. The three perspectives I outlined at the beginning of this chapter do not give electoral institutions a large role in understanding who votes in the contemporary United States.[9] How should institutions be incorporated into the theory of electoral influence?

Chapter 7 explores contemporary election policies, finding limited evidence that the turnout gap is contingent on a specific set of electoral rules even when such policies are designed and implemented with discriminatory intent. However, electoral institutions do play one major role in structuring the turnout gap: cleaving the population into electoral jurisdictions. Since the *Baker* v. *Carr* (1962) and *Reynolds* v. *Sims* (1964) decisions, most electoral districts are required to be roughly equal in population within states or localities. The most dilutionary forms of districting are thus in the past. Yet in most places politicians still exercise significant leeway in the drawing of election boundaries. The 1982

---

[9] Though studies in the history of voter turnout give institutions a much larger role (e.g. Keyssar 2009), as do comprehensive analyses of Black political behavior (Walton 1985, 1994).

Voting Rights Act Amendments added a further wrinkle to redistricting, as today states are often required to demonstrate that their districting choices do not impede minority influence in elections. The usual outcome of interest is minority officeholding, but a common pre-election proxy is a measure of the relative size of ethnic groups within the jurisdiction; the same measure I employ to determine electoral influence. Thus, electoral institutions could play a significant role in structuring participation by modifying the size of groups within a district or jurisdiction, a feature that I explore in greater depth in Chapter 6.[10]

Briefly returning to the historical record, institutions also had the greatest impact on the turnout gap when they were designed and implemented to not only dilute, but *eliminate* political participation by minority voters. Alt (1994) indicates that the main goal of disenfranchising institutions in the 1950s and 1960s South was to ensure White numerical dominance on election day. Outside of a few Black-majority counties in the Deep South, therefore, such measures would not have been necessary to ensure continued White dominance. Again, the size of the ethnic group in question was key. As articulated by Wright (1987), a fear of Black political influence was also the primary reason for Redeemer-era restrictions on the franchise. White politicians would (and indeed, did) cater to the Black electorate even in the context of *de facto* disenfranchisement when African Americans were perceived to have sway in elections, thus indicating that the relationship between group size and political participation could only be broken by reducing the size of the Black electorate that is eligible to participate. Contemporary restrictions on the franchise, such as felon disenfranchisement and voter identification laws, pale in comparison to the *de facto* barriers faced by minority groups prior to the Voting Rights Act.[11] Nonetheless, insofar as these policies serve to limit who can participate, they may influence the decisions of elites to seek minority votes in the first place.

---

[10] In a far more extreme form, Posner (1994) demonstrates that the *same* ethnic group in Africa is politically relevant only when the size of the group has political ramifications. While not dealing with explicitly electoral boundaries (Posner uses national boundaries), this does imply that institutions can play a key role in structuring how and when groups gain or lose political salience.

[11] Voter identification laws and other policies perceived as "suppressing" minority voting may also elicit anger among voters, stimulating participation (Valentino and Neuner 2017). Voter identification laws and other contemporary restrictions on voting are discussed in greater detail in Chapter 7.

Partisanship and Electoral Capture

The theory outlined above gives political parties a role as mobilizing agents in service of election-seeking candidates. As with the elite mobilization framework, partisan candidates and their allies will seek to mobilize groups that are relevant for election outcomes (Rosenstone and Hansen 1993; Leighley 2001). Parties decide who to target and mobilize (Aldrich 1995), and often do not employ a strategy of mobilizing all potential voters. Hersh (2015) indicates that contemporary campaigns rely on two pieces of information when designing mobilization strategies: the propensity to vote and the propensity to be a supporter. Individuals are most likely to be targeted when they fall into the "low turnout, base voter" category or "high turnout, swing voter" categories. On its face, therefore, current partisan strategy does *not* appear to fit neatly into the theory of electoral influence.

Parties become even more challenging to fully include in the theory when considering the strategic behavior of partisan mobilizers regarding race. Stevens and Bishin (2011) suggest that minority voters who are otherwise prime candidates for mobilization appear to be targeted less than Whites. As noted by Fraga and Ramírez (2003, 2004), the demographic growth of the Latino population did not (and does not) necessarily translate into electoral influence given established party allegiances and the dominance of White voters in both parties' coalitions. In what they term "symbolic mainstreaming," Fraga and Leal (2004) describe scenarios where a growing Latino electorate is catered to by the parties only as a symbolic appeal to win *White* votes. Instead of seeking to mobilize fast-growing minority groups, parties may thus appear to advocate without any real effort at either including minority issues in the broader partisan agenda or mobilizing non-White groups to vote.

Frymer (1999) describes an even more pernicious scenario, termed "Electoral Capture." Focusing on African Americans, Frymer characterizes party competition as generating a scenario where Black voters are taken for granted by Republicans (in the Reconstruction and post-Reconstruction eras) and then Democrats (from the Civil Rights era to today) while being given few policy benefits in exchange for their party loyalty. Electoral capture mirrors Bartels's (1998) assertion that Black potential voters are limited in their influence as they are not considered a swing electorate worthy of attention. Yet there is another side of electoral capture, a side that manifested clearly in the Reconstruction era and in recent elections: African American voters were mobilized at high rates by the parties that "captured" them. Since at least the 2000s, campaigns have shifted attention to mobilizing base voters in the wake of polarized national elections (Panagopoulos 2016), perhaps mirroring the polarized climate of the Reconstruction-era South. Even in the Hersh (2015) framework, voters with strong partisanship and low rates of turnout in previous elections are prime targets for GOTV efforts. This tendency may help to explain high African American voter turnout in recent elections (Fraga 2016a), though the 2016 election could demonstrate the consequence of straying too far from the "low turnout, base voter" category.

When considering subnational levels of electoral geography, the mechanics of electoral capture do not preclude the mobilization of racial/ethnic minority voters. Focusing on national party dynamics, Frymer (1999: chs. 3–4) tells us that regional dominance in one part of the country, driven by minority voters, could detract from party success in other regions where White voters are numerically dominant. For instance, northern Republicans eventually abandoned enforcement of Black voting rights in the South in the pursuit of the Southern White electorate. Hood, Kidd, and Morris (2012) find that the national Democratic Party's focus on the mobilization of African Americans in the South after full enfranchisement in the 1960s contributed to Southern White Democrats' decline in the party and their eventual alignment with the Republican Party. However, for the enterprising candidate in a state or congressional election, recognition would be paid to the district context: in an area where minority voters have the potential to dominate politics, there is less downside to turning out racial/ethnic minority groups. Leighley (2001) notes that party elites recognize the incentives candidates have to mobilize racial/ethnic groups when the groups are large. Party resources also allow for campaign coordination across jurisdictions, meaning that otherwise largely White parties can tailor strategies to district-level context.

Given the above, would racial/ethnic groups be better off as swing electorates? While White voters have the advantage of being relatively high turnout swing voters in many, though not all parts of the contemporary United States, they also have greater electoral influence in most states and districts in the country. Latinos are a more instructive counterfactual. Low Latino turnout and inconsistent partisanship is, according to Hersh (2015), the worst scenario for GOTV targeting. It is also probably not coincidental that Latinos and Asian Americans have lower rates of party affiliation than Whites or African Americans (Hajnal

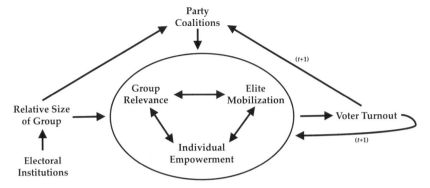

FIGURE 4.2 Relationship between group size and voter turnout

and Lee 2011), and also lag behind in turnout by at least 20 percentage points.

IMPLICATIONS OF THE THEORY

Figure 4.2 adds to Figure 4.1, indicating both the cyclical nature of the three turnout perspectives noted earlier in the chapter and the relationship of this endogenous turnout pattern to relative group size (our key indicator of electoral influence), electoral institutions, party coalitions, and finally, voter turnout itself. As the diagram indicates, the relative size of a given racial/ethnic group within a jurisdiction contributes to the relevance of the group, elite mobilization of said group, and/or the individual empowerment of the group. Each of these three mechanisms reinforces the other, and produces greater rates of voter turnout for the racial/ethnic group in question. This increased voter turnout then facilitates the perceived relevance, mobilization, and empowerment of groups, shaping rates of voter turnout in a future election,[12] making each of these turnout-stimulating phenomena more likely and perpetuating a cycle of heightened voter turnout going forward. While the challenging task of adjudicating these mechanisms is largely left to other researchers,[13] Figure 4.2 suggests that future analysts should be cautious when attempting to study any of these self-reinforcing factors in isolation.

[12] As indicated by the *t*+1 notation.
[13] See Fraga (2016a) and Chapter 6 in this volume for discussions of how we can distinguish between conventional operationalizations of empowerment and elite mobilization.

Party coalitions are also included in Figure 4.2, and help to shape the dynamics of turnout. However, both the relative size of ethnic groups in a jurisdiction and previous rates of voter turnout contribute to the structure of party coalitions, as both large and high turnout groups are more likely to be incorporated into party coalitions.[14] Party coalitions on their own cannot structure the relative size of groups nor rates of voter turnout, at least at the jurisdiction level.[15] Finally, electoral institutions are included as a factor shaping turnout through the electoral rules that impact the relative size of groups within a jurisdiction. Fitting this placement with the findings of Chapter 2, we can see that *de jure* disenfranchisement through electoral institutions could be seen as reducing the size of disenfranchised groups to zero, while *de facto* disenfranchisement did not necessarily preclude some minority participation when the racial/ethnic group was particularly relevant to election outcomes in the post-Reconstruction era and later again in the 1950s. After the Voting Rights Act, institutions shape turnout through the drawing of electoral jurisdictions, which define electorates and in the process determine the distribution of racial/ethnic groups. Chapter 6 tests various ways in which district composition can impact and manipulate the turnout gap, but aside from this feature of our electoral system, political factors are largely unable to shape the fundamental force that I theorize as crucial for producing and sustaining the turnout gap: the group size-based electoral influence held by a racial/ethnic group. Again, many factors impact the individual decision to vote. However, as it pertains to differences in participation across groups, once defined the relative size of groups in a jurisdiction both influences participation and is exogenous to the cyclical forces theorized to impact turnout and perpetuate the turnout gap.

Another important implication of the theory of electoral influence is that the forces producing the turnout gap are zero-sum. As one group increases in relative size, the combined electoral influence of other groups must diminish. Conceptualizing of relative group size as a percentage of the total eligible population, as is done in the rest of this book, facilitates

---

[14] This relationship bears some resemblance to Browning, Marshall, and Tabb's (1984) notion of political incorporation, which focused on minority representation in governing coalitions in the 1970s and 1980s.

[15] As indicated in Chapter 2, parties played a major role in structuring *de jure* and *de facto* barriers to voting. Today parties have limited control over the electoral institutions that impact relative group size, perhaps outside of districting. The role of districts in shaping the turnout gap is addressed earlier in this chapter and in Chapter 6.

our understanding of the tradeoffs and shifts in perceptions made by mobilizers and voters, respectively. This is not to say that turnout always rises for one group as it falls for another, as many other characteristics structure rates of turnout across groups. Rather, the only implication is that insofar as the relative size of groups structures mobilization, empowerment, and group relevance, group-level averages in turnout produced by these forces will vary as a function of relative group size. Moreover, the turnout gap itself is a zero-sum measure of participation: a measure of political (in-)equality between groups. With a zero-sum measure of electoral influence and voting rates used in this volume, a new perspective is given to the demographic trends outlined in Chapter 1. The non-White population in the United States is growing, but at present, the U.S. electorate is approximately 70 percent non-Hispanic White. In nearly every jurisdiction in the country, and in presidential elections, Whites dominate electoral politics. The persistence of the national-level Minority–White turnout gap coincides with continued high levels of electoral influence for Whites and relatively low levels of electoral influence for minority groups, and is thus not at all surprising even with the dramatic demographic change we have seen since the 1960s. Again, turnout itself is not a zero-sum phenomenon: Chapter 2 indicated that voting rates across groups have often shifted in sync. The political impact of such turnout, though, is zero-sum. If Black voter turnout increases, but White turnout does as well, what is the political relevance of the change in turnout witnessed for both groups? The turnout gap is thus relevant both as an observational reality and as a measure of the persistent political inequality at the heart of this book.

It is also worth noting what is *not* included in the theory of electoral influence I describe in this chapter. First, the theory does not indicate a primary role for socioeconomic factors. As demonstrated in Chapter 3, education, income, and age are associated with voter turnout, but cannot account for the turnout gap today or changes in the gap over the last forty years. The historical record also seems to contradict a simple relationship between socioeconomics and participation. As demonstrated in Chapter 2, turnout for the freedmen was roughly equivalent to that of southern Whites during the early 1870s, despite no measure of social equality between the groups. Latino turnout during the machine era in South Texas may also have exceeded Latino voting in the same areas today. Finally, Asian American turnout lags far behind African Americans and Whites despite higher socioeconomic status for

Asians according to many measures. The relationship between sociode-mographic resources and participation in immigrant enclaves may be somewhat clearer (Ramakrishnan 2005: 99), but the need for natural-ization makes the relationship between SES, group concentration, and turnout more complex.[16]

The second idea not directly incorporated into the framework is the theory of racial or group threat. Such understandings trace their lin-eage to a finding in Key (1949), wherein White turnout was higher in counties with a large number of African Americans. Notably, this took place despite the effective disenfranchisement of all African Americans in such counties (Key 1949; Enos 2016). In Chapter 2, it was made clear that the response to an actual political threat was disenfranchisement of the Black population (Alt 1994: 359), which fits with the theory of electoral influence as the relative size of the group was reduced to zero. While Enos (2016) finds a racial threat effect in reduced White turnout after the *removal* of a large Black population in Chicago, the remain-ing research on a turnout effect of group proximity is far more mixed. Indeed, an emerging consensus in the literature is that the attitudinal effects of racial threat are conditional on interpersonal contact (Bobo and Hutchings 1996; Oliver and Wong 2003; Oliver 2010; Enos 2017): voting behavior may be similarly conditional. Leighley (2001: 26), for instance, notes that an increased minority population concentration may decrease White turnout on average, and while efforts have been made to tie policy threat to Latino voter turnout (Bowler, Nicholson, and Segura 2006; White 2016), evidence for a pure racial threat–participation link for Whites interacting with Latinos has not presented itself. A more promising avenue for future research may be to expand the notion of threat to the voting behavior of non-Whites, with Bowler, Nicholson, and Segura (2006) and Towler and Parker (2018) finding evidence that resistance to anti-Latino and anti-Black political movements can be an effective mobilization tool for minority citizens.

---

[16] The decision to naturalize is beyond the scope of this volume, but may be driven by a desire to participate in politics (Cho 1999; Pantoja, Ramirez, and Segura 2001; Ong and Nakanishi 2003; Pantoja and Gershon 2006). See Ramakrishnan (2005) for an extended discussion of generational differences in voter turnout.

TURNING OUT WHEN THEY COUNT

Questions regarding who takes part in American democracy have been central to the scientific understanding of politics, and within that tradition, race and voter turnout have been inextricably linked. In this chapter, I consolidated existing perspectives on race and voter turnout into the theory of electrol influence. Unlike most understandings of voter behavior, the theory of electoral influence indicates that forces largely external to the individual create and perpetuate the substantial racial/ethnic differences in turnout that we continue to witness today. Also, unlike much recent work on race and politics, I establish a more limited role for policy and institutional barriers in structuring the turnout gap. Instead, relative rates of voter turnout are a function of the relative size of ethnic groups within a jurisdiction. Both minority and White voters turn out when they count in the electoral process, as groups holding influence in election outcomes are more likely to be mobilized, feel empowered, and determine that their racial/ethnic group has political relevance and motivates their participation. The Minority–White turnout gap exists because White voters are, in almost all circumstances, far more likely to matter for election outcomes than minority citizens.

As noted in Chapter 1, an explanation of the turnout gap is critical for understanding the distribution of power in American elections and American politics more broadly. Chapter 2 investigated the roots of the turnout gap, finding that minority voters would turn out even under conditions of *de facto* disenfranchisement, but also that the elimination of these barriers did not necessarily lead to an increase in voting. Similarly, Chapter 3 demonstrated that sociodemographic factors do not explain away racial/ethnic differences in who turns out to vote. In the next chapter I evaluate evidence for the theory of electoral influence, studying geographic variation in the contemporary turnout gap.

5

The Political Geography of the Turnout Gap

The Voting Rights Act of 1965 (VRA) celebrated its fortieth anniversary in 2005, and key provisions of the act were scheduled for expiration in 2007. At the time, Republicans held sizable majorities in both the House and the Senate, and Republican President George W. Bush had just begun his second term in office. Voting rights advocates were concerned that portions of the VRA, including the Section 5 preclearance mandate discussed in Chapter 2, might be allowed to expire. Instead, Section 5 and other vital parts of the act were extended for twenty-five years, until 2032. Wide, bipartisan majorities in both the House and the Senate approved of the extension, citing thousands of pages of research demonstrating the success of, and continuing need for, the VRA (Becker 2007: 248). Scarcely three years later, however, the Supreme Court raised concerns about the coverage formula used to determine which jurisdictions would be subject to preclearance. In the words of Chief Justice John Roberts:

> Things have changed in the South. Voter turnout and registration rates now approach parity. Blatantly discriminatory evasions of federal decrees are rare. And minority candidates hold office at unprecedented levels . . . It may be that these improvements are insufficient and that conditions continue to warrant preclearance under the Act. But the Act imposes current burdens and must be justified by current needs.[1]

Citing the academic scholarship,[2] the Chief Justice questioned the need to single out the mostly Southern covered jurisdictions. In the Court's

---

[1] *Northwest Austin Municipal Utility District Number One v. Holder,* 557 U.S. 193 (2009): 7–8.
[2] Including published work by Persily (2007).

view, the Black–White turnout gap had closed in the South, or at least diminished to such a degree that special protections for Black voters were no longer necessary. In other words, the VRA had done its job, and it was now time to focus on undefined "current needs" in the area of voting rights.

The analyses presented so far indicate that the turnout gap has persisted over time, across groups, and despite changes in the oft-identified socioeconomic or *de facto* political barriers experienced by minority citizens. Yet we also know that overall turnout varies a great deal across geographic areas in the United States (McDonald 2002, 2017b), and Chapter 2 demonstrated that there were once large regional differences in rates of voter turnout within racial/ethnic groups. Using the same Current Population Survey data found in Chapter 2, a 5–4 majority in the Supreme Court struck down the formula used to determine coverage under the preclearance provisions, pointing to Black turnout exceeding White turnout in Southern states.[3] Where do we see continued racial/ethnic disparities in who turns out to vote? Is the turnout gap larger or smaller in the South than in other parts of the country? Are there areas of the country where Latino and Asian American turnout is closer to that of Whites?

In this chapter, I evaluate initial evidence for the theory of electoral influence outlined in Chapter 4. I study geographic variation in the turnout gap in an effort to identify the kinds of places where racial/ethnic differences in voter turnout are less pronounced. Such variation is difficult to measure with traditional surveys as sample sizes for small geographic units, such as counties, are correspondingly quite small as well; the analysis of subgroups within these geographies exacerbates the problem even further.[4] To overcome these problems, I draw on individual-level data derived from voter registration records. As discussed in greater depth below, I make use of turnout figures from Catalist, LLC, a data vendor that compiles state-level voter files to construct a national database of all registrants (and many non-registrants) nationwide. Information drawn from Catalist closely mirrors the best available estimates

---

[3] *Shelby County v. Holder*, 570 U.S. 2: 2.

[4] Recent advances in the analysis of survey data, in particular, multilevel regression and poststratification (MRP), present an opportunity for researchers to analyze behavior or opinions for relatively small demographic groups at ever-finer geographic levels (Ghitza and Gelman 2013). However, as I will demonstrate in this chapter, such techniques still rely on assumptions about the validity of survey measurements of behavior, assumptions that are violated when examining voter turnout for racial/ethnic groups.

of voter turnout, as it is not dependent on self-reports of voter turnout. However, the most important feature of the Catalist data is the availability of highly accurate predictions of individual race/ethnicity, information not usually found in public voter files. Combining the Catalist data with estimates of the voting eligible population, I find that the Latino–White and Asian–White turnout gaps are much larger than what is suggested by survey data. Furthermore, I demonstrate that the Black–White turnout gap has *not* closed in recent years, as even in the historic 2008 and 2012 elections Black turnout lagged White turnout by as much as 10 percentage points.

With a more complete understanding of persistent racial/ethnic disparities in voting rates, I map the turnout gap and find that the gap between minority and White turnout is smaller in places where minority groups compose a larger portion of the potential electorate. This suggests a striking change from the patterns found in the pre-VRA era, where heavily African American areas of the Deep South saw the lowest rates of voter turnout. Today, the Black–White turnout gap is smallest in southern states with relatively large African American populations, and in counties where Black citizens make up a large share of the pool of potential voters. Examining Latinos and Asian Americans, I find a similar pattern in southwestern and western states both overall and at the county level. The chapter thus indicates that geographic variation in the turnout gap conforms to the theory of electoral influence outlined in Chapter 4.

WHO ACTUALLY VOTED?

The analyses featured in earlier chapters relied on survey measures of who turned out to vote. A key reason for using such data is the fact that a pair of national surveys have queried voter turnout for decades: the American National Election Study (ANES) since 1948 and the Current Population Survey Voting and Registration Supplement (CPS) since 1964. The ANES has a dramatically lower sample size than the CPS, providing information on only a handful of individuals in some states. The CPS seeks to poll over 100,000 households nationwide each month, and is better suited for studying national trends in participation. Yet, even the CPS does not have the geographic coverage to allow us to inspect state-by-state differences in voter turnout by race: the CPS itself uses *regional*, rather than state-level estimates of participation in their press releases (File 2013). Some of this is due to the household sampling employed by the CPS, though other studies have suggested that this does not bias turnout estimates significantly when comparing demographic subgroups (Highton 2005). Instead, the larger issue is the fact that for relatively small populations within states, such as African Americans in the Mountain West, Asian Americans in the South, and Latinos in New England, the CPS estimates would be constructed from fewer than a dozen individuals.[5] Measures of the turnout gap below the national level are thus not reliably estimated by even the largest surveys.

Misreporting is a second, more substantial flaw plaguing studies relying on self-reported voter turnout. For some time, political scientists have "widely recognized, though not always highly publicized" the fact that surveys tend to overstate the share of the population that takes part in elections (Sigelman 1982: 47). For instance, the 2008 ANES reported that approximately 78 percent of the eligible population voted in the November election, while estimates based on official vote totals place turnout closer to 62 percent (McDonald 2017b). Scholars have attributed this deviation to the "overreporting" of participation by individual survey respondents since at least the 1980s (Sigelman 1982; Abramson and Claggett 1984; Hill and Hurley 1984).[6] The leading explanation for overreporting is an eagerness on the part of respondents to report socially desirable behavior; in this case, political participation (Silver, Anderson, and Abramson 1986). In what is perhaps a troubling sign for researchers, social desirability seems to be most forceful in producing overreporting for individuals who are older, have high levels of education, are interested in politics, and attend church (Silver, Anderson, and Abramson 1986; Bernstein, Chadha, and Montjoy 2001; Belli, Traugott, and Beckmann 2001; Fullerton, Dixon, and Borch 2007; Ansolabehere and Hersh 2012). As a result, our models of voting may overstate the role of these demographic factors or "resources" (e.g. Verba, Schlozman, and Brady 1995) in predicting who participates (Ansolabehere and Hersh 2012).

Overreporting is an especially acute concern given the potential for minority groups to misreport at higher rates than Whites. Early studies also noted that African Americans appeared to systematically overstate the rate at which they took part in elections (Sigelman 1982; Abramson and Claggett 1984). However, findings soon became mixed as to whether

---

[5] For instance, in the November 2016 CPS, only ten African Americans were polled in Wyoming, four Asian Americans were polled in Mississippi, and nine Latinos were polled in Maine.

[6] Note that earlier work attributed the deviation to either biases in sample construction, or a potential turnout stimulating effect of selection into the sample (Clausen 1968–1969).

racial differences in overreporting were attributable to the distribution of the aforementioned traits among ethnic groups (Silver, Anderson, and Abramson 1986; Ansolabehere and Hersh 2012) or to a more clearly race-linked factor (Fullerton, Dixon, and Borch 2007; Deufel and Kedar 2010; McKee, Hood, and Hill 2012). As Deufel and Kedar (2010) note, we would expect African Americans to overreport participation less than Whites simply because Black turnout is lower than White turnout: there is a larger share of Black voters who could misstate that they voted. Drawing on the same ANES data, Cassel (2002) determines that Latinos overreport at a rate similar to non-Hispanic Whites, yet lower overall turnout for Latinos means that greater proportion of the Latino population misreports. Studies of self-reported voter registration reach similar conclusions, as validated Latino registration lags significantly behind self-reports (Shaw, de la Garza, and Lee 2000). Despite this dynamic, Deufel and Kedar (2010) continue to find that Black ANES respondents overreport at a higher rate even accounting for the increased nonvoting proportion of the population, attributing the persistent racial effect to increased social pressure to vote in the Black population. McKee, Hood, and Hill (2012) align with such an understanding, asserting that Barack Obama's candidacy contributed to overreporting among African Americans in 2008, while Fraga (2016a) suggests circumstances associated with heightened minority electoral influence may exacerbate turnout overreporting by Black and Latino citizens.

A solution to the above concerns is to use "official," or state-generated, information on who turns out to vote. The gold standard is generally considered to be reports from county and state election administrators, public officials who are tasked with recording and reporting the vote totals that decide election outcomes. Yet, when it comes to determining *how many* citizens voted, the goal of reporting election outcomes trumps the creation of precise estimates of overall voter turnout. As McDonald (2017b) notes, some states do not provide figures on the total number of individuals who voted; elections are decided by the number of votes cast for each candidate, not the number of voters arriving at the polls. Individual-level data is even more difficult to come by. In the wake of the contested 2000 presidential election, Congress passed the Help America Vote Act (HAVA) of 2002, mandating that states create and maintain voter registration lists, or *voter files*, with individual-level records of the geographic and electoral information of every registrant in a state (McDonald 2010: 137). Beyond information about the precinct and electoral districts of every registrant, contemporary voter file data often includes information about turnout in past elections. However, voter files are often challenging to acquire and have restrictions on use for academic purposes (McDonald 2017a). That said, since turnout as recorded in the voter file is not subject to overreporting, scholars have increasingly realized the potential inherent in voter file data (Gimpel, Dyck, and Shaw 2004; McDonald 2007), and voter file-based analyses have become common in the political science scholarship on who votes (Enos 2016; Fraga 2016a, 2016b).

Catalist Data

Given concerns about geographic coverage and misreporting, voter file data offers many advantages over traditional surveys. Beyond the difficulty of acquisition, however, public voter file data has another significant drawback: modern voter registrars only gather a limited amount of information about each registrant. The name, address, age, and gender of each registrant is generally available. In some states, individuals register with political parties and thus party affiliation can be inferred from voter file records. A much smaller number of states (eight) also provide space for individuals to indicate their race/ethnicity, a legacy of Jim Crow-era voting restrictions. As noted by Hersh (2015: 49), candidates have used printed voter registration lists for campaign mobilization since at least the late 1800s (Harris 1929), and continue to be the primary users of such information today. Thus, for political scientists interested in topics such as the demographics of who turns out to vote, a tradeoff must be made when using public voter file data.

In the wake of HAVA implementation, campaigns were able to access voter registration lists on a large scale in machine-readable format. Yet, inconsistencies between states in the format of their databases made it difficult for campaigns to effectively use this new information. Campaign consulting firms stepped in and offered to assist with contact efforts using voter file-based data, such that vendors began appearing who specialized in aggregating, organizing, verifying, and distributing (for a fee) an approximation of a "national" voter file (Kreiss 2012). While often affiliated with one of the two major political poles, these firms now serve as a resource to campaigns across the political spectrum. The voter turnout information I use in this chapter is provided by Catalist, LLC.[7] Hersh (2015: ch. 4) discusses the history and campaign use of Catalist in greater

7 www.catalist.us

detail, but for the purposes of this project, there are two points to keep in mind. First, Catalist has every incentive to produce an accurate representation of the voter file and to provide any and all data that can be used by campaigns (Ansolabehere and Hersh 2014). While primarily vending to left-leaning causes in addition to academic researchers, the data I extract from Catalist is unlikely to be biased in a manner systematically favoring a political persuasion. Second, the Catalist database is designed to track both registered *and* unregistered voters for targeting purposes, such that unlike the public file, individuals who are dropped or "purged" from the registration list are kept in the database. Catalist organizes its database by state, such that separate registration records are maintained for each person in both their "new" and "old" state if they were to move and duplicate records of turnout are avoided to the extent possible.

In this chapter I draw on counts of the voting population in the 2006, 2008, 2010, 2012, 2014, and 2016 elections. These counts are based on data entry by poll workers and election officials at the county level, which are then linked to the state voter files, acquired by Catalist, and finally merged with the existing Catalist database. States vary in the quality of their voter file data (Ansolabehere and Hersh 2014). Yet, Table 5.1 demonstrates the high accuracy of the Catalist data in providing individual-level information regarding the voting population. Contrasting the number of voters nationwide as indicated by Catalist with state counts of total ballots cast as estimated by McDonald (2017b), we can see that in nearly every election the Catalist count of voters deviates less than three-quarters of one percent from McDonald's estimate of the individuals casting ballots.[8] For comparison, I also provide the

---

[8] The Catalist count of voters in Table 5.1 reflects the total number of individual records flagged as having voted in the Catalist database as of summer 2017. Per correspondence with data analysts from Catalist, this number may be an overestimate of the number of voters Catalist has records for as some individuals are duplicated due to name changes, in-state movers, or other changes in registration records that would cause Catalist to treat an existing registration record as a new record within a state. This issue appears particularly severe for the 2008 election, where the deviation from McDonald's (2017b) count may be as much as 2 percent once accounting for duplicate records. For Tables 5.1, 5.2, and 5.3, along with Figure 5.1, statistics reflect Catalist estimates that can be drawn from the 2017 iteration of the database. For the state, county, and district-level analyses in Chapters 5 and 6, I use custom versions of the Catalist database contemporaneous to each election in order to avoid biases caused by in-state movers, name changes, and other issues inducing mismatching.

TABLE 5.1 *Comparison of ballots counted to Catalist and CPS estimates*

		Catalist		CPS	
Year	Ballots counted	Count	Difference (%)	Count	Difference (%)
2006	85,769,132	85,223,008	−0.64	96,118,886	+12.07
2008	132,609,063	132,969,285	+0.27	131,143,947	−1.10
2010	90,912,015	90,497,901	−0.46	95,987,029	+5.58
2012	130,292,355	129,699,025	−0.46	132,948,229	+2.04
2014	83,262,122	83,100,029	−0.19	92,251,444	+10.80
2016	138,846,571	137,310,169	−1.11	137,536,547	−0.94

Note: "Ballots counted" represents an estimate of the total number of ballots cast across states in the general election for each year, as computed by McDonald (2017b). "Catalist Count" is the number of records in the Catalist database flagged as having voted in the general election. "CPS Count" is the estimate of the number of voters published by the CPS (e.g. File 2013). "Difference" is the deviation from the McDonald (2017b) estimate for the Catalist and CPS estimates, expressed as a percentage of the McDonald (2017b) estimate. Catalist figures for the number of voters deviate from the McDonald (2017b) estimates by an average of 0.52 percent, while the CPS figures deviate by an average of 5.42 percent.

CPS-weighted estimates of the number of voters in each year, based on the November Supplement data also used in Chapter 2. Deviations are ten to twenty times larger when comparing the CPS to McDonald's estimates, and in line with research suggesting substantial overreporting of voter turnout in surveys, the CPS figures on how many adults voted are, on average, 4.7 percent higher than McDonald's (2017b) totals.

Modeling Individual Race

Firms began adding proprietary information as soon as digitized voter files became available (Hersh 2015). Given the importance of race/ethnicity as a predictor of vote choice in the 2000s, campaigns soon demanded such information as well. As noted above, eight states[9] do record self-reported information on race/ethnicity. Scholars have leveraged this publicly available data on race/ethnicity to conduct research on the predictors of voter turnout for African Americans (Whitby 2007; Keele et al. 2014) or used surname matching to Census lists of Spanish names in order to distinguish Latinos from non-Latinos outside of

[9] Alabama, Florida, Georgia, Louisiana, North Carolina, and South Carolina require that registrants list their race, while Mississippi and Tennessee provide space for registrants to do so, but do not mandate completion of this section of the form.

these states (Barreto, Segura, and Woods 2004; Henderson, Sekhon, and Titiunik 2016).

Catalist, however, uses a proprietary algorithm incorporating full name and Census block group or tract demographic information to predict the race/ethnicity of every person in their database. While proprietary, the method of linking individual names with data on the composition of the individual's neighborhood in a Bayesian framework is a well-understood method of race prediction (Elliott et al. 2008; Enos 2016; Imai and Khanna 2016). Where available, Catalist also incorporates self-reports of race from commercial and nonprofit databases to improve their estimates. Using this information, I am able to isolate voters from each of the five racial/ethnic groups I examine in the book, eliminating the possibility of overreporting while providing the geographic coverage necessary to make firm inferences about the relationship between my measure of relative group size-based electoral influence and voter turnout.

How accurate are Catalist's measures of individual race/ethnicity? Catalist provides some metrics as to the quality of their race coding, and in previous work I put their prediction rate at over 90 percent (Fraga 2016a).[10] Accuracy is lower for minority groups, especially in areas where they compose a small proportion of the population. In fact, the distribution of racial/ethnic groups across the country present a special challenge to the theoretical framework I outline in Chapter 4: our best measures of Black, Latino, and Asian voter turnout are found in exactly the kinds of places where I would expect minority turnout to be *highest*. Careful construction of the turnout gap is thus of utmost importance when seeking to understand geographic variation in turnout differences, and thus I discuss Catalist's race modeling and my method of aggregating the race/ethnicity of voters in Appendix A.3.

Who Could Have Voted?

Catalist provides highly accurate estimates of the number of individuals who voted in recent elections. In addition, Catalist's race modeling allows us to understand the racial/ethnic composition of the voting population. Despite the value of these datapoints, when constructing turnout *rates* we again confront the issue of defining the denominator as discussed in

---

[10] See Appendix A.3 for updated estimates and a breakdown of prediction accuracy by information source and race/ethnicity.

Chapter 2 (p. 37). In that chapter, I discussed the importance of taking into account voting eligibility. These concerns are exacerbated when analyzing state or substate variation in voter turnout, as for instance, Holbrook and Heidbreder (2010) demonstrate that inferences about what impacts state-level voter turnout vary depending on whether one uses the voting-age population or the voting-eligible population (VEP) as the measure. As the Catalist database is principally composed of voter registration lists, it may seem attractive to use registrants as the denominator in turnout calculations. Yet, once again, this approach creates complexities when comparing state-level turnout, as states vary in the extent to which they keep their registration databases updated (Ansolabehere and Hersh 2014).

Instead, I turn to information from the U.S. Census Bureau to estimate the voting-eligible electorate by state, and later county. Two Census products are used to approximate the VEP by state and county. First, I use the American Community Survey (ACS) one-, three-, and five-year surveys to determine the proportion of voting-age adults in each geographic unit who are citizens. The ACS is a survey, albeit a very large survey, and uses estimates of the adult population to weight the sample and produce estimates of how many adults should be included in the sampling frame. Non-response could create significant variation in the number of self-reported citizens in small geographic units, and thus I make use of a non-survey-based Census product, the Population Estimates Program (PEP), to determine the voting-age population in each unit. The PEP program, and related Intercensal Estimates, track births, deaths, and migration on a monthly basis to provide researchers with counts of the adult population at specific points in time. However, the PEP program does not include estimates of citizenship, and thus I multiply the PEP estimate with the ACS citizen to non-citizen ratio to generate an estimate of the citizen voting-age population (CVAP) in the midpoint of each year. Interpolation is used to convert these figures to the November of each election year.[11] When estimating rates of turnout by race, these steps are repeated for each race plus sex combination to ensure that variation in citizenship rates by sex and differences in the size of the CVAP by sex and race are accounted for.

The third source of data I use is information regarding disenfranchised felons and incarcerated individuals. In all states aside from Vermont

---

[11] More details regarding the procedure used to combine multi-year ACS estimates, intercensal estimates, and PEP data may be found in the Online Appendix to this book.

TABLE 5.2 *Comparison of turnout rate estimates*

Year	McDonald (%)	Catalist		CPS	
		Turnout (%)	Difference	Turnout (%)	Difference
2006	42.20	42.29	+0.08	47.80	+5.60
2008	63.65	64.53	+0.88	63.64	−0.01
2010	42.77	42.99	+0.22	45.53	+2.77
2012	59.95	60.23	+0.28	61.81	+1.87
2014	37.54	37.83	+0.29	41.94	+4.41
2016	61.48	61.36	−0.11	61.38	−0.09

Note: "McDonald" represents estimates of voter turnout as a share of the US-resident VEP in the general election for each year, as computed by McDonald (2017b). Note that McDonald (2017b) includes estimates of the "Overseas Eligible" population when calculating turnout, a population not included here as it is not part of the denominator in the Catalist or CPS-based estimates. "Catalist" turnout is the number of records in the Catalist database flagged as having voted in the general election, divided by the estimate of the CVAP minus the disenfranchised incarcerated and felon populations as detailed in this section. "CPS" turnout is the estimate of the turnout rate of the CVAP published by the CPS, which counts non-respondents as non-voters (see File 2013). "Difference" is the deviation from the McDonald (2017b) rate for the Catalist and CPS estimates, expressed in whole percentage points. Catalist figures for the turnout rate deviate from the McDonald (2017b) rate by an average of 0.31 percentage points, while the CPS rates deviate by an average of 2.46 percentage points.

and Maine, individuals who are currently incarcerated are ineligible to vote. In addition, nearly all states restrict the voting rights of those with felony convictions, in some instances for life. There are considerable racial disparities in who loses voting rights due to these policies (Manza and Uggen 2008), and the impact of felon disenfranchisement laws on political participation is well documented (Burch 2013). Thus, I draw on information from the Sentencing Project (Uggen, Shannon, and Manza 2012; Uggen, Larson, and Shannon 2016) and exclude disenfranchised felons and incarcerated individuals from the denominator when calculating turnout. In 2016, approximately 2.5 percent of otherwise eligible adults were excluded from the franchise due to state laws barring convicted felons from voting.

Table 5.2 is similar to Table 5.1, but now compares *rates* of voter turnout as estimated by McDonald (2017b), the combination of a Catalist-based numerator and Census-based denominator, and the CPS estimates of voter turnout rates. Note that McDonald uses ACS and PEP figures as the base for his computation of the VEP, though he also incorporates information about disenfranchised felons and overseas residents to provide a more precise measure of who could vote (McDonald 2017b). Yet, as in Table 5.1, the voter turnout rates using Catalist and Census data are far closer to the estimates produced by McDonald. On average, Catalist plus Census rates are an overestimate of the true turnout rate by 0.31 percentage points, while the CPS overestimates turnout by more than 2 percentage points.[12]

THE TRUE MAGNITUDE OF THE TURNOUT GAP

Table 5.2 confirms that the use of Catalist data for the numerator and Census data for the denominator allows for an approximation of the "true" turnout rate as estimated by McDonald (2017c). Yet, the quasi-official turnout estimates produced by McDonald (2017b) are not disaggregated by race; he, like other researchers, has been forced to rely on the overreport-prone CPS to estimate national rates of turnout by race/ethnicity. However, as Catalist provides estimates of the number of voters by race, we are able to use these estimates of who voted to better understand racial/ethnic differences in voter turnout. As noted above, the denominator in my turnout estimates subtracts individuals who are ineligible to vote due to a felony conviction. The potential for felon disenfranchisement to exacerbate the turnout gap is addressed in greater detail in Chapter 7, but briefly, nearly 8 percent of otherwise eligible African American citizens are removed from the denominator due to felon disenfranchisement.[13]

Table 5.3 presents estimates of turnout by race and the Black–White, Latino–White, and Asian–White turnout gaps for elections from 2006–2016. Chapter 2, specifically, Figure 2.4 already indicated substantial turnout gaps over time. When using a combination of Catalist data (which is not subject to self-report) and Census information (which is not subject to geographic coverage issues), we get a much clearer indication as to the *severity* of the contemporary turnout gap across minority groups. Latino and Asian American turnout was less than half that of Whites in recent midterm elections, and fewer than 18 percent of eligible

---

[12] Again, due to the potential for record linkage errors in the Catalist database, these figures may overestimate the number of "voters" in the Catalist database and thus overestimate turnout rates. See note associated with description of Table 5.1 for more details.

[13] The aforementioned Sentencing Project reports are used here, along with estimates of Latino disenfranchisement (Demeo and Ochoa 2003) and contemporaneous Black and non-Black disenfranchisement rates (Manza and Uggen 2008). Due to limited data, the Asian disenfranchisement rate is calculated as the same as the non-Hispanic White disenfranchisement rate. For more details, see Chapter 7.

TABLE 5.3 *Estimate of turnout and the turnout gap by race, 2006–2016*

Year	White turnout %	Black turnout %	Gap	Latino turnout %	Gap	Asian turnout %	Gap
2006	48.4	28.3	−20.1	23.7	−24.7	22.3	−26.1
2008	70.3	59.7	−10.6	45.2	−25.1	39.2	−31.2
2010	49.3	33.1	−16.2	23.6	−25.7	22.6	−26.7
2012	66.6	56.4	−10.2	39.2	−27.5	34.7	−31.9
2014	44.5	29.6	−14.9	17.7	−26.8	17.6	−27.0
2016	69.2	51.3	−17.9	43.4	−25.8	37.9	−31.2

Note: "Turnout %" calculated as the number of records in the Catalist database flagged as having voted in the general election, by race, divided by an estimate of the voting eligible population, by race, as detailed in this section. "Gap" is the gap between the indicated group's rate of turnout and White turnout, expressed in whole percentage points.

citizen Latinos and Asians voted in the 2014 election. The most striking finding, however, pertains to African American turnout. Even in the historic presidential elections of 2008 and 2012, Black turnout continued to lag behind the non-Hispanic White turnout rate by a large margin. Midterms look even worse, as despite recent gains African American voting rates are 15 percentage points behind that of the White population nationally. Consistent with an older scholarship (Sigelman 1982; Abramson and Claggett 1984; Deufel and Kedar 2010; McKee, Hood, and Hill 2012), but in contrast to some more recent work (Ansolabehere and Hersh 2012), survey estimates appear to overstate African American turnout to a large degree.[14]

The magnitude of the turnout gap in Table 5.3 provides a very different picture of contemporary political inequality than what was suggested in Chapter 2. When using voter file-based data and estimates of the eligible population, turnout rates are dramatically lower for racial/ethnic minority groups, including African Americans, than surveys indicate. In Figure 5.1, I compare the estimate of the turnout gap in the 2006–2016 CPS surveys[15] to the Catalist plus Census estimates I used to construct

[14] As discussed in Appendix A.3, alternative methods of aggregating the Catalist data yield a persistent, but smaller Black–White turnout gap. However, even under the most generous estimates of Black turnout using voter file data, Black turnout did not reach parity with White turnout during the period examined here.

[15] Note that the CPS estimates I use here remove missing responses, unlike the CPS-reported estimates in Table 5.2. Appendix A.2 details why this is the case: non-Whites are far more likely to complete the Voting and Registration Supplement questions in recent elections. Chapter 2 also removes missing responses from the CPS estimates (see p. 37).

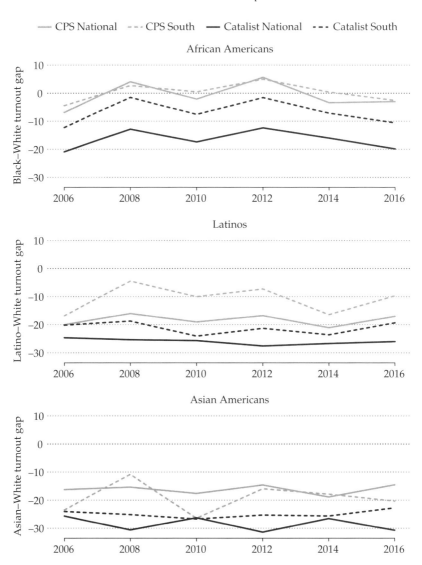

FIGURE 5.1 Comparison of estimates of the turnout gap

Note: CPS figures remove missing responses when calculating the turnout gap. Catalist estimates are based on the number of records flagged as having voted in the database, by race, and remove individuals who are imprisoned from estimates of the CVAP for each racial/ethnic group. "South" restricts data to the six states with self-reported race data on registration records.

Table 5.3.[16] The figure indicates that the Black–White turnout gap is 12 to 18 percentage points larger when using Catalist data as opposed to statistics from the CPS. Instead of Black turnout approximating White turnout in recent elections, disparities of 10 to 20 percentage points persist. For Latinos, the difference between the CPS estimates and Catalist estimates are smaller, but surveys may underestimate the Latino–White turnout gap by as much as 10 percentage points. The Asian–White turnout gap is similarly wider in the CPS: the CPS estimates Asian American voter turnout to lag that of Whites by 14.5 percentage points for 2016, but Catalist plus Census estimates put the Asian–White turnout gap at over 30 percentage points.

As noted above, and discussed in further detail in Appendix A.3, Catalist estimates the race/ethnicity of nearly every registrant nationwide. However, in the eight states where registrants may self-report their race/ethnicity, Catalist uses what registrants themselves indicated about their racial/ethnic identity instead. Focusing on the six southern states where 90 percent or more of registrants self-reported their race as either White, Black, Latino, or Asian,[17] the dashed lines in Figure 5.1 indicate that the actual voter file records of who turned out by race vary from CPS estimates for these states. Unlike the CPS, which reported Black voter turnout to be as much as 5 percentage points higher than White turnout in 2012, voter file data indicates Black turnout lagged White turnout in every election from 2006 to 2016. Notably, the CPS also reports that turnout disparities for African Americans in the six southern states were essentially the same as disparities in the rest of the country: a small Black–White turnout gap in four of the six elections and Black turnout slightly greater than White turnout in 2008 and 2012. Voter file data indicates that this is not the case: the Black–White turnout gap is indeed smaller in the South. For Latinos and Asian Americans, we also see that the CPS is not able to reliably approximate the actual state records of racial differences in voter turnout, underestimating the gap by as much as 14

---

[16] In order to provide a fair comparison of these two data sources, I align estimates of the VEP based on Census data as closely as possible to the CPS population of interest. The CPS may poll disenfranchised ex-felons, but does not seek to cover institutionalized populations, such as those in prisons (who, outside of Maine and Vermont, are ineligible to vote). Therefore, I only remove prisoners from the citizen voting-age population estimates by race, using yearly state-level figures from the Bureau of Justice Statistics (DOJ 2017). For the 2016 election, 2015 estimates of imprisonment by race/ethnicity are used.

[17] These states are AL, FL, GA, LA, NC, SC. See Hersh (2015: ch. 6) for more details regarding the history of and variation in self-reported race on voter registration files.

percentage points for Latinos and Asian Americans. Again, Appendix A.3 contains details of how Catalist models individual race/ethnicity when necessary. However, the fact that the CPS underestimates the turnout gap even for states where we know the "correct" gap may help to assuage concerns that the estimates in Table 5.3 result from vagaries of the race modeling procedure.

While the CPS tends to underestimate the turnout gap, we may recover some utility for the survey-based statistics. Variation in the Black–White turnout gap from 2006 to 2016 appears to be consistent across the CPS and Catalist estimates, with the gap shrinking in 2008 and 2012 but changes in the gap tracking together using both data sources. It is plausible that the strong gains in relative turnout for African Americans in Figure 2.4 prior to the 1970s are not simply an artifact of biases in the CPS. For Latinos and Asian Americans, where a double digit gap manifested even using survey data, there is a less close relationship between the two gap measures in recent elections. In the absence of non-survey data on turnout for preceding decades, survey estimates indicating any sizable variation in the Latino–White and Asian–White turnout gap over time should perhaps be taken with a grain of salt. A broad story regarding persistent, large disparities in voter turnout between minority voters and non-Hispanic Whites overall, though, is difficult to dispute. Furthermore, the CPS and other survey data are invaluable for understanding the relationship between race, sociodemographics, political preferences, and turnout, and changes in these relationships over time. Absent the recovery of historical voter file data,[18] surveys will continue to be a necessary tool for understanding political participation in America.

STATE-LEVEL VARIATION IN THE TURNOUT GAP

The substantial racial/ethnic disparities in Table 5.3 conform to the theory of electoral influence as outlined in Chapter 4: minority groups are a smaller share of the electorate in nearly every jurisdiction nationwide, and thus a persistent gap in participation with Whites is to be expected. In Chapter 2, we saw disaggregated rates of voter turnout by race and region, indicating the collapse of regional differences in the turnout gap and motivating the declaration that "things have changed in the South." Opinions of Chief Justice Roberts notwithstanding, the ANES and CPS

---

[18] See Spahn (2017) for ongoing research in this area.

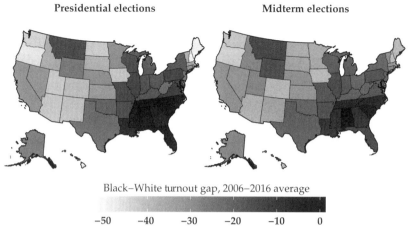

Presidential elections   **Midterm elections**

Black–White turnout gap, 2006–2016 average

−50   −40   −30   −20   −10   0

FIGURE 5.2 State-level Black–White turnout gap, 2006–2016
Note: Averages over presidential and midterm elections, respectively. States where Black turnout exceeded White turnout in presidential elections (on average) are Alabama, the District of Columbia, Florida, Mississippi, North Carolina, South Carolina, and Tennessee.

TABLE 5.4 *Black turnout gap by state proportion Black, 2006–2016*

	State Black CVAP	
	<15%	≥15%
Midterm	−26.5	−9.8
presidential	−28.4	−4.9

Note: Cells reflect average turnout gap with non-Hispanic Whites in states where the African American proportion of the enfranchised citizen voting-age population is greater than or equal to 15 percent, or less than 15 percent. Rows average over midterm and presidential elections, respectively.

data do not allow us to examine state-level variation in a reliable manner given their relatively small minority samples in most states; misestimation of the turnout gap exacerbates these issues even further. Using the Catalist and Census-derived estimates of voter turnout, Figures 5.2 through 5.4 map the turnout gap at the subregional level in recent elections, displaying state-by-state differences in the turnout gap. I average over presidential and midterm elections for ease of presentation.

Beginning with Figure 5.2, which documents the Black–White turnout gap, we see considerable variation across states. Here the more darkly

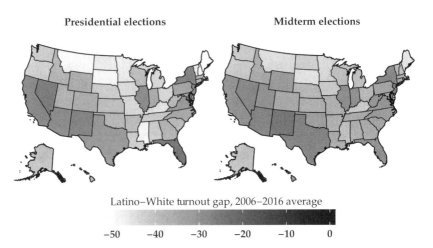

Presidential elections   **Midterm elections**

Latino–White turnout gap, 2006–2016 average

−50   −40   −30   −20   −10   0

FIGURE 5.3 State-level Latino–White turnout gap, 2006–2016
Note: Averages over presidential and midterm elections, respectively. In no state
did Latino turnout exceed White turnout.

shaded states have a smaller, or even reversed, Black–White turnout gap.
States fitting such a description are found not in the North, but rather, the
states of the Deep South where racial barriers to voting were most viru-
lent, most recent, and in the view of many voting rights advocates, persist
today. Lower turnout midterms also show similar state-level patterns to
presidential contests. Table 5.4 documents the relationship between the
Black–White turnout gap and the percent Black in states. Black turnout
lags White turnout by over 26 percentage points in states where African
Americans make up less than 15 percent of the population, even in
presidential elections. However, in states where the Black population is
15 percent or more of statewide eligible voters, Black turnout is sharply
higher relative to Whites in both midterms and Presidential contests.[19]

The Latino–White turnout gap is not smaller in states of the Deep
South, but instead, follows a pattern consistent with the theory of electoral influence outlined in Chapter 4. Figure 5.3 uses the same color
gradient as maps of the Black–White turnout gap, but here all states
are much lighter, indicating that on average Latino turnout lags White

[19] Table 5.3 indicates that the Black–White gap was smaller in 2008 and 2012 as compared to 2016. Figure 5.2 provides estimates of the Black–White gap in nine southern
states with relatively large African American populations, presenting the same pattern
of smaller gaps in heavily Black states even for 2008 and 2012. For important caveats
about estimating Black turnout in heavily Black states, see Appendix A.3.

TABLE 5.5 *Latino turnout gap by state proportion Latino, 2006–2016*

	State Latino CVAP	
	<15%	≥15%
Midterm	−33.2	−23.4
Presidential	−37.4	−24.1

Note: Cells reflect average turnout gap with non-Hispanic Whites in states where the Latino proportion of the enfranchised citizen voting-age population is greater than or equal to 15 percent, or less than 15 percent. Rows average over midterm and presidential elections, respectively.

turnout by a greater margin than for African Americans. Yet, once again, states where Latinos make up a larger portion of the potential electorate have a smaller Latino–White turnout gap. In no state does Latino turnout exceed White turnout on average, but the southwestern states, Florida, Illinois, and New York all see a smaller gap than the rest of the country. Table 5.5 indicates that the Latino–White turnout gap is smaller in states where Latinos could have a larger impact on election outcomes; while still lagging far behind Whites, Latino turnout is 13 percentage points closer to White turnout in presidential contests with a sizable Latino population.

The Asian–White turnout gap is featured in Figure 5.4 and Table 5.6. Disparities are large in every state and for every election, except in Hawaii. Hawaii is unique in that it is the only state where Asian Americans make up more than 15 percent of the state's population; combined with multiracial Asians and non-Hawaiian Pacific Islanders, Asian Americans are a majority of Hawaii's population. Not surprisingly, the Asian–White turnout gap is smaller in this state. In the continental U.S., it appears that the Asian–White turnout gap is smaller in the southeast. National origin differences may account for some of this, as South Asians make up a plurality of the Asian American population in many southern states and had the first Indian American governor in South Carolina's Nikki Haley. Yet, California and New York also see a smaller Asian–White turnout gap, despite the fact that Filipinos and Chinese, respectively, make up the plurality of the Asian American population in each of these states. Asian Americans make up less than 4 percent of the VEP today, and far less than that in most states. However, if Hawaii is indicative of a general pattern, when the Asian American population

Presidential elections   **Midterm elections**

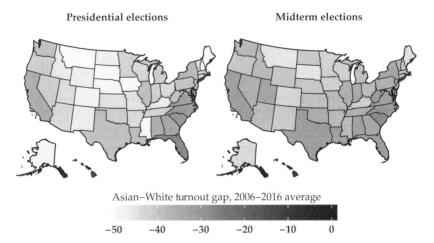

Asian–White turnout gap, 2006–2016 average

−50   −40   −30   −20   −10   0

FIGURE 5.4 State-level Asian–White turnout gap, 2006–2016
Note: Averages over presidential and midterm elections, respectively. Asian turnout exceeded White turnout in Hawaii in presidential and midterm elections on average.

TABLE 5.6 *Asian turnout gap by state proportion Asian, 2006–2016*

	State Asian CVAP	
	$<15\%$	$\geq15\%$ *(Hawaii)*
Midterm	−34.5	+4.6
Presidential	−41.0	−2.4

Note: Cells reflect average turnout gap with non-Hispanic Whites in states where the Asian proportion of the enfranchised citizen voting-age population is greater than or equal to 15 percent (the State of Hawaii), or less than 15 percent. Rows average over midterm and presidential elections, respectively.

is larger the Asian–White turnout gap may be proportionally smaller as well.

COUNTY-LEVEL VARIATION IN THE TURNOUT GAP

The preceding section offered evidence that Black, Latino, and Asian American turnout is consistently closer to White turnout in states where these groups make up a larger portion of the potential electorate. Yet, non-Hispanic Whites are an overwhelming majority of most state populations; an analysis of this level of geography may not be sufficient to characterize the demographics–turnout relationship. With the Catalist data and appropriate Census estimates, we can examine *county*-level variation in the turnout gap, enhancing our understanding of which places are likely to have a smaller difference between minority and White voter turnout.

Previous work has studied county-level variation in minority turnout using data from the CPS (Jang 2009). However, the aforementioned shortcomings of the CPS when analyzing state-level data are even more severe when looking at counties. Even large, urban counties have only a handful of minority respondents in the yearly CPS. Voter file-based data and information from the Census allows for a detailed analysis of sub-state trends in turnout. Unfortunately, shifting to the county level still necessitates appropriate care to avoid spurious relationships. The first concern regards the ACS data used to generate estimates of the proportion of voting-age adults who are citizens. The ACS has uncertainty as to citizenship rates by race and county in each election year, and as a result, counties with few citizens of a certain race may produce highly inaccurate estimates of turnout as small (numerical) errors in the denominator are magnified when converting turnout to a rate. As a result, I exclude counties with fewer than 1,000 voting-age citizens from the minority group in question and non-Hispanic Whites when producing the charts and tables below. The second major caveat regards data on the disenfranchisement of convicted felons and incarcerated individuals. The Sentencing Project does not provide county-level data, and given the fact that incarceration and crime does not necessarily occur in the county in which a potential registrant lives, it may be impossible to know the full extent of felon disenfranchisement at the substate level.[20] Chapter 7 provides a more extensive exploration of the role of felon disenfranchisement in the Black–White turnout gap, but for the analyses below, it is important to note that many of the states where disenfranchisement has its largest impact (the South) are exactly the places where parity between Black and White turnout is reached even *without* accounting for the large disenfranchised Black population.

With these limitations in mind, Figure 5.5 documents the relationship between the county-level Black–White turnout gap and the percent Black

---

[20] One option is to impute the statewide average of felon disenfranchisement on all counties within a state. Doing so produces results with the same substantive outcome as those featured here.

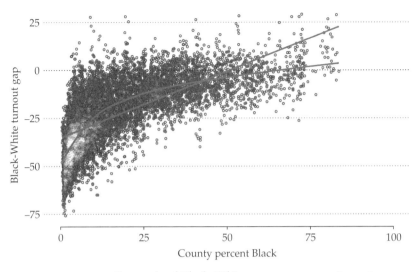

FIGURE 5.5 County-level Black–White turnout gap, 2006–2016
Note: Each point indicates a county-election observation. Black–White turnout gap is in whole percentage points. Gray lines indicate bivariate regression line and locally weighted smoother fit to the range of the data. Counties with fewer than 1,000 Black citizens and 1,000 White citizens not included.

in the county. Each point in the figure represents a single county-election observation; the clustering of points between 0 percent and 15 percent indicates that the vast majority of counties have a relatively small African American population percentage. In these places, Black voter turnout tends to lag White turnout by 20, 40, or even 60 percentage points. On the other hand, counties where a greater proportion of the population is African American see a substantially smaller turnout gap, or even a reversal of the gap. To make this relationship more clear, the gray, straight line plots the bivariate relationship between the Black–White turnout gap and the proportion Black within each county. Crossing over the zero threshold at approximately 50 percent Black, we see strong evidence that the Black–White turnout gap is smaller in places with a large Black population. A second, curved line accounts for the nonlinearity in the data, and indicates a moving average of the turnout gap as the county percent Black increases. A large change is visible when going from less than 1 percent Black to greater than 15 percent Black, with diminishing returns afterward. However, the most heavily Black counties in the country are exactly where the turnout gap has reversed.

Table 5.7 uses the same data as Figure 5.5, indicating the average Black–White turnout gap for counties within the specified proportion

TABLE 5.7 *Black turnout gap by county proportion Black,*
2006–2016

	County Black CVAP		
	<15%	15%–50%	>50%
Midterm	−29.3	−12.4	−5.5
Presidential	−35.3	−10.3	+1.2

Note: Cells reflect average turnout gap with non-Hispanic Whites in counties where the African American proportion of the citizen voting-age population is less than 15 percent, between 15 percent and 50 percent, or greater than 50 percent. Rows average over midterm and presidential elections, respectively. Counties with fewer than 1,000 Black citizens and 1,000 White citizens not included.

African American. Because of the greater range of demographic compositions available when examining counties, we can now see what turnout is like on average in majority-Black areas of the country. While Black turnout lags far behind White turnout in areas with a small Black population share, counties with 15 percent to 50 percent Black CVAP are much closer to parity. In majority-Black counties, however, Black turnout *exceeds* White turnout in recent presidential elections.[21]

Latino turnout at the county level displays a similar, if muted, relationship as that found for African Americans. Figure 5.6 and Table 5.8 indicate that Latino turnout and White turnout inch toward parity in places with a large Latino population. Again, large gains in relative Latino turnout are made up to approximately 15 percent Latino, with diminishing returns afterward. Yet in counties with a Latino majority, the turnout gap is cut by more than half. The turnout gap is even smaller in areas where Latinos make up more than 75 percent of the citizen voting-age population.

Asian Americans make up a small, but growing proportion of states other than Hawaii. However, county-level variation in the percent Asian American is great enough to evaluate whether correlations are consistent with what is suggested by the theory of electoral influence. Figure 5.7 indeed demonstrates that, on average, the Asian–White turnout gap is smaller in counties where Asian Americans make up a larger

[21] One intriguing possibility is that the CPS disproportionately samples African American respondents from heavily African American counties, producing turnout estimates reflecting the much higher turnout of Black citizens living in such places. The fact that Black turnout is higher than White turnout, on average, in heavily Black counties for presidential elections fits with the overall CPS estimates for the "historic" 2012 election.

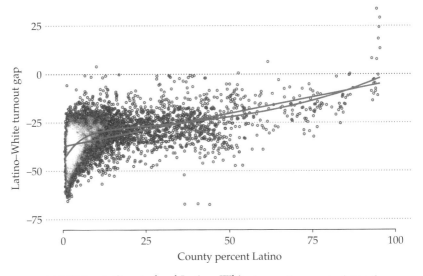

FIGURE 5.6 County-level Latino–White turnout gap, 2006–2016
Note: Each point indicates a county-election observation. Latino–White turnout gap is in whole percentage points. Gray lines indicate bivariate regression line and locally weighted smoother fit to the range of the data. Counties with fewer than 1,000 Latino citizens and 1,000 White citizens not included.

TABLE 5.8 *Latino turnout gap by county proportion Latino,*
2006–2016

	County Latino CVAP		
	<15%	*15%–50%*	*>50%*
Midterm	−32.3	−25.3	−16.1
Presidential	−38.4	−28.8	−18.0

Note: Cells reflect average turnout gap with non-Hispanic Whites in counties where the Latino proportion of the citizen voting-age population is less than 15 percent, between 15 percent and 50 percent, or greater than 50 percent. Rows average over midterm and presidential elections, respectively. Counties with fewer than 1,000 Latino citizens and 1,000 White citizens not included.

proportion of the potential electorate. The few observations where the Asian population makes up more than 40 percent of the population are in Hawaii, where the statewide results also indicated Asian turnout exceeded White turnout. Table 5.9 shows that about half of the Asian–White turnout gap disappears when looking at counties where at least 15 percent of the population is Asian American.

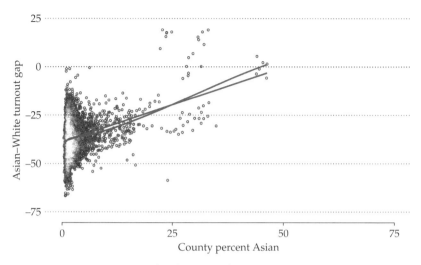

FIGURE 5.7 County-level Asian–White turnout gap, 2006–2016
Note: Each point indicates a county-election observation. Asian–White turnout gap is in whole percentage points. Gray lines indicate bivariate regression line and locally weighted smoother fit to the range of the data. Counties with fewer than 1,000 Asian American citizens and 1,000 White citizens not included.

TABLE 5.9 *Asian turnout gap by county proportion Asian, 2006–2016*

	County Asian CVAP	
	<15%	*≥15%*
Midterm	−33.1	−16.3
Presidential	−40.1	−21.9

Note: Cells reflect average turnout gap with non-Hispanic Whites in counties where the Asian proportion of the citizen voting-age population is less than 15 percent or greater than 15 percent. Rows average over midterm and presidential elections, respectively. Counties with fewer than 1,000 Asian citizens and 1,000 White citizens not included.

Electoral Influence or Urban Enclaves?

The theory of electoral influence outlined in Chapter 4 indicates that the correlations found here between a group's increased relative size and a diminution of the turnout gap are the result of the group having greater influence in the electoral process. In the next chapter, I explore the relationships found in this chapter at the congressional district level, which serves as a clearer test of the theory. That said, there are alternative explanations for the state and especially county-level relationships I find above. Prominent among these is the chance that places with a high proportion of non-White eligible voters are distinctive arenas for both intergroup contact and electoral coordination across underrepresented groups (Kaufmann 2004). As noted in Chapter 4, partisan coalitions are formed on a strategic basis with the relative size of groups usually determinative of such coalitions; these processes should not be seen as in direct conflict with the theory of electoral influence. However, if the relationship between relative group size and the turnout gap is unique to the kinds of places where cross-minority group coalitions could form, then we would need to shift our attention to mechanisms rooted more fully in the urban politics literature (Browning, Marshall, and Tabb 1984; Bobo and Hutchings 1996; Hajnal 2010; Oliver 2010).

Fortunately, we see little evidence that the relative size of *other* minority groups is determinative of the Black–White, Latino–White, or Asian–White turnout gaps. Once accounting for the relative size of the racial/ethnic group of interest at the county level, there is generally no diminution of the turnout gap associated with the relative size of any other racial/ethnic group. The one exception appears to be the Latino–White turnout gap, which is smaller in counties with both a large Latino population relative to other groups and a large Asian American population relative to other groups. When interacting these factors, though, only the size of the Latino population remains determinative. In all other cases, there is either no change or an *increase* in turnout disparities for a group when the relative size of any other group is increased.

Furthermore, the relationship between relative group size and the turnout gap persists in both urban and rural areas. One sign suggesting rural minority population concentrations can lead to a diminished turnout gap is the fact that non-urban counties in the Black Belt and along the U.S.-Mexico Border have relatively small Black–White and Latino–White turnout gaps, respectively. A regression analysis controlling for the logged population size of counties also indicates that the relationship between the Black–White, Latino–White, and Asian–White turnout gap is not influenced by the county's population size once accounting for a group's population share. As Ramakrishnan (2005: 99) discusses, the concentration of immigrant-origin voters in urban enclaves has been seen as an important mechanism for the political incorporation of said immigrant groups. However, it is the relative *size* of the racial/ethnic group's population that better predicts the turnout gap. Of course, consideration should be given to the unique politics of urban areas, which are not fully explored in this work. Furthermore, national origin distinctions within pan-ethnic groupings may mean that a measure of the overall pan-ethnic population is less efficient at predicting the turnout gap than origin-specific measures. That said, data limitations hamper such an investigation using the methodologies I employ in this volume (see Appendix A.1), and thus this must be left to future work.[22]

A Final Look at the South

As a final note, let us once more consider Chief Justice Roberts's assessment of the Black–White turnout gap in the South. The state-level analysis featured in Figure 5.2 indicated a surprising reversal from the pre-1965 situation discussed in Chapter 2, as even when using voter file data the smallest disparities in Black and White turnout appear in states of the Deep South. Yet, both the state and county-level analyses that followed revealed that in heavily Black parts of the country, the turnout gap is smaller. Do we see the same pattern *within* the southern states referenced by Chief Justice Roberts?

Figure 5.8 presents the Black–White turnout gap at the county level (left panel) and the proportion African American of each county's citizen voting-age population (right panel) in the eight southern states where data on race/ethnicity is available on the voter file. For each county, I average turnout and the percent Black for the six federal elections from 2006 to 2016. Note that, in the aggregate, Black voter turnout was nearly equal with turnout for Whites in presidential elections in this region. However, when examining county-level patterns *within* these states, we again see a relationship between the Black–White turnout gap and heavily Black parts of the Deep South. The southern counties that tend to have the largest disparities between Black and White turnout are areas with fewer African Americans as a share of the total county population; the Black Belt region stands out as having especially high Black voter turnout relative to Whites. The bivariate relationship between the turnout gap and county percent Black in these states produces an R^2 value of 0.3, indicating that nearly one-third of the variation in the Black–White turnout gap within the South is accounted for by variation in the percent Black

---

[22] See Ramakrishnan (2005); Wong et al. (2011) and Fraga et al. (2012) for recent analyses of national origin differences in participation.

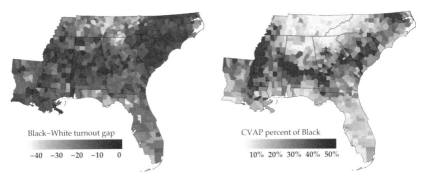

FIGURE 5.8 Black–White turnout gap and Black CVAP in the South
Note: Averages over both presidential and midterm elections. Counties where
Black turnout exceeds White turnout are topcoded as having zero gap. Counties where the Black population exceeds the White population are topcoded at
50 percent Black.

of counties.[23] While "things have changed in the South," this initial evidence suggests that they have changed in places where Black voters have
the power to influence electoral outcomes the most.

THE NEW GEOGRAPHY OF THE TURNOUT GAP

In *Shelby County* v. *Holder*, Chief Justice Roberts indicated that the special protections of the VRA must be justified based on "current needs."
In this chapter, I determine where such "needs" exist, quantifying the
turnout gap at the state and county levels. What we see is a pattern
dramatically different from the pre-1965 reality. As implied by the analysis in Chapter 2, Black turnout has increased considerably in the South,
approaching and occasionally exceeding White voter turnout despite considerably lower rates of Black voting nationally versus what appeared to
be the case based on survey data. In other parts of the country, Black
turnout lags far behind Whites. Latino turnout is also much lower than
White turnout almost everywhere in the country, as is Asian American
turnout.

In Chapter 4, I introduced the theory of electoral influence as a key
explanation for why the turnout gap exists. With the state and county-level analysis contained here, we can see patterns that conform to this
theory. Black turnout is higher in Southern states because Southern states

---

[23] Introducing state fixed effects increases the R^2 to 0.4.

have higher concentrations of African Americans. Similarly, in Southwestern states Latinos are more likely to vote, relative to non-Hispanic Whites, in part due to the impetus put upon campaigns and organizations to mobilize Latinos in places where they are likely to have an impact on election outcomes. Finally, Asian American turnout only approaches White turnout in Hawaii, the nation's most heavily Asian state. Investigating county-level patterns, we can see that *even within states* counties having a higher concentration of a given racial/ethnic group see a smaller turnout gap for that group with Whites. Latino and Asian American turnout may even exceed that of Whites in counties where Latinos dictate election outcomes or Asian Americans have substantial sway.

States are relevant political units for federal election outcomes, but in every state non-Hispanic Whites are the plurality group. More variation is present at the county level, though counties are not relevant units for major national elections. Therefore, if it is *electoral* influence that impacts the turnout gap, we may need to shift our attention. In the next chapter, I examine congressional districts to offer a more direct test of the impact of electoral influence on the turnout gap. While county-level group size is associated with a smaller turnout gap for African Americans, Latinos, and Asian Americans, the next chapter will demonstrate that it is the electoral jurisdictions within states that drive this relationship.

6

How Electoral Districts Shape Turnout Rates

Few controversies in electoral politics generate as much bipartisan unity as *gerrymandering*. With an etymology dating back to a salamander-shaped district approved by Massachusetts Governor Elbridge Gerry in 1812, the creation of electoral districts that advance a group's political interests is a longstanding tradition in American elections (Cox and Katz 2002: 3). Yet, this custom is derided by elites from both sides of the aisle, with former Attorney General Eric R. Holder calling gerrymandering "the biggest rigged system in America," (Schneider 2017), and Senators John McCain (R-AZ) and Sheldon Whitehouse (D-RI) similarly criticizing the practice as "rigging our political system to favor special interests" (McCain and Whitehouse 2017). These arguments are not new: President Reagan stated that "gerrymandering has become a national scandal" in 1987.[1] What may be new is the public's concern about the representative outcomes of districting. According to a 2017 poll commissioned by the bipartisan Campaign Legal Center, 90 percent of likely voters found it "Concerning" or "Very Concerning" that "politicians get to choose their own voters instead of the voters choosing them."[2] Despite complaints from citizens, and a plethora of social science tools identifying the partisan advantage granted by strategic redistricting (Gelman and King 1994; Kousser 1996; Cox and Katz 2002; McGhee 2014; Stephanopolous and McGhee 2015), the courts have struggled to determine how much gerrymandering is too much for representative democracy to tolerate.

---

[1] Remarks at the Republican Governors Club Annual Dinner, October 15, 1987. Washington, DC.

[2] Poll details available at www.campaignlegalcenter.org/document/partisan-redistricting-new-bipartisan-national-poll

The intersection of race and districting has produced clearer legal guidelines. As discussed in Chapter 2, African American voter registration and voter turnout increased considerably in the years immediately preceding and following passage of the Voting Rights Act of 1965 (VRA). VRA-related litigation quickly shifted from removing racial barriers to participation to ensuring minority votes would have an impact on political outcomes (Grofman, Handley, and Niemi 1992; Gerken 2001). Building on precedent set in *Baker* v. *Carr* and *Reynolds* v. *Sims*, which established the "one person, one vote" standard and eliminated malapportionment (Ansolabehere and Snyder 2008), the Supreme Court's 1969 ruling in *Allen* v. *State Board of Elections* made it clear that any election practices or procedures constituting "a dilution of voting power" for African Americans would be suspect for the courts. While *partisan* gerrymandering may persist, *racial* gerrymandering intended to reduce minority group influence was not to be permitted.

Subsequent VRA amendments and related court rulings reinforced the notion that electoral institutions, especially electoral boundaries, are important determinants of the representation and influence minority groups hold (Grofman, Handley, and Niemi 1992). Much research demonstrates that changing the way districts are drawn affects which racial/ethnic groups can influence who wins office (Lublin 1997; Canon 1999; Epstein and O'Halloran 1999; Grofman, Handley, and Lublin 2001; Branton 2009; Bullock and Gaddie 2009; Grose 2011). Therefore it is not surprising that the creation of majority–minority districts has become a standard way of ensuring racial/ethnic minorities' representation in Congress and state legislatures (Barreto, Segura, and Woods 2004; Levitt 2010). The theory of electoral influence presented in Chapter 4 predicts a diminution of the Minority–White turnout gap in places where African American, Latino, or Asian American voters have more sway in election outcomes. With the VRA, electoral districts are often created to ensure that such influence manifests in a meaningful way. Do we see a relationship between the presence of these districts and racial/ethnic differences in who turns out to vote?

The chapter that follows explores the relationship between the turnout gap and the racial/ethnic composition of electoral districts. Building on previous work (Fraga 2016a), I use voter file-based data to track rates of voter turnout at the congressional district level for every federal election from 2006 to 2016. As with counties, I find a strong effect of relative group size on the turnout gap; Black, Latino, and Asian American turnout is sharply higher in places where these groups form a substantial share of the potential electorate. I also find similar correlations for Whites. These relationships persist even after accounting for the presence (or absence) of co-ethnic candidates, electoral competition, or the sociodemographic variables examined in Chapter 3. Then, leveraging panel data tracking *individual* rates of voter turnout before and after the 2012 round of redistricting for over 5 million registered voters, I demonstrate a causal impact of assignment to districts where a voter's ethnic group is in the majority, as the Black–White and Latino–White turnout gap shrinks for registrants placed in majority-Black or majority-Latino districts, respectively. Whites also turn out at much higher rates when placed in majority-White districts for the first time, suggesting that high White turnout overall may result from the fact that Whites control actual election outcomes in nearly every electoral jurisdiction nationwide. The final section of the chapter evaluates the implications of these findings, exploring the district-associated mechanisms that underly the theory of electoral influence, as I demonstrate that citizens are aware of the makeup of their congressional districts even immediately after redistricting and that circumstances where elites have little incentive to mobilize minority voters *despite* their group size, no increase in turnout results. While there are notable exceptions, particularly for Latinos, the findings in this chapter provide the strongest support yet for the theory of electoral influence.

COUNTIES OR DISTRICTS?

The previous chapter indicated that the turnout gap is smaller in places where minority groups make up a sizable portion of the potential electorate. States located in the Deep South, which saw the greatest restrictions on African American political participation, now have the smallest Black–White turnout gap. Heavily Latino counties in the Southwest are the only part of the country where Latino turnout approaches White turnout. Asian Americans vote at higher rates in Hawaii, the single state with an Asian plurality, but also in urban mainland counties where Asian Americans are concentrated. On its face, the political geography of the turnout gap would thus indicate that where minority groups have greater electoral influence, and conversely, Whites have less of a say in political outcomes, the turnout gap is smaller.

Yet, a careful reader would note that the patterns found at the county level may not be definitive evidence for the theory of electoral influence outlined in Chapter 4. As discussed therein, it is the *electoral* relevance of racial/ethnic groups that is determinative of turnout rates, indicating that the theory should be tested with units that pertain to elections. With every state in the nation currently holding a plurality White voting-eligible population (VEP), states do not have the sort of variation necessary to witness what happens when minority populations drive election outcomes. Counties do offer greater variation in racial/ethnic composition, and indeed, counties are important units of analysis for understanding the impact of racial context on local legislative outcomes (Hopkins 2010) and the actions of local elected officeholders (Farris and Holman 2017). Furthermore, counties are of critical importance for election administration, as in nearly every state, county officials control voter registration, polling place operation, and many other facets of elections known to be associated with racial/ethnic turnout disparities (Kimball and Kropf 2006; White, Nathan, and Faller 2015; Pettigrew 2017). Yet, counties are generally not considered salient *electoral* units to voters or candidates, a tension recognized by scholars of minority political participation. For instance, Leighley (2001) uses counties as the units of analysis for understanding the role of group size and officeholding on minority political participation, but acknowledges that counties may not be the appropriate geographic area to analyze given race-based legislative districting (170). Jang (2009) also recognizes this fact, though as he relies solely on the relational goods framework (Uhlaner 1989a, 1989b), counties may be more fitting. If we want to explore the impact of relative group size on electoral participation versus other plausible factors, it will be necessary to isolate the effect of group size when holding alternative electoral factors constant.

Here I shift the analysis of political geography to the congressional district level. Congressional districts offer similar variation in the size of racial/ethnic groups to counties, but are also electoral jurisdictions relevant to federal elections. Each of the 435 congressional districts elects a single representative to the U.S. Congress, and represents a discrete geographic area composed of, on average, 725,000 individuals. In addition, congressional districts are salient to voters in biennial elections, as victorious candidates spend over $1,000,000 on average to win a U.S. House seat. Partisanship drives U.S. House outcomes (Ansolabehere and Fraga 2016), but a sizable literature indicates that voters see House elections as more than just a referendum on the party in power (Jacobson and Kernell 1983; Ansolabehere and Jones 2010). Furthermore, candidates for Congress are strategic in both the decision to seek office (Banks and Kiewiet 1989; Bond, Covington, and Fleisher 1985; Jacobson 1987; Stone and Maisel 2003; Thomsen 2014) and ensure reelection (Mayhew 1975; Fenno 1978), with race often playing a significant role (Canon, Schousen, and Sellers 1996; Highton 2004; Branton 2009; Grose 2011). Finally, the presence of majority and near majority–minority congressional districts serves as a sharp contrast to most electoral jurisdictions nationwide: instead of non-Hispanic Whites holding the balance of electoral power, minority voters have substantial electoral influence. As recognized by Hajnal and Trounstine (2005) and Hajnal (2010), disparities in participation matter most in places where minority citizens are numerous enough to sway outcomes. Congressional districts thus provide an ideal testing ground for the theory of electoral influence.

DISTRICT-LEVEL VARIATION IN THE TURNOUT GAP

In this chapter I use two methodological approaches to determine the effect of congressional district composition on the turnout gap. The first builds on the analysis in Chapter 5, as I aggregate data from Catalist, LLC to the congressional district level over the six federal elections from 2006 to 2016. Combining this information with racial/ethnic group percentages of the citizen voting-age population (CVAP) from the contemporaneous American Community Survey (ACS), I calculate rates of turnout for each racial/ethnic group in each of the 435 congressional districts nationwide.[3] As with the county-level analysis, I remove congressional districts with fewer than 1,000 voting-age citizens from the minority group and fewer than 1,000 voting-age non-Hispanic White citizens. I also remove districts where intercensal redistricting or court-mandated changes to district boundaries mean that the denominator in my turnout estimates and the racial/ethnic composition of the district cannot be precisely measured. This includes five districts in Texas for the 2016 election[4] along with districts in the states of Florida, Virginia, and North Carolina for the 2016 election. Inclusion of these cases does not impact the main results shown in this chapter, but does reduce precision as the Census information does not line up with the actual district composition.

---

[3] Statistics on the disenfranchised felon population are not available at the congressional district level, so estimates of the CVAP are my primary measure of group size. More details regarding the procedure used to combine multi-year ACS estimates may be found in the Online Appendix to this book.

[4] TX-15, TX-21, TX-23, TX-25, and TX-28.

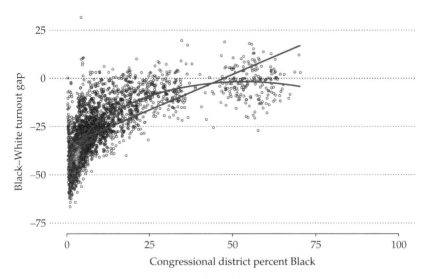

FIGURE 6.1 District-level Black–White turnout gap, 2006–2016
Note: Each point indicates a district-election observation. Black–White turnout gap is in whole percentage points. Gray lines indicate bivariate regression line and locally weighted smoother to the range of the data. Districts with fewer than 1,000 Black citizens and 1,000 White citizens not included.

Figure 6.1 indicates the relationship between the district-level Black–White turnout gap and the percent Black in the congressional district. As with the county-level analysis in the previous chapter, each point represents a single district-election observation, and the dense clustering of points between 0 percent and 15 percent Black indicating that the overwhelming majority of congressional districts have very few African American residents. Keep in mind that congressional districts are of a much larger magnitude, on average, than counties; there are a far smaller number of points in Figure 6.1 beyond 25 percent Black as compared to Figure 5.5 (in Chapter 5). Furthermore, as of the 2016 election no congressional district has an African American share of the CVAP higher than 73 percent, and few districts lie between the 40 percent and 50 percent range, making it difficult to make a direct comparison with the county-level data. However, the same general pattern manifests with congressional districts as with counties: districts where African Americans have greater electoral influence also see a smaller Black–White turnout gap. The curved gray line displays a moving average of the turnout gap as the percent Black within the congressional district increases, and suggests a leveling off of the turnout gap diminution beyond 50 percent

TABLE 6.1 *Black turnout gap by district proportion Black, 2006–2016*

	District Black CVAP		
	<15%	15%–50%	>50%
Midterm	−29.5	−11.9	−5.3
Presidential	−33.6	−8.4	+1.2

Note: Cells reflect average turnout gap with non-Hispanic Whites in districts where the African American proportion of the CVAP is less than 15 percent, between 15 percent and 50 percent, or greater than 50 percent. Rows average over midterm and presidential elections, respectively. Districts with fewer than 1,000 Black citizens and 1,000 White citizens not included.

African American that is not implied by the least-squares fit indicated by the bivariate regression line.

Table 6.1 again uses the same data as featured in the scatterplot, showing the average Black–White turnout gap in three midterm and three presidential elections at varying district compositions. When binning the percent African American into these three categories, we again see that in both midterm and presidential elections Black voter turnout lags White voter turnout by a large margin in districts that are less than 15 percent Black. Again, this finding is notable given the high rate of Black turnout reported in the CPS (see Chapter 2) and the much narrower turnout gap we witness with national data (see Chapter 5). In districts that are 15 to 50 percent African American, the Black–White turnout gap is cut by two-thirds, and in majority-Black districts in presidential elections the turnout gap reverses as Black turnout exceeds White turnout.

The relationship between the percent Latino in congressional districts and the Latino–White turnout gap is shown in Figure 6.2. As with African Americans, the magnitude of congressional districts makes it such that we are unable to observe the Latino–White turnout gap in places where the Latino share of the electorate exceeds 75 percent. The county-level analysis in Figure 5.6 indicated that the most heavily Latino counties (> 90 percent Latino) saw a consistent reversal of the Latino–White turnout gap. It is possible that congressional districts with such a high Latino percentage would also see a complete elimination of the gap, though that is beyond the scope of the actual data presented in Figure 6.2. Yet despite this caveat we again see a clear diminution of the Latino–White turnout gap in heavily Latino districts. Table 6.2 indicates that Latino turnout and White turnout are 15 to 20 percentage points

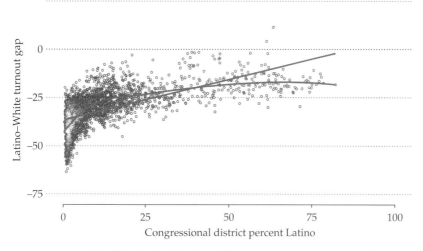

FIGURE 6.2 District-level Latino–White turnout gap, 2006–2016
Note: Each point indicates a district-election observation. Latino–White turnout gap is in whole percentage points. Gray lines indicates bivariate regression line and locally weighted smoother fit to the range of the data. Districts with fewer than 1,000 Latino citizens and 1,000 White citizens not included.

TABLE 6.2 *Latino turnout gap by district proportion Latino, 2006–2016*

	District Latino CVAP		
	<15%	*15%–50%*	*>50%*
Midterm	−32.3	−22.7	−17.1
Presidential	−37.5	−23.8	−16.5

Note: Cells reflect average turnout gap with non-Hispanic Whites in districts where the Latino proportion of the CVAP is less than 15 percent, between 15 percent and 50 percent, or greater than 50 percent. Rows average over midterm and presidential elections, respectively. Districts with fewer than 1,000 Latino citizens and 1,000 White citizens not included.

closer to each other in Latino majority districts versus districts where Latinos make up less than 15 percent of the population.

Asian Americans also turn out at higher rates, as compared to Whites, in congressional districts with a larger Asian American population. Figure 6.3 documents this situation, and roughly mirrors the county-level analysis found in the previous chapter. Hawaii's congressional district 1, the most heavily Asian American district in the country and the

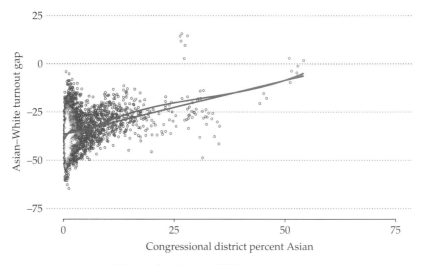

FIGURE 6.3 District-level Asian–White turnout gap, 2006–2016
Note: Each point indicates a district-election observation. Asian–White turnout gap is in whole percentage points. Gray lines indicate bivariate regression line and locally weighted smoother fit to the range of the data. Districts with fewer than 1,000 Asian citizens and 1,000 White citizens not included.

TABLE 6.3 *Asian turnout gap by district proportion*
Asian, 2006–2016

	District Asian CVAP		
	<15%	*15%–50%*	*>50%*
Midterm	−31.8	−23.5	+1.1
Presidential	−38.2	−27.2	−6.0

Note: Cells reflect average turnout gap with non-Hispanic Whites in districts where the Asian proportion of the CVAP is less than 15 percent, between 15 percent and 50 percent, or greater than 50 percent. Rows average over midterm and presidential elections, respectively. Districts with fewer than 1,000 Asian citizens and 1,000 White citizens not included.

only congressional district with a clear Asian American majority,[5] has approximately zero Asian–White turnout gap across federal elections from 2006 to 2016. The similarity between the nonparametric moving average and the least-squares fit, both indicated with overlapping gray

---

[5] HI-2 is plurality Asian American, and could be considered majority Asian American depending on how one allocates the multiracial population. See Appendix A.1 for more details as to how racial/ethnic categories are aggregated.

lines, demonstrates a somewhat consistent effect of increases in the percent Asian American within a congressional district; while the relatively
small size of the Asian American population in the United States pre-
cludes firm conclusions, it is possible that future efforts to construct
majority-Asian districts in the continental United States will result in a
smaller Asian–White turnout gap.

One notable divergence between Asian Americans and the other
racial/ethnic minority groups appears in Table 6.3. Again, there is only
one congressional district where single-race Asians make up more than
50 percent of the CVAP: Honolulu's HI-1. Yet, in this district, *midterm*
elections see a reversal of the Asian–White turnout gap, not presidential
elections where minority turnout is usually presumed to be higher.

Candidates or Districts?

Figures 6.1 through 6.3 indicate that the Minority–White turnout gap is
smaller in places where minority groups compose a substantial portion
of the potential electorate. In line with the theory of electoral influence
introduced in Chapter 4, in districts where minority empowerment, elite
mobilization, or group-level incentives are aligned with political participation, we see a shift from the overall national trend where White
turnout is consistently higher. Unlike the county-level analysis in Chapter 5, evidence that congressional jurisdictions with large minority shares
of the population see a diminution of the turnout gap points more clearly
to a set of *electoral* mechanisms. But which mechanisms produce this
effect?

Previous work has found that African American and Latino turnout is
higher in places where these groups have gained, or *could* gain, co-ethnic
representation. As discussed in Chapter 4, minority officeholding and
candidacy have been used to operationalize the empowerment hypothesis, in that citizens will be more likely to vote when "representation
and influence" for the group is embodied as descriptive representation.
Minority elected officials are more common in heavily minority electoral jurisdictions, in part due to racial bloc voting (Swain 1993; Lublin
1997; Thernstrom and Thernstrom 1997). The 1982 VRA amendments,
and the *Thornburg v. Gingles* (1986) Supreme Court decision, compelled legislators to produce districting plans that concentrated Black,
and later, Latino voters in congressional and state legislative districts
where they could elect candidates of their own choosing. Thus, the *creation* of the districts where I found the turnout gap was the smallest often

also resulted in co-ethnic representation elected by empowered minority groups. Minority candidacy and officeholding in Congress is indeed far more common in heavily minority districts (Fraga 2014), indicating that a plausible mechanism behind the turnout gap diminution found above is increased minority voting due to co-ethnic candidates. Existing empirical work examining the impact of co-ethnic candidates has produced mixed findings. Minority candidates and elected officials boost turnout by co-ethnic voters in some instances (Bobo and Gilliam 1990; Griffin and Keane 2006; Washington 2006; Barreto 2007; Whitby 2007; Barreto 2010; Rocha et al. 2010), but have no effect on minority voting in other work (Gay 2001; Keele and White 2011; Henderson, Sekhon, and Titiunik 2016). Notably, many of these analyses also indicate that non-Hispanic White turnout is *depressed* in the presence of minority candidates.

In an earlier study I demonstrated that, for primary and general congressional elections from 2006 to 2010, the presence of co-ethnic candidates on the ballot did not significantly alter turnout after accounting for the size of racial/ethnic populations within a district (Fraga 2016a). Does this null finding hold for elections from 2012 to 2016, and is it reflected in the turnout gap? Building on this previous work, here I again distinguish between the racial/ethnic makeup of the district and the race/ethnicity of candidates who seek office by combining district-level turnout data with information about the race/ethnicity of general election congressional candidates. Appendix A.4 contains more information about the candidate data I use.

I visualize the impact of the racial/ethnic composition of congressional districts on raw rates of voter turnout for Whites, African Americans, Latinos, and Asian Americans with a parametric regression model. Separate regressions are run for each racial/ethnic group, with year fixed effects included to account for significant variation in raw rates of turnout across midterm and presidential elections. The decision to visualize these effects using raw rates of turnout, instead of the turnout gap, stems from the desire to isolate the specific impact of group size and co-ethnic candidacy on each racial/ethnic group, without conflating the relative contribution of changes in White and non-White turnout. Details of the estimation procedure may be found in Appendix A.4, but to briefly summarize the approach, I model raw rates of voter turnout using a generalized estimating equation (GEE) that accounts for the correlation between turnout rates within a single jurisdiction over time (Liang and Zeger 1986; Zorn 2006; Gardiner, Luo, and Roman 2009). Modeling the relationship between relative group size and these turnout measures with a least-squares fit line, I then plot the predicted rate of turnout for each group and accompanying bootstrapped 95 percent confidence intervals. Co-ethnic candidacy is operationalized as a binary indicator variable, taking a value of 1 if at least one general election candidate was from the racial/ethnic group in question, zero if not.[6] This variable is interacted with group size, and then the conditional effect of group size in the presence of a co-ethnic candidate or with no co-ethnic candidate is estimated using the *Zelig* package in R (Imai, King, and Lau 2007; Lam 2007).

Figure 6.4 provides four panels, reflecting the result of separate regressions run for each racial/ethnic group. The unit of analysis is the congressional district in an election year.[7] The lines in the panel indicate the change in the predicted voter turnout rate for the indicated group as a function of the group's percent of the CVAP. Gray lines indicate the turnout rate when a co-ethnic general election candidate was on the ballot, black lines the turnout rate when a co-ethnic candidate was not on the ballot. Consistent with the nonparametric visualizations of the turnout gap in Figures 6.1 through 6.3, turnout rises where groups are a larger share of the potential electorate. Importantly, this extends to districts *without* a co-ethnic candidate, and for African Americans and Latinos, on average turnout may be *higher* in heavily minority jurisdictions without Black or Latino candidates.[8]

The results displayed in Figure 6.4 help to clarify how features of electoral districts shape turnout rates. First, we see little evidence that voter turnout for a group is stimulated in the presence of co-ethnic candidates for office, after accounting for the racial/ethnic composition of the district. This is in line with the aforementioned research exploring a more limited set of elections (Fraga 2016a).[9] The county-level results in Chapter 5 are also unlikely to be caused by co-ethnic officeholding,

---

[6] For alternative operationalizations of candidate race/ethnicity, including accounting for candidate quality and incumbency, see Fraga (2016a).

[7] Districts with fewer than 1,000 citizens from the racial/ethnic group in question are not included due to imprecision in the estimate of the turnout rate in such places. Exclusion of these cases produces a conservative estimate of the marginal effect of group size, as turnout is lower in heavily non-minority jurisdictions, on average.

[8] For Asian Americans, the regression line for co-ethnic candidate districts overlaps with the line modeling the relationship for districts with no candidate, and is therefore obscured.

[9] As in Fraga (2016a), there is suggestive evidence of a turnout-boosting impact of co-ethnic candidacy on the rare occasion that minority candidates seek office in heavily White jurisdictions. The empowering effect of a minority candidate where one has never been present before may lead to a unique boost in turnout, as for example the primary candidacy of Jesse Jackson and general election candidacy of Barack Obama were thought to be moments leading to higher African American turnout (Tate 1991; Philpot,

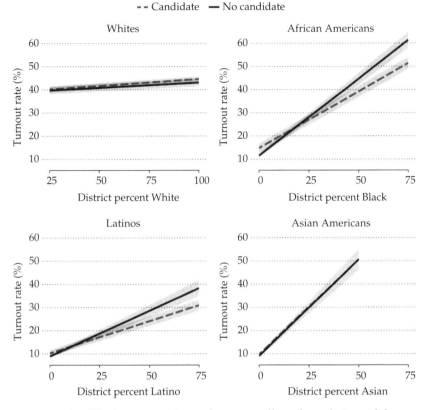

FIGURE 6.4 District composition and turnout, effect of co-ethnic candidates
Note: Values generated from a GEE regression model with year fixed effects and variance clustered at the district level, covering elections from 2006 to 2016. $N \approx$ 2500. Shaded areas are 95 percent confidence intervals generated via parametric bootstrapping.

as Leighley (2001) finds that "empowerment" operationalized as county officeholders does not predict Latino turnout and only occasionally predicts mobilization. The lack of a minority candidate boost to minority turnout indicates that previous researchers may have been operationalizing the wrong variable. Second, recalling previous work that found White

Shaw, and McGowen 2009). Similar effects may be found for Latinos with mayoral candidates (Barreto 2007). Past work searching for a distinct effect of "novel" minority congressional candidates versus entrenched incumbents has been less clear (Gay 2001), but we might imagine that non-White politicians who seek office in majority-White areas are attuned to the need to mobilize their (small) minority base and act accordingly.

voter turnout is depressed in the presence of minority candidates (Gay 2001; Keele and White 2011; Henderson, Sekhon, and Titiunik 2016), we see that a major reason for this effect may have been the fact that other analyses have almost exclusively studied minority candidates *in majority–minority districts*.[10] As with other groups, White turnout is lower in places where Whites hold less electoral influence. The effect is much smaller for Whites, however, with a 10 percentage point increase in the White population leading to approximately half a percentage point increase in White voter turnout rates. Recall discussions in Chapters 4 and 5 regarding White electoral influence: in every state and nationwide, non-Hispanic White voters dominate the electoral arena. It is not surprising, therefore, that district-level variation in racial/ethnic context has less of an effect for Whites than for racial/ethnic minority groups.

Connecting the diminution of the turnout gap as shown in Figures 6.1 through 6.3 to the evidence in Figure 6.4 of a limited co-ethnic candidate effect, we again see signs of the theory of electoral influence outlined in Chapter 4. Officeseekers running in heavily minority districts have a strong incentive to focus mobilization efforts on minorities (Rosenstone and Hansen 1993; Leighley 2001), such that politicians of any race should tailor their campaign strategies to district conditions (Uhlaner 1989a). This does not mean that all candidates can do so equally well; minority candidates may be able to tap into previous experience to mobilize co-ethnic constituents more easily (Shaw, de la Garza, and Lee 2000; McConnaughy et al. 2010; Rocha et al. 2010), perhaps leveraging shared ethnicity in order to build a connection with voters (Barreto 2010) or using racially inclusive get-out-the-vote strategies to mobilize otherwise low turnout groups (García Bedolla and Michelson 2012). Yet, once again the primary mechanism producing turnout increases for Black, Latino, and Asian American citizens is not individual-level empowerment stemming from co-ethnic representation, but a response to an empowering environment that may be conducive to targeted mobilization activities by aspiring politicians. Influence and representation can manifest in multiple ways, but district composition appears to be a superior predictor of increased political participation across racial/ethnic groups.

A Role for Electoral Competition?

If we accept that electoral districts are the relevant geography for measuring factors related to turnout it stands to reason that the electoral

---

[10] See Fraga (2016a) for a listing of past studies that demonstrates this point.

conditions within the district influence rates of voting. The existing literature indicates that electoral competition is a key predictor of rates of
voter turnout within a nation (Franklin 2004; Geys 2006). In the United
States, the prevailing interpretation is that heightened turnout in competitive contexts is a product of increased elite mobilization (Rosenstone
and Hansen 1993; Wielhouwer and Lockerbie 1994). Indeed, mechanisms linking competition to turnout in American elections focus on
mobilizing agents as the instigators of participation, not citizen perceptions of closeness (Enos and Fowler 2014, 2017). There may even be a
reason to expect citizens to be *less* likely to participate absent mobilization in competitive contexts, as work by Lipsitz (2011) indicates that the
most highly competitive elections may *decrease* citizen engagement as
a focus on candidate-to-candidate interactions dissuades participation.
As outlined in Chapter 4, elite mobilization is a key component in the
theory of electoral influence used in this book, arguing that when mobilization takes place, large groups will be disproportionately targeted for
mobilization.

As discussed in Chapter 4, the pivotality of minority groups is also
thought to lead to higher levels of mobilization and increased rates of participation. The logic is that even when minority groups are small, if they
could "make the difference" in election outcomes at least one party will
seek to mobilize them, producing electoral influence and mobilization
that is only conditionally dependent on group size (Barreto, Collingwood, and Manzano 2010). An implication of this understanding is that
group size should matter more in competitive elections, inducing both an
intercept and slope shift versus non-competitive contests and implying
that group size only impacts turnout conditional on electoral closeness.
Therefore, it is worth exploring whether or not the effect of relative
group size holds even in places where election outcomes are not in doubt.

As in Figure 6.4, each panel of Figure 6.5 indicates the result of a
separate regression by racial/ethnic group. Here each line in the panel
indicates the modeled change in the predicted voter turnout rate for
the group as a function of the group's percent of the CVAP and the
amount of electoral competition in the district for each year. More details
regarding the competition measure I use can be found in Appendix A4,
but here the gray line indicates the turnout rate when the general election had a margin of victory of less than 10 percentage points, and
the black line the turnout rate when the election had a margin of victory greater than 10 percentage points. We see no statistically significant
difference in the marginal effect of relative group size when comparing
uncompetitive and competitive districts, and few substantive differences

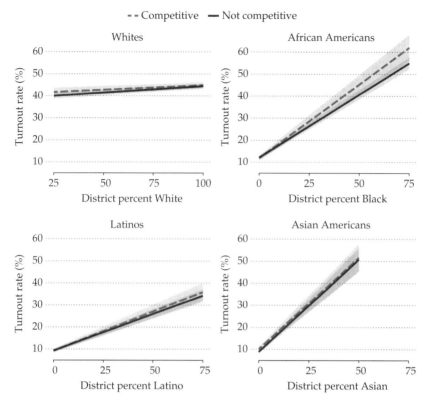

FIGURE 6.5 District composition and turnout, effect of competitiveness
Note: Values generated from a GEE regression model with year fixed effects and variance clustered at the district level, covering elections from 2006 to 2016. $N \approx$ 2500. Shaded areas are 95 percent confidence intervals generated via parametric bootstrapping.

implying mechanisms like pivotality are at work. Turnout is, on average, approximately 1 percentage point higher in competitive elections for Whites, as expected, given the previous literature. However, we see no measurable impact of competition on turnout rates for minority groups, implying that this is not a key determinant of participation for minority citizens after accounting for the relative size of the group in the district.

Again, the fact that competitiveness has no measurable effect on the relationship between group size and voter turnout clarifies mechanisms. First, low competition in districts with minority candidates (which are also majority–minority) has been cited as one reason why these districts did not appear to lead to higher rates of voter turnout (Tate 1991, 1994;

Gay 2001). We see some evidence of an interactive effect suggesting a lack of competition in majority–minority districts may depress turnout, as competition seems to increase turnout slightly, though not significantly more in districts with few Whites for both Whites and minority citizens. Could this be the result of shifts in candidate behavior? Cox and Munger (1989) find a role for urbanization in understanding the competition–turnout relationship, in that urban districts interfere with elite mobilization as these areas are more difficult to mobilize. While not characterizing their findings in this fashion, it is plausible that a part of the omitted variable bias brought by urbanicity is due to the racial/ethnic composition of urban districts: the urbanicity of districts and the percent minority of districts are highly correlated, especially in contemporary elections.[11] Perhaps elites are not effective mobilizers in heavily minority districts, but this small effect is swamped by the effect of group size.

Second, and perhaps more importantly if we seek to evaluate the utility of the theory of electoral influence, we see little evidence to support the notion that minority turnout is structured primarily by the group's size relative to election margins. From a theoretical perspective, a hypothesized relationship between pivotality and increased turnout has major drawbacks: any group larger than the margin of victory would be mobilized under this logic, indicating that large groups are always more likely to be mobilized than small groups irrespective of competition. The state-level turnout gap maps in Chapter 5 support this conclusion, as some "Red" or "Blue" states that are not competitive still see smaller turnout gaps. Again, competitiveness may increase turnout for *all* groups through a variety of mechanisms (Franklin 2004).[12] Yet, these mechanisms do not appear to produce an effect that accounts for the relative group size–turnout relationship I find in this book. The empirical evidence presented in Figure 6.5 also contradicts the notion that pivotality is critical,

---

[11] Though see evidence in Chapter 5 suggesting more densely populated counties do not lead to a smaller turnout gap, on average.

[12] Self-reported measures of campaign contact are an indicator of mobilization in Rosenstone and Hansen (1993) and Leighley (2001). However, there does not appear to be a consistent relationship between group size or competition and self-reported campaign contact at the congressional district level when using data from the Cooperative Congressional Election Study. The connection between self-reported contact and actual contact is not clear, though with actual targeting data we do see evidence of a mobilizing effect of campaign contact (Enos and Fowler 2017).

suggesting once again that the relative size of racial/ethnic groups within a jurisdiction is sufficient to explain *differences* in turnout rates, versus a more complicated interaction with electoral closeness.

Multivariate Regression Analysis

Although co-ethnic candidacy and electoral competition are the two most likely confounders based on the previous literature, we could imagine that other characteristics influence the relationship between district composition and voter turnout. For instance, Chapter 3 indicated that income, education, and age do influence rates of voter turnout across groups, even if not accounting for changes in the turnout gap. In contrast to the nonparametric modeling techniques used in previous chapters, in this section I use multivariate regression analysis to test whether the estimated effects found above hold even after removing the average effect of a host of factors related to turnout. To do so I extend the GEE least-squares fit regression approach taken to estimate the impact of co-ethnic candidates and electoral competition, extracting predictions of the change in the raw turnout rate or turnout gap when a racial/ethnic group's share of the CVAP increases by 20 percentage points. Parametric bootstrapping is used to generate 95 percent confidence intervals around this marginal effect of relative group size, indicating the amount of observed uncertainty in the estimated effect. Again, details of the variables I use and the regression models I employ may be found in Appendix A.4.

Table 6.4 summarizes the results of the multivariate regression analysis when a variety of variables are included in the model. All of the regressions include fixed effects for the election year, as we see vastly different raw rates of voter turnout in midterm and presidential elections. Results are broken down by racial/ethnic group, with the change in the raw turnout rate indicated for all groups and the change in the gap between the minority group's turnout rate and the White turnout rate within the congressional district also shown for Black, Latino, and Asian American citizens. Bracketed values below the average effects indicate the 95 percent confidence interval constructed via parametric bootstrapping. The first model, labeled "Bivariate," is based on the patterns shown in Figures 6.1 through 6.3 earlier in the chapter; only the group's share of the CVAP and year fixed effects are included in the model. Across groups, we see significantly higher rates of voter turnout when the group is a larger share of the potential electorate. The effect is smallest for White voters, where an increase of 20 percentage points results in, on average, a 1.2 percent increase in White voter turnout. Again, given the fact that all White voters (outside of Hawaii) live in states where their racial/ethnic group forms a plurality of the population, Whites always have electoral influence and thus congressional district context may have little added significance. For African Americans, the effect is ten times as large, as a 20 percentage point increase in the Black CVAP within a district predicts an 11.5 percentage point increase in Black voter turnout. Latino turnout also increases by 6.7 percentage points on average, demonstrating that non-Whites feel a greater impact of changing demographic composition than the White population. Figure 6.3 indicated that there are few districts with an Asian American population greater than 20 percent, meaning that heavily Asian districts in California, New York, and Hawaii may be unrepresentative leverage points in estimating the effect on Asian American turnout. However, on average Asian voter turnout is 16.7 percentage points higher when the Asian CVAP increases by 20 percentage points.

For Black, Latino, and Asian American citizens, we can also examine the change in the Minority–White turnout gap. Recall that here the dependent variable is the difference in the rate of voter turnout at the district level: district-level factors that should impact turnout for all groups are accounted for in what could be characterized as a difference-in-differences estimation. Rows indicating the average effect of a 20 percentage point increase in Black, Latino, or Asian American population size suggest a robust increase in a group's rate of voter turnout relative to Whites in the same district, and thus a decrease in the turnout gap, when the group's share of the potential electorate increases. For African Americans and Latinos, we see decreases that are very similar to the increase in raw rates of minority turnout. Thus, most of the diminution of the turnout gap may be attributed to increased *minority* voter turnout that is correlated with district racial/ethnic makeup, *not* variation in White voter turnout. For Asian Americans the story changes somewhat, as the reduction in the turnout gap is 10.1 percentage points versus the raw rate increase of 16.7 percentage points. White turnout *is also higher* in heavily Asian districts, muting some of the effect of Asian population size on the Asian–White turnout gap but still establishing a clear effect of district composition on inequalities in voting participation.

TABLE 6.4 *District composition and turnout, modeled effects*

	Model specifications, *Effect of 20ppt increase in group %*			
	Bivariate	Co-ethnic candidates	Competitiveness	Full specification
White turnout				
Turnout rate	1.2	1.1	1.2	1.2
	[0.67,1.7]	[0.6,1.7]	[0.6,1.7]	[0.7,1.7]
N	2554	2547	2554	2547
Black turnout				
Turnout rate	11.5	12.9	11.7	10.5
	[10.7,12.3]	[11.9,13.9]	[10.9,12.5]	[9.4,11.6]
Turnout gap	14.0	15.2	14.1	11.5
	[13.0,15.0]	[14.1,16.3]	[13.1,15.1]	[10.4,12.7]
N	2554	2547	2554	2547
Latino turnout				
Turnout rate	6.7	7.7	6.7	5.0
	[5.8,7.6]	[6.6,8.7]	[5.6,7.6]	[3.9,6.0]
Turnout gap	8.11	8.9	8.1	5.8
	[7.4,8.8]	[8.1,9.7]	[7.3,8.8]	[4.8,6.8]
N	2554	2547	2554	2547
Asian turnout				
Turnout rate	16.7	16.7	16.7	13.5
	[14.5,19.0]	[14.7,18.7]	[14.5,19.0]	[11.4,15.5]
Turnout gap	10.1	9.8	10.1	8.9
	[8.0,12.1]	[7.8,11.8]	[8.0,12.1]	[6.8,10.9]
N	2553	2546	2553	2546

Note: Table indicates modeled first differences when comparing turnout rates as the indicated group's population share increases by 20 percentage points. *Turnout rate* is the change in the raw turnout rate for each group in percentage points, *Turnout gap* uses the [group]–White turnout gap as the dependent variable and indicates the increase in the group's turnout rate relative to Whites. Bracketed values are parametric bootstrapped 95 percent confidence intervals calculated at 30 percent to 50 percent transition points for Whites, African Americans, and Latinos, and 10 percent to 30 percent transition for Asian Americans. All models include year fixed effects and are estimated with a GEE-based unstructured district-level variance estimator. "Bivariate" model includes only the group percent of district, "Co-ethnic candidates" includes a co-ethnic candidate interaction, "Competitiveness" an interacted binary 10 percent margin of victory indicator, and "Full specification" all of the prior variables plus controls for group-level age, education, and income in each district.

Do these results change when additional district-level covariates are added to the model? Figures 6.4 and 6.5 suggested that co-ethnic candidates and the competitiveness of districts did not attenuate the effect of district racial/ethnic composition. Indeed, the second and third columns of Table 6.4 confirm these findings, as adding controls for candidate race and electoral competition do not lead to substantive or statistically significant differences in the relationship between a group's CVAP and a group's rate of voter turnout. Once accounting for the relative size of a racial/ethnic group within a congressional district, these electoral factors do not have a clear impact on turnout rates. Chapter 3 indicated that, at the individual level, income, education, and age showed significant, though heterogeneous, effects on voter turnout across racial/ethnic groups. The fourth column of Table 6.4 seeks to determine whether variation in these sociodemographic factors might change the group size–turnout relationship. Using district-level estimates of each group's income, education, and age distribution drawn from the ACS, the "full specification" model controls for these traits, co-ethnic candidacy, and electoral competition, holding all of these at their mean level and again simulating the impact of relative group size on raw rates of voter turnout and the turnout gap.[13] For Whites and African Americans, a fully specified model produces results that are essentially the same as the simple bivariate relationship in the first column of Table 6.4. For Latinos and Asian Americans, where the relationship between income, education, age, and turnout was less consistent at the individual level, the impact of relative group size diminishes somewhat when accounting for district and group-level averages of these factors. The estimated effect of a 20 percentage point increase in the percent Latino within a congressional district is now a 5 percentage point increase in voter turnout and a 5.8 point diminution of the Latino–White turnout gap. For Asian Americans, the changes are 13.5 points and 8.9 points, respectively. However, a robust relationship is still witnessed between relative group size and turnout rates.

A thorough investigation of the observed relationship between relative group size and voter turnout supports the theory of electoral influence as outlined in Chapter 4. Extending earlier work by Fraga (2016a), these effects cannot be explained by co-ethnic candidacy, electoral competition, or other district-level characteristics generally thought to be associated with voter turnout. While there is some heterogeneity in these effects, perhaps even beyond the scatterplots in Figures 6.1–6.3, the evidence of a robust correlation between a group's share of the potential electorate and rates of voter turnout is clear.

---

[13] Further details of how district and group-level variation in age, income, and education were accounted for may be found in Appendix A.4.

ESTABLISHING CAUSALITY THROUGH REDISTRICTING

The previous section demonstrated that Black and Latino voter turnout is higher in heavily African American and Latino congressional districts, exactly the kinds of districts often formed to ensure minority influence on election outcomes. Therefore, districting policies designed to avoid minority vote dilution (Grofman, Handley, and Niemi 1992; Grofman, Handley, and Lublin 2001; Lublin 1997) are also associated with increased minority voting. Asian American, and to a lesser degree, White voter turnout is also substantially higher in places where these groups hold greater electoral influence, providing observational evidence for the unified theoretical framework outlined in Chapter 4. These effects hold even after accounting for the presence of co-ethnic officeseekers, electoral competitiveness, or sociodemographic factors, and when combined with results from previous chapters, the finding that majority–minority districts boost minority turnout provides the clearest evidence yet that the influence an ethnic group has on election outcomes structures the turnout gap.

Yet we may have reason to be skeptical of such a claim. Individuals may prefer to live in areas where their ethnic group is a sizable portion of the population (Boustan 2011), and people with greater socioeconomic resources, political interest, or partisan preferences may be more likely to actualize their preference for residential homogeneity (Burns 1994; Massey and Denton 1998; Tam Cho, Gimpel, and Hui 2013). All of these factors are likely correlated with higher rates of voter turnout, indicating that self-selection may contaminate our estimates of the relationship between group size and turnout. The connection between individual residential selection and political behavior or preferences is likely complicated and beyond the scope of this analysis, and Mummolo and Na!l (2016) suggest that claims about residential sorting are overstated. However, Enos (2016, 2017) finds that racial neighborhood context and contact with other racial/ethnic groups are important determinants of political dispositions, including voting. Combining these perspectives, perhaps the district-level effect found above does not reflect electoral influence at all, but instead is produced by a more nuanced relationship between where individuals live and which individuals vote. In other words, does greater relative group size within one's congressional district *cause* higher turnout, or is group size instead only *correlated* with any number of turnout-inducing factors present in such districts?

At the beginning of this chapter, I noted the important role played by redistricting in ensuring Black and Latino citizens have substantial influence in electoral politics. Current interpretations of the VRA see the act as generally mandating the creation of majority–minority districts where possible, particularly when such districts are necessary to ensure non-dilution of minority votes (Hasen 2015). Beyond this requirement, every ten years states are tasked with redrawing district configurations to account for population shifts (Levitt 2010). Thus, the boundaries of congressional districts are fluid, with citizens generally not having direct control over the district that they are assigned to. Redistricting thus provides an important opportunity to identify the impact that district-driven changes in the electoral influence a racial/ethnic group holds have on behavior, removing the possibility of self-selection. Establishing causality with observational data is often challenging (Morgan and Winship 2007), but under a specific set of circumstances, longitudinal analyses of electoral data that happen to be intersected by redistricting can estimate causal effects (Ansolabehere, Snyder, and Stewart 2000; Dunning 2012; Sekhon and Titiunik 2013; Fraga 2016b).

The goal of examining the causal effect of relative group size leads to the second methodological approach I employ in this chapter: tracking individual-level patterns of voter turnout before and after the 2012 round of redistricting. Previous literature attempting to use redistricting to study race and voter turnout has produced somewhat mixed results. For instance, Keele and White (2011) find no causal impact of assignment to districts with Black incumbents on Black turnout in Louisiana, and Henderson, Sekhon, and Titiunik (2016) find similar null results for Latinos in California. However, a ten-state analysis of voter registration records demonstrated that the racial/ethnic composition and representation of congressional districts does have a causal impact on voting, increasing turnout for African Americans (Fraga 2016b). Here I extend this prior work, covering elections from 2012 to 2016 and focusing on how changes in relative group size at the district level influence individual rates of voting.

Panel Data Spanning a Redistricting Cycle

To establish the causal impact of district composition on the turnout gap, I draw on individual-level panel data tracking the behavior of a sample of registered voters nationwide. As noted earlier, Catalist records information about every registered voter and keeps information on voter turnout for each individual in each election. The aggregate data used above and in Chapter 5 uses this information, but does not allow us to differentiate *individual*-level changes in behavior over time. Fortunately, Catalist provided a 1 percent sample of individual records from their entire database approximately once each year, providing a "snapshot" of the national file. Combining samples drawn in 2014, twice in 2015, and 2016, I am able to track the behavior of a total of 5,022,792 non-Hispanic White, African American, Latino, or Asian American registered voters who were registered to vote continuously from the 2006 midterm election through at least the 2012 presidential election.[14]

Given the time frame covered by the samples, I can measure the impact of substantial changes in district racial/ethnic composition that were induced by the redistricting that set boundaries for 2012 congressional elections. The 2012 round of redistricting was based on the results of the 2010 Census, with a number of shifts in congressional apportionment meaning that some states were forced to make wholesale changes to district boundaries. Even for states that did not add or subtract congressional seats, however, changes in the population distribution across districts meant that all states with more than one congressional district saw at least *some* change in district boundaries. Using redistricting methodologies similar to those mentioned earlier, we may examine how individuals responded to these changes by tracking their behavior before redistricting and after redistricting. Thus, the panel data I use focuses on individual participation in the 2012, 2014, and 2016 elections, three federal elections that were held using the district boundaries created after the 2010 elections.[15]

In order to evaluate the effect of redistricting, we must know which districts individuals reside in and which districts they were in prior to redistricting. The current congressional district of a registered voter can be extracted from data in the state voter file. However, most state

---

[14] Individuals not identified as White, Black, Latino, or Asian by Catalist are excluded from the analysis. The strategy I employ relies on tracking individual registrants over time, and thus misclassification of individual race is less likely to influence the results than in Chapter 5 or the previous section of this chapter. To the extent that misclassification exists, it would likely mean that I produce conservative estimates of the effect of redistricting.

[15] By 2016, Florida, North Carolina, and Virginia had modified their congressional districts in some fashion since the 2012 election. As a result, individuals from these three states who were in the 2016 sample are removed from the analysis of 2012, 2014, or 2016 turnout. However, residents from these states are included in the analysis of 2012 and 2014 turnout if they were in the 2014 or 2015 samples.

voter files do not retain information linking individuals to their pre-redistricting districts after a cycle was completed, and since the samples that were created by Catalist are all based on post-redistricting voter files, we might expect that they do not retain this geographic data either. Fortunately, Catalist was able to link post-redistricting records to their previous congressional districts based on the ZIP-9 postal code from each person's registration address. I rely on these indicators to determine the previous district a registrant was assigned to.[16] As a further check, individuals whose registration record indicates that they are no longer registered at the same address that they were for the 2010 election are removed, as their ZIP-9 based previous district information may be unreliable.[17]

Testing the Turnout Effect

In order to evaluate the impact of relative group size on voter turnout using redistricting, I construct *treatment* and *control* groups of registered voters who started in the same district before redistricting but ended up in different districts after redistricting. The choice of terminology here is not accidental: as indicated in Dunning (2012) and demonstrated by Sekhon and Titiunik (2013), under a particular set of conditions redistricting-based research designs have features similar to a true experiment. Notably, redistricting provides the potential for *as-if* random assignment, as voters are not in direct control of the boundary-making process and thus comparing differences in behavior across those who were placed in new districts and those who were not may help us estimate the causal impact of redistricting (Dunning 2012: 44–45, 59–60). As our interest is in the effect of relative group size, the treatment group consists of those assigned to a 2012 district where a given racial/ethnic group is in the majority and the control group as those whose 2012

[16] As a result, the small number of individuals who do not register with a ZIP-9, or where the ZIP-9 is not enough information to determine which district an individual was assigned to, are not included in the analysis.

[17] While every effort was made to identify individuals who moved from their 2010 address after redistricting took place, some individuals may have moved into their *pre-redistricting* district from another district in the state in between the 2006 and 2010 elections. Some of these within-state movers may have previously resided in a district with a racial/ethnic composition that is different from their immediate pre-redistricting district, interfering with the treatment and control assignments discussed below. To the extent that these pre-redistricting changes in districts reduce the "novelty" of post-redistricting districts to individuals, they will push the estimated effects of redistricting toward zero.

district continues to have said group in the minority. Separate analyses are conducted for assignment to majority-Black, majority-Latino, and majority-White districts, and in order to approximate the impact of redistricting on the turnout gap, changes in the behavior of Whites when assigned to majority-Black and majority-Latino districts and non-Whites when assigned to majority-White districts will also be examined.[18]

The treatment and control groups are distinguished based on the voting-age population (VAP) found in congressional districts before and after the 2012 round of redistricting. The decision to use VAP, and not the CVAP or other proxies for the VEP is primarily driven by data precision: the VAP for pre-redistricting congressional districts and post-redistricting congressional districts can be reconstructed from publicly available 2010 Census bloc-level data[19] that is also used by those in charge of the districting process to construct districts. Furthermore, by using data generated in April 2010, instead of after district boundaries were constructed, we can be sure that self-selection related to redistricting is as minimal as possible.[20] As outlined in Sekhon and Titiunik (2013), and first implemented to study race and turnout by Henderson, Sekhon, and Titiunik (2016) and Keele and White (2011), valid redistricting-based designs must compare those who experience a "change" versus "no change" resulting from redistricting. Thus, for registrants to be included in the study, they must have resided in a district where the racial/ethnic group in question was not in the majority, and where a comparison can be made between those who remained in such a district and those whose district makeup changed a considerable amount. The control group consists of those whose pre-redistricting and post-redistricting districts had the racial/ethnic group of interest's population at less than 30 percent. The treatment group is made up of registrants

---

[18] No congressional districts in the continental United States have an Asian American majority, and the average percent Asian American in a congressional district is approximately 1.5 percent. In Hawaii, both congressional districts have a relatively high Asian American population, depending on how multiracial individuals are counted. Thus, the effect of redistricting to majority-Asian districts cannot be examined using the framework employed in this chapter.

[19] Available at www.census.gov/rdo/data/2010_census.html

[20] 2011 ACS one-year estimates could provide a rough measure of the CVAP by race/ethnicity for most groups as of July 2011. Analyses run using the CVAP instead of the VAP yield similar conclusions to those found here for African Americans. However, for Whites and Latinos the set of qualifying districts is cut a great deal. There are a number of congressional districts where Latinos are a majority of the VAP, but appear to be between 40 percent and 50 percent of the CVAP in 2011.

whose pre-redistricting district met the same condition, but where their "new" district post-redistricting had the racial/ethnic population at more than 50 percent.[21]

In the 2012 round of redistricting, there were 1,463 unique combinations of pre-redistricting districts and post-redistricting districts with more than 1,000 voting-age adults nationwide. Most of these combinations do not see a contrast in the racial/ethnic composition of the districts, however: the vast majority of districts are heavily White, and most individuals who resided in a heavily non-White district before redistricting continue to do so afterwards as well. After filtering the data to valid comparisons, we can estimate the impact of a large change in racial/ethnic composition for individuals residing in approximately fifty-eight unique congressional districts prior to redistricting.

Redistricting-based designs account for one major confound when studying the impact of district conditions on voter turnout: self-selection. Yet redistricting itself is only an *as-if* random process from the perspective of everyday citizens, as politicians draw district boundaries. We know that elected officials will seek to draw jurisdictions to their advantage when possible; in other words, they gerrymander (Friedman and Holden 2008; Levitt 2010). How much of a problem will gerrymandering be for the study of minority turnout? Both Henderson, Sekhon, and Titiunik (2016) and Fraga (2016b) cite evidence that districtors take into account a myriad of electoral data when creating districts, including examining rates of turnout for minority groups and "packing" or "cracking" minority populations in ways that may introduce bias in our estimates.[22] To account for this possibility, I ensure that voter turnout rates for those who end up in treated districts and those who end up in control districts *post*-redistricting are equal *pre*-redistricting. This is achieved through exact matching individuals on rates of voter turnout across treatment and control conditions. To ensure other information available to redistrictors is not producing any effects I detect, I

---

[21] The decision to use 30 percent as the lower threshold is driven by data availability. Thresholds lower than 30 percent curtail the number of available treatment–control pairings considerably, as few people experienced such a large change in relative group size as a result of the 2012 round of redistricting. It is plausible that larger effects would be found with a more substantial shift in relative group size, especially given the threshold effects found in the observational analyses earlier in this chapter. The Online Appendix to this book provides alternative estimates when varying the thresholds used in the redistricting analysis.

[22] See Li (2012) for suggestive evidence of this process at work in Texas.

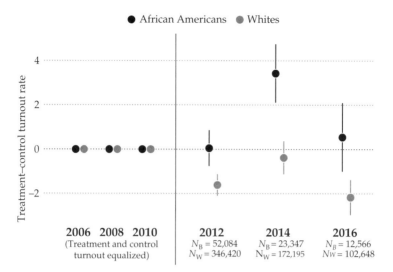

FIGURE 6.6 Effect of assignment to majority-Black district
Note: Points indicate the average treatment effect on the treated (ATT) of assignment to a majority-Black congressional district for those previously residing in a district that was less than 30 percent Black. Black points indicate the ATT for African Americans, gray points the ATT for Whites, with 95 percent confidence intervals extend outward from the points. Control group remained in a 30 percent Black or less district. Registrants are exact matched across treatment and control groups by pre-redistricting district, race, turnout in the 2006, 2008, and 2010 elections, age group, and gender. N_B indicates the number of Black registrants remaining after matching, N_W the number of White registrants remaining.

also add additional conditioning variables to the exact matching process: age group,[23] gender, and as required by the redistricting design, pre-redistricting congressional district.[24]

Results

Figure 6.6 documents the impact of assignment to a majority-Black district on voter turnout for African Americans and Whites. The figure indicates the difference in the rate of voter turnout between individuals

[23] Binned into categories of 24–34, 35–54, and 55–90, based on age in the 2012 election. Individuals under 24 are excluded as they could not vote in the 2006 election, and registrants over 90 are excluded as the likelihood that these records reflect deceased individuals is relatively high.
[24] Additional details regarding the estimation procedure and matching methodology may be found in Appendix A.5.

whose congressional district after redistricting was at least 50 percent Black, and those whose post-redistricting congressional district remained 30 percent Black or less. Recall that exact matching ensures the treatment and control groups are distributed equally in old districts, have the same pattern of voter turnout in 2006, 2008, and 2010, the same age distribution, and the same gender distribution. Thus, no variation is observed in turnout in pre-redistricting elections by design.

The black points in Figure 6.6 indicate the difference in the turnout rate for African Americans who ended up in majority-Black districts after being in majority non-Black districts pre-redistricting, compared to African Americans who remained in majority non-Black districts. Comparisons are based on individuals starting in the same set of forty-four non-Black congressional districts covering sixteen states. For turnout in the 2012 election, we see no significant difference in Black turnout depending on assignment to a majority-Black district. Previous work had indicated a small increase when using a ten-state sample and population data instead of a sample (Fraga 2016b). However, here we fail to see a measurable change in turnout until the 2014 election. In 2014, when congressional elections were more salient, turnout for Black registered voters is 3.4 percentage points higher as a result of assignment to a majority-Black district, a substantial effect that indicates that increased electoral influence at the district level does indeed shift the behavior of registered voters. For 2016, uncertainty increases as a result of the fact that estimates are based on only one sample of the Catalist voter registration database, and the necessary exclusion of three states with majority-Black districts due to court-ordered redistricting.[25] However, the results look more similar to the 2012 presidential election than the 2014 midterm, suggesting that the most prominent effects of district composition on turnout manifest in situations where mobilization at the congressional district level may have a greater impact on participation.

Contrast may be provided by examining White registrants. The gray points in Figure 6.6 indicate turnout differences for Whites, comparing turnout for those who started in non-majority Black districts, but some of whom remained in non-Black districts and some were assigned to majority-Black districts. Again, the same matching procedure ensures that the treatment and control groups are balanced on a set of observable characteristics, except for the district they ended up in. In each election, but most clearly for the 2012 and 2016 elections, White voter turnout

---

[25] FL, VA, and NC

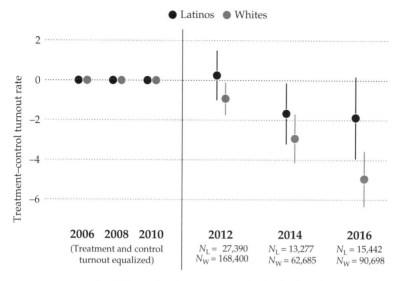

FIGURE 6.7 Effect of assignment to majority-Latino district
Note: Points indicate the ATT of assignment to a majority-Latino congressional district for those previously residing in a district that was less than 30 percent Latino. Black points indicate the ATT for Latinos, gray points the ATT for Whites, with 95 percent confidence intervals extending outward from the points. Control group remained in a 30 percent Latino or less district. Registrants are exact matched across treatment and control groups by pre-redistricting district, race, turnout in the 2006, 2008, and 2010 elections, age group, and gender. N_L indicates the number of Latino registrants remaining after matching, N_W the number of White registrants remaining.

decreases as a result of assignment to a majority-Black district. Because the matching procedure is conducted at the racial/ethnic group level,[26] direct comparison of the 95 percent confidence intervals should not be used to imply thresholds for statistical significance. That said, Black turnout is 1–3 percentage points higher than White turnout for voters assigned to majority-Black districts. The Black–White turnout gap, therefore, narrows for those assigned to exactly the kinds of districts where we saw the smallest Black–White gap in the observational data.

The impact of assignment to a majority-Latino district is presented in Figure 6.7. As with the analysis of turnout after assignment to

---

[26] One might be tempted to match across racial/ethnic groups to estimate the effect of redistricting on the turnout gap. Such a procedure creates unrealistic sets of Black and White voters that likely would not generalize to the populations of interest. See Sen and Wasow (2016) for a more extended discussion of difficulties in estimating the causal effect of race.

majority-Black districts, exact matching on previous participation means that voter turnout differences between the treatment and control group in 2006, 2008, and 2010 are removed. Covering twenty-three districts in seven states, the findings here provide greater geographic coverage than recent analyses of the causal impact of majority-Latino districts on Latino turnout (Henderson, Sekhon, and Titiunik 2016; Fraga 2016b). However, as in those studies, little evidence emerges for a positive impact of assignment to Latino-majority districts for Latino voters. A null finding for Latino turnout in the 2012 election transitions to a more clearly negative impact for the 2014 and 2016 elections of approximately 2 percentage points. Again, these estimates ensure balance on previous congressional district, previous rates of voter turnout, age, and gender. If Latinos who are prone to low turnout are more likely to be redistricted, the research design should remove this effect.

At first glance, the findings for Latino turnout in Figure 6.7 would seem to challenge the theory of electoral influence outlined in Chapter 4. The short-term impact of placement in majority-Latino districts appears to be negative. Yet, as with assignment to majority-Black districts, the gray points indicate differences in voter turnout for Whites that can be attributed to the Latino-majority status of treatment districts. Here it becomes clear that White turnout is negatively impacted by placement in majority-Latino districts to a much greater degree than Latino turnout: turnout is 0.9 percentage points lower in 2012, 2.9 percentage points lower in 2014, and nearly 5 percentage points lower in 2016 for Whites redistricted into majority-Latino districts. Again, these results do not match previous turnout across Latino and White registrants, but by 2016 Latino turnout is, on average, three percentage points higher than White turnout for those who are experiencing a Latino-majority district for the first time. This aligns with the early-cycle findings in Barreto, Segura, and Woods (2004), where they found that the difference between Latino and non-Latino turnout (that is, the Latino–White turnout gap) was smaller in majority-Latino districts even for newly created Latino majority districts, implying that whatever negative effect new Latino-majority districts have on Latino turnout is shared by non-Latino citizens. Thus, as with African Americans, the Latino–White turnout gap decreases in majority-Latino districts.

The analysis of African American and Latino voter turnout after assignment to majority-Black and majority-Latino districts provides mixed evidence for an immediate causal impact of increased group size on voter turnout. However, when comparing turnout of these groups to

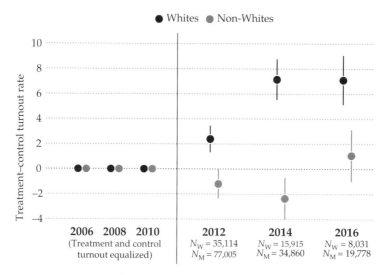

FIGURE 6.8 Effect of assignment to majority-White district
Note: Points indicate the ATT of assignment to a majority-White congressional district for those previously residing in a district that was less than 30 percent White. Black points indicate the ATT for Whites, gray points the ATT for non-Whites, with 95 percent confidence intervals extending outward from the points. Control group remained in a 30 percent White or less district. Registrants are exact matched across treatment and control groups by pre-redistricting district, race, turnout in the 2006, 2008, and 2010 elections, age group, and gender. N_W indicates the number of White registrants remaining after matching, N_M the number of non-White registrants remaining.

Whites in the same districts, the effects are clearer: the Black–White and Latino–White turnout gaps decline for those placed in districts where Black and Latino voters, respectively, hold sway in elections. What happens when the situation is reversed, and White and minority voters find themselves in majority-White jurisdictions for the first time?

The vast majority of congressional districts nationwide are majority-White, and more than 85 percent of non-Hispanic White adults live in congressional districts where they are a majority of the potential electorate. That said, for seventeen majority–minority congressional districts pre-redistricting, a nontrivial number of White registrants found themselves in majority-White districts after the redistricting process had taken its course. These individuals, and their non-White[27] counterparts placed into the same set of districts, are examined in Figure 6.8. Somewhat

---

[27] Including Black, Latino, and Asian American registered voters.

surprisingly given the correlational analyses earlier in the chapter, turnout increases a large amount for Whites placed in majority-White districts for the first time. In 2012, White turnout is 2.4 percentage points higher for Whites who compose a majority of the district versus Whites remaining in majority–minority districts, an effect growing to over 7 percentage points in 2014 and 2016. This far outstrips the average impact of increased White electoral influence indicated in Table 6.4, perhaps indicating that the rare experience of *not* having control of electoral fortunes at the congressional level deflates White turnout to a much greater degree than previously thought.

We do not see clear turnout increases for non-White voters when placed into majority-White districts for the first time. Black, Latino, and Asian registrants are not significantly more likely to vote in any of the elections I study here, and aside from 2016, appear significantly less likely to vote. This aligns with the findings in Figures 6.6 and to a lesser degree 6.7, but given the magnitude of the increase for White turnout caused by such districts, it is worth noting the markedly larger minority–White turnout gap that opens even immediately after minority and White voters are reassigned to majority-White districts. These effects persist even in the third election after redistricting, suggesting again that in (very common) circumstances where Whites have substantial electoral influence voter turnout is higher and racial/ethnic differences in participation are sharpened.

Leveraging redistricting to estimate the causal effect of relative group size on voter turnout, I find that the minority–White turnout gap can be reduced or enhanced with changes in the relative size of groups in the potential electorate. Note that the research design I employ here only allows us to understand the effect of changes in relative group size conditional on an individual being registered to vote; any effects of district composition on *registration* rates are masked in this analysis (Nyhan, Skovron, and Titiunik 2017). Given the prominence of voter registration drives for low-turnout-prone groups, the correlational analyses featured earlier in the chapter may better reflect the total, cumulative effect of majority-minority districts on the turnout gap. Despite this caveat, however, we see increases in voter turnout for Whites and African Americans when assigned to contexts where their group is a majority of the population, and a diminution of the Black–White turnout gap and Latino–White turnout gap attributable to assignment to majority-Black and majority-Latino districts, respectively.

THE LIMITS OF DISTRICTS

The confirmation that congressional district racial/ethnic composition is related to the turnout gap has important implications for our understanding of why these disparities persist. Nearly every congressional district nationwide has a majority-White population, along with nearly every state and, of course, the nation as a whole. The scatterplots in Figures 6.1–6.3 and linear models in Table 6.4 indicate that, on average, districts where Black, Latino, and Asian voters make up a majority or near-majority of the CVAP see virtually no turnout gap with Whites. The *causal* effect of changing district composition is more muted, on the order of a 2–3 percentage point reduction in the Black–White or Latino–White turnout gap for those redistricted into majority-Black or majority-Latino districts. However, these effects are comparable to mobilization efforts such as a "civic duty" mailer (Gerber, Green, and Larimer 2008) or other electoral mail (García Bedolla and Michelson 2012), and larger than receipt of a text message (Malhotra et al. 2011) or social media notification (Bond et al. 2012). In addition, contested election reforms such as early voting, strict photo ID requirements, and election day registration only appear to increase turnout by 1–2 percentage points per reform (McDonald, Shino, and Smith 2015). With this perspective, the finding that simply changing the electoral context around an individual may have an immediate effect, and perhaps larger impacts after many election cycles as indicated by the correlational analysis, should not be understated.

The strongest effects also appear for Whites, suggesting that an appreciable part of high relative turnout for Whites may be the preponderance of heavily White electoral jurisdictions. Turnout increases a large amount (7 percentage points) for Whites when assigned to majority-White districts for the first time. While the research design employed above does not provide definitive evidence for situations where individuals *lose* electoral influence, turnout for Whites who transition from a majority-White district to a majority-Latino district indicates a sharp decrease that nearly mirrors the increase seen with placement into a majority-White district. Of course, this leads us to consider the one instance that seems to deviate from the patterns found for other groups: when Latinos are assigned to a majority-Latino district for the first time, their rate of voter turnout is on average two percentage points *lower* than Latinos left in a majority-non Latino district. On the one hand, the drop in White turnout implies that political equality is indeed improved in majority-Latino districts relative to non-majority Latino places. On the other hand, any number of factors

that coincide with placement into a majority-Latino district may be at
work, challenging the practical applicability of the theory of electoral
influence for Latino voter turnout.

To determine the lessons of these findings for our broader understanding of the turnout gap, we must again broach the subject of potential
mechanisms. In Chapter 4 I establish that at least one of two processes
must be occurring for relative group size to impact the turnout gap:
individuals having knowledge of the racial/ethnic composition of their
electoral district, or elites focusing mobilization efforts on racial/ethnic
groups most relevant to election outcomes. The former is most closely
associated with individual-level psychological processes as outlined in
empowerment theory (Bobo and Gilliam 1990), the latter, notions of elite
mobilization (Leighley 2001; Fraga 2016a), and both pertain to shifts in
the calculus of voting as discussed in Uhlaner (1989a, 1989b) and Morton (1991). As noted in Chapter 4, these likely occur in the same places
and at the same time, but below I examine evidence for the presence of
either of these critical processes.

Do Citizens Know About Their Districts?

The above results suggest not only that the racial/ethnic composition of
electoral jurisdictions is correlated with rates of voter turnout, but that a
causal relationship is likely to exist. There are multiple mechanisms that
could connect relative group size within an electoral jurisdiction to political participation, mechanisms that depend at least to some degree on
perceptions of electoral influence. The strongest role for perceptions may
be found in the empowerment framework, where individuals must know
when they form a larger share of the potential electorate and feel that they
have greater "representation and influence in political decision making"
(Bobo and Gilliam 1990: 378) in such contexts. Is it plausible that citizens know the racial/ethnic composition of their congressional districts?
We have good reason to be skeptical of such an assertion, as innumeracy
regarding the racial/ethnic makeup of the population is a well-known
phenomenon (Sigelman and Niemi 2001; Wong 2007; Lawrence and
Sides 2014; Velez and Wong 2017; Landy, Marghetis, and Guay 2017).
Furthermore, given that there was a correlational, but not causal impact
of higher Latino group size on Latino turnout, we may want to pay
particular attention to perceptions for this group.

To approach this question, I make use of data from the Cooperative Congressional Election Study's 2010–2012–2014 panel. The CCES

panel queried approximately 20,000 individuals in the month before and months after the 2010 and 2012 elections, with half of the sample contacted again in the months surrounding the 2014 election. For the 2012 and 2014 surveys, respondents were asked to indicate the race/ethnicity of "most people" in the district they were assigned to after the 2012 round of redistricting, or to note that their district is a "mix with no single dominant group."[28] Linking these perceptions of relative group size to the actual racial/ethnic configuration of congressional districts, we can examine the extent to which respondents accurately understand the demographics of their electoral jurisdiction. Furthermore, as the panel data indicates respondents' pre-redistricting congressional district, we can determine whether individuals who found themselves in a district where their racial/ethnic group was in the majority for the first time perceive this shift.

Figure 6.9 separates non-Hispanic White, African American, and Latino CCES respondents, indicating their perceptions of the racial/ethnic composition of their post-redistricting congressional district as a function of the actual composition of their district. The leftmost and rightmost sets of estimates indicate districts where the respondent's racial/ethnic group was less than 30 percent or more than 50 percent of the district both pre- and post-redistricting. As each panel of the figure indicates, across groups, more than half of respondents living in districts where their racial/ethnic group is 30 percent or less of the district report that "most people" in their district are of a racial/ethnic group *other than their own*. If we include individuals who state that the district is mixed, we see that well over 80 percent of respondents from each group correctly understand that their group does not dominate the district. Similarly, for respondents whose pre- and post-redistricting districts had their racial/ethnic group in the majority, less than 10 percent of respondents think that "most" people in their district are *not* from their group and clear majorities of Whites, African Americans, and Latinos correctly indicate that "most" in their district are White, Black, or Latino, respectively.

The sets of results at the center of each panel in Figure 6.9 test whether a change in the racial/ethnic composition of one's congressional district is known to respondents. Recall that innumeracy regarding racial/ethnic

[28] The question wording for this item was as follows: *How would you describe the new Congressional District you live in?* Response options: "Most people are white," "Most people are African American (black)," "Most people are Hispanic or Latino," "Most people are Asian," or "My district is a mix with no single dominant group."

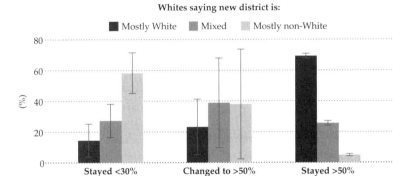

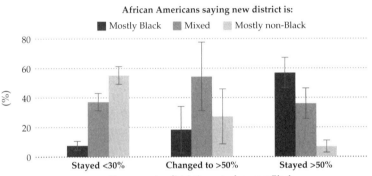

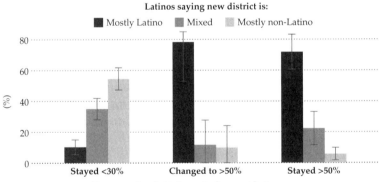

FIGURE 6.9 Knowledge of congressional district racial/ethnic composition
Note: Bars are weighted percent of respondents from each group indicating that their post-redistricting district had the indicated racial/ethnic composition, as a function of the actual composition of their pre- and post-redistricting districts; 95 percent confidence intervals extend from bars.

groups is relatively common, with some asserting that individuals may use heuristics when asked to judge the demographic makeup of a place. For instance, Wong (2007) finds that the local context, which in her case is understood as the racial makeup of respondent's county and neighboring counties, drives respondents' perceptions of the racial composition of the entire United States. Perhaps citizens simply think of their neighborhood as an indicator for their entire district, which given segregation would likely produce an accurate guess but would indicate these questions do not probe the demographic indicator most closely linked to the *electoral* influence a racial/ethnic group holds in the district.[29] The redistricting process allows us to account for this possibility, as the neighborhood the individual lives in does not change, only the congressional district.[30] The amount of random error in these estimates is significant, as a very small number of CCES panelists experienced a large change in the composition of their district.[31] However, on average, White and Black respondents are more likely to describe their new district as mostly White or Black (respectively) or "mixed" when compared to those who remained in a < 30 % White or Black district, and less likely to describe their district as mostly non-White or non-Black.

For Latino respondents, a change in district composition appears to be particularly salient, as the vast majority of Latinos assigned to heavily Latino districts for the first time note this shift when probed about their new district's makeup. These results indicate that, if anything, Latino respondents are *more* likely to perceive that their racial/ethnic group has gained substantial electoral influence when redistricted into a majority-Latino district. One reason for such a large percentage of

---

[29] Landy, Marghetis, and Guay (2017) suggest that error in demographic projections is part of a broader pattern whereby respondents provide a "moderate" answer under conditions of uncertainty that will consistently overestimate the proportion *any* relatively small group composes in a population. Thus, where bias does exist, it would be in overestimating the perceived share of the population that is not in the majority and thus biasing judgments of electoral influence made by individuals toward greater equality between racial/ethnic groups.

[30] Individuals who moved to a different county or whose location post-redistricting suggests a change in pre-redistricting congressional district were removed from the analysis. However, it is possible that some individuals changed their neighborhood of residence with counties and congressional districts between the 2010 and 2012 waves of the survey.

[31] 67 non-Hispanic White respondents were reassigned from a < 30 % White district to a > 50 % White district; 48 Black respondents were reassigned from a < 30 % Black district to a > 50 % Black district; 16 Latino respondents were reassigned from a < 30 % Latino district to a > 50 % Latino district.

Latinos identifying their district correctly could be that individuals living *near* a majority-Latino district already think that they are in a majority-Latino district before redistricting. However, we do not see the same effect for Whites and African Americans, where most districting also involves the reassignment of "edges" of existing districts into a different district. The finding in Figure 6.7, where Latino turnout appears to *decrease* as a result of assignment to a majority-Latino district, is not caused by particularly low salience of this district change for Latinos as compared to Whites or African Americans. Thus, while the salience of district characteristics provides evidence for a key mechanism that accords with the theory of electoral influence, other factors need to explain the dissimilarity of Latino turnout.

Candidates and Constituent Responses

The second set of mechanisms tying relative group size in electoral jurisdictions to turnout focuses on elite behavior. When using self-reported measures of campaign contact, survey respondents who indicate that they were contacted by campaigns are significantly more likely to report voting (Rosenstone and Hansen 1993), including minority voters (Wong, Lien, and Conway 2005). While the effect of any single mobilization activity appears to be small (Green, McGrath, and Aronow 2013), Enos and Fowler (2017) demonstrate that the aggregate effect of a large-scale campaign, such as a presidential contest, can be on the order of a 7 to 8 percentage point boost in turnout in recent elections. It is difficult to measure the mobilization efforts of congressional campaigns, and harder still to determine their targeting efforts. Yet as suggested by the theory of electoral influence outlined in Chapter 4, we have strong reason to believe that the mobilization of racial/ethnic minority groups will be more common in places where they control electoral outcomes. State and county-level evidence supports the assertion that group size impacts mobilization (Oberholzer-Gee and Waldfogel 2005), and Leighley (2001) finds that party chairs are more likely to state that they targeted minorities for mobilization when minority groups are a larger share of the potential electorate (26, 40–42, 93–95). Practical considerations may also play a role: given the power of race as a predictor of vote choice in contemporary elections, campaigns may be more likely to target potential minority voters using large-scale voter files when it is easy to find such voters (Hersh 2015). With base mobilization playing an increasingly large role in presidential campaigns (Panagopoulos 2016), the more clear partisan learnings of racial/ethnic minority groups may lead candidates to pay particular attention to these groups when designing GOTV efforts.

Despite these motivating factors, minority voters may be *less* likely to be contacted by campaigns even when the incentives are present to do so (Osborn, McClurg, and Knoll 2010; Stevens and Bishin 2011; Ramírez, Solano, and Wilcox-Archuleta 2018). The 2008 election seemed to counter this tendency, as the Obama campaign's mobilization of African Americans led to a robust increase in Black turnout (Philpot, Shaw, and McGowen 2009; McKee, Hood, and Hill 2012). Might some elites be better at mobilizing minority candidates than others? Operationalizations of Bobo and Gilliam's (1990) empowerment theory often focus on the race/ethnicity of officeholders and candidates as producing a turnout-boosting effect (Gay 2001; Barreto 2007), but shared ethnicity could facilitate elite mobilization through appeals that make use of shared identity (Barreto 2010). Recall that Figure 6.4, Table 6.4, and previous work (Fraga 2016a) all indicated that candidates have little impact on minority voter turnout or the turnout gap on average after accounting for the share of the electorate composed by each racial/ethnic group. Upwards of 90 percent of constituents know the race/ethnicity of their member of Congress (Ansolabehere and Fraga 2016), with minority citizens particularly likely to know when they have co-ethnic representation (Branton, Cassese, and Jones 2012), so the reason for this non-effect after accounting for relative group size is not likely to be lack of knowledge on the part of voters. Given the prominence of this notion for Latino voters, and the fact that the causal impact of assignment to a majority-Latino district did not appear to be positive with regard to raw turnout, it is worth revisiting the possibility that candidate traits and mobilization strategies play a unique role in structuring Latino turnout.

In Figure 6.7, I found evidence that turnout was lower for Latinos redistricted into majority-Latino districts. Though the correlational analyses found in Figure 6.2 and Table 6.4 demonstrated that, on average, Latino turnout is *higher* in heavily Latino districts, the lack of a clear causal impact accords with some recent work (Fraga 2016b; Henderson, Sekhon, and Titiunik 2016) and provides tentative evidence of heterogeneity in the applicability of the theory of electoral influence. A lack of knowledge about the new district composition does not appear to produce this effect (see Figure 6.9), motivating a deeper look at what happened in majority-Latino districts. Drawing on the redistricting-based analysis used earlier in the chapter, I identified sets of congressional districts where voter turnout for Latinos was consistently lower or consistently higher than for redistricted Latinos who remained in non-majority Latino districts. Using the same matching procedure detailed earlier in the chapter, I account for pre-redistricting differences in turnout in 2006, 2008, and 2010, along with variation in the age and gender of registrants.

Where Latino Turnout Increases

Urban areas have long been the most common location for majority–minority districts, with districts in Chicago and New York City being the first to elect African Americans to Congress after 1900. The racial/ethnic diversity of urban areas means that one may encounter districts that share boundaries and have vastly different racial/ethnic compositions. It is for Latinos moving from majority-Black districts to majority-Latino districts that we see the clearest positive impact of redistricting on Latino voter turnout. There are two examples of this occurring as a result of the 2012 round of redistricting. The first is in Chicago, where a substantial number of Latino voters were redistricted from African American Democrat Danny K. Davis's majority-Black district (IL-7) to Latino Democrat Luis Gutiérrez's majority-Latino district (IL-4). In the 2016 election, turnout by registered Latinos was 7.5 percentage points higher for those who were assigned to Gutiérrez's district versus those who remained in Davis's district. In 2012, Latino turnout was 3 percentage points higher for those moved to Gutiérrez's district, but 2.7 percentage points lower in 2014. The second set of districts, covering areas of the New York metropolitan area in New Jersey, consists of those who were assigned to Latino Democrat Albio Sires's majority-Latino district (NJ-8) compared to those who remained in African American Democrat Donald Payne's, and later Payne's son Donald Payne, Jr.'s, majority-Black district (NY-10). Turnout was 4 percentage points higher in 2016 for Latinos who switched to Sires's district, and unlike with Gutiérrez's district, turnout was also higher in both 2012 (1.2 percentage points) and 2014 (1.9 percentage points).

In no other set of districts do we see a clear increase in turnout for Latinos placed into a majority-Latino district. In both of these cases, this involved moving from a majority-Black district with a Black representative to a majority-Latino district with a Latino representative. Other researchers document circumstances where Black and Latino citizens may come to see themselves as being in competition (Browning, Marshall, and Tabb 1986; McClain and Karnig 1990; Bobo and Hutchings 1996), and while this may not extend to the realm of behavior in Congress (Hero and Preuhs 2013), the theory of contact, context, and identification offered by Wilkinson (2015) would suggest that the shift from representation by an African American to a Latino could be particularly salient (180–184). What else might explain these results? Competition or the pivotality of Latino voters cannot play a role: Gutiérrez was uncontested in 2016 and Davis won by nearly 70 points. Both Sires and Payne, Jr. won by at least 50 points in 2016. None of the four candidates have faced serious opposition since redistricting. Fraga (2016b) also indicates that a lack of competition does not account for reduced Latino turnout in majority-Latino districts as a result of redistricting, as the same non-impact of competition on the group size–turnout relationship found in the earlier chapter manifests for Latinos redistricted into majority-Latino districts. We are left considering the possibility that being redistricted out of a majority-Black district provides more of a turnout boost than being redistricted in to a majority-Latino district.

Where Latino Turnout Decreases

When is Latino turnout lower after assignment to a majority-Latino district? In some ways, the story is similar to what we see above: circumstances where Latinos are represented by African Americans lead to lower Latino turnout. However, as qualifying cases for the redistricting comparison must be majority-Latino districts, these places are unique instances where electoral influence does not appear to translate into candidates of choice. The first place where this occurs is African American Democrat Marc Veasey's majority-Latino and heavily Democratic district (TX-33). For Latinos redistricted into his district, and comparing to Latinos remaining in uncompetitive districts represented by White Republicans, Latino turnout was 4 percentage points lower in 2012, 4.5 percentage points lower in 2014, and approximately 5 percentage points lower in 2016. Echoing the possibilities for coalition building identified by Hero and Preuhs (2013), Veasey has taken strongly pro-immigration stances that would seem to cater to a majority of his district. However, Veasey came into office in this newly created majority-Latino district by narrowly defeating a Latino Democrat in the 2012 primary runoff, and defended his seat by defeating another Latino primary challenger in 2016. Strong Black turnout in the primary, runoff, and general meant that Veasey could win without mobilizing Latino voters (Gonzales 2013): Texas 33 may be a majority-Latino district in name only. A slightly more complicated story presents itself in California District

44, a supermajority-Latino district where a White Democratic incumbent (Janice Hahn) defeated a Black Democratic incumbent (Laura Richardson) in the 2012 election. Hahn was the pre-redistricting incumbent for the area, winning a special election in 2011. Comparing to Latinos who were instead assigned to Ted Lieu's mostly White district (CA-33), Latino turnout was 3 percentage points lower in 2012, and 6 percentage points lower in 2014 and 2016. Unlike in Veasey's district, the opportunity for Latino representation emerged, as Hahn did not seek reelection. Nanette Barragán, a Latina, defeated African American state senator Isadore Hall in the 2016 election, but turnout for Latinos in this supermajority-Latino district was still 6 points lower than Latinos who ended up in Ted Lieu's majority-White district.

There are other instances where Latino turnout is lower for those redistricted into a majority-Latino district. Some of these cases involve departures from districts that are already nearly 30 percent Latino, or where turnout was usually lower but rose in one of the three post-redistricting elections. In each of these districts, though, we witnessed patterns of decreased participation by Latinos contributing to a failure of these districts to elect a Latino representative. In legal parlance, this is called an "underperforming" majority–minority district. Yet, underperformance in one election may carry over to the next election from an elite perspective, as politicians decide not to run if they feel they would depend on the support of low turnout Latinos (Gonzales 2013). Thus, a history of non-participation perpetuates a cyclical pattern of non-mobilization as discussed in Chapter 4. These districts also highlight the importance of *perceived* electoral influence for turnout to increase. In their study of Latino voting patterns in majority-Latino districts, Barreto, Segura, and Woods (2004) indicate that turnout for Latino registered voters residing in Latino majority districts is *lower* than turnout for Latinos in non-Latino majority districts until multiple elections into a redistricting cycle (72). However, where Latinos proved to hold the balance of power in electoral outcomes, turnout was robustly higher. Though Barragán's election seems to defy that trend, we might imagine that persistent indications that Latino voters have influence produces long-run outcomes more similar to the correlations found in Figure 6.2.

TURNING OUT *WHERE* THEY COUNT

In this chapter I examined the impact that electoral jurisdictions have on turnout disparities, focusing on congressional districts as a key test of the theory of electoral influence. As the racial component of the redistricting process is designed to ensure that minority groups can impact election outcomes, do the resulting districts also reduce the turnout gap? The association between a group's share of the potential electorate and heightened rates of voter turnout is clear, and robust to a variety of potential confounds. Unlike national or state-level elections, where the number of minority voters is far exceeded by the number of non-Hispanic White voters, in places where minority voters could control election outcomes they turn out to vote at higher rates. Leveraging the very same redistricting process that produces these districts, I also demonstrated a causal effect at the individual level, whereby registrants were more likely to vote when assigned to districts where their racial/ethnic group is in the majority. The Black–White and Latino–White turnout gaps shrink upon placement in majority-Black and majority-Latino districts, and White turnout increases dramatically for those who find themselves in the conventional majority-White district. However, the Latino–White turnout gap only shrinks in majority-Latino districts due to an even sharper decline in White turnout in such places, challenging the theory of electoral influence. Citizens seem to know when they have gained influence, but politicians may not mobilize a large Latino population when the opportunity presents itself. Future work should investigate these cases and determine the extent to which a lack of candidate effort to mobilize Latinos structures the turnout gap, but in this critical test of the main theoretical framework in the book, we see evidence that political equality comes with demographic equality.

Comparison of the county-level results in Chapter 5 and district-level results in this chapter also indicates an important limit to districts as a panacea for the turnout gap: few districts are so heavily minority that they ensure a reversal of the turnout gap. An important tradeoff must also be made with representation of minority groups, as the creation of majority–minority districts has already been questioned as potentially reducing substantive representation (Cameron, Epstein, and O'Halloran 1996; Lublin 1997; Epstein and O'Halloran 1999; Lublin 1999). The pursuit of ever more electoral influence may in fact limit descriptive representation if districtors create one supermajority–minority district instead of two "influence" districts where minority voters can elect candidates of choice (Grose 2007; Engstrom 2011). Tradeoffs with descriptive representation may be overstated in contemporary elections (Shotts

2001), but in a world where the creation of new majority–minority districts is not always feasible, we should be cognizant of the limited power of redistricting to effect the turnout gap.

Gerrymandering is derided as one of our most undemocratic traditions. However, this chapter demonstrated that district boundaries could be manipulated in a manner that shifts, and indeed ameliorates, racial/ethnic differences in participation. Therefore, enhanced participation should be added as a potential benefit to modifying districts in a manner conducive to gains in minority descriptive representation. A plurality system of elections will generally lead to diminished influence of minority (racial or otherwise) voices (Guinier 1993), but majority-minority districts provide a window to how things look when minority groups are political minorities no longer. The way district boundaries are drawn is almost entirely shaped by the policy process, and every ten years states make policy decisions that we now know to have a demonstrable impact on who votes. Do other policies impact the turnout gap? An analysis of the effect of these policies is where we turn next.

7

Do Modern Election Policies Exacerbate the Gap?

People try to make this political thing really complicated. Like, what kind of reforms do we need? And how do we need to do that? You know what, just vote.

— Pres. Barack Obama, May 7, 2016

The Voting Rights Act 1965 (VRA) continues to frame our understanding of minority political participation. As noted in Chapters 1 and 2, the removal of *de facto* racial barriers to voting was the initial aim, and clearest achievement, of the VRA. While African American voter turnout was already on the rise prior to enactment of the VRA, it is difficult to dispute the notion that federal action was necessary to ensure that minority Americans could access the ballot everywhere in the United States (Alt 1994; Davidson and Grofman 1994; Valelly 2006; Thernstrom 2009). Yet, the history of voting rights in the United States indicates periods of expansion followed by renewed restrictions that, while different in form, often seek to achieve the same goals as prior efforts by limiting who can vote (Keyssar 2009). In recent years, the specter of federal *in*action has returned and given greater latitude to states to implement measures that could have a disparate racial impact (Rhodes 2017). Subsequent to the *Shelby County v. Holder* decision, which effectively deactivated federal preclearance for election law changes under the VRA, states that had restricted African American and Latino voting prior to the VRA quickly passed measures labeled by opponents as "voter suppression" (Lopez 2014; Weiser 2014; Hajnal, Lajevardi, and Nielson 2017). The result has been a protracted battle in the courts as to what constitutes unfair burdens imposed on voters and how clear racially discriminatory intent must be to strike down such laws (Hasen 2014; *Veasey* v. *Abbott* 2017).

This pattern of renewed barriers to voting has been tied to the very same demographic changes that give minority voters more influence than ever before. As Berman (2015a) notes in *Give Us The Ballot: The Modern Struggle for Voting Rights in America*, more "routine and sophisticated" efforts to restrict voting rights came in the wake of high Black voter turnout in 2012 and the reelection of the nation's first African American president (11). Some of this effort may be misdirected, as the role of non-White voters in producing recent presidential election outcomes is overstated (Cohn 2016). However, empirical analyses of restrictive voting measures find that the share of the electorate that is African American and/or Latino is a strong predictor of state legislatures passing such measures (Bentele and O'Brien 2013; Biggers and Hanmer 2017), often with the express purpose of removing the electoral influence of a heavily Democratic constituency on outcomes (Hicks et al. 2015).

Do modern policies that restrict access to the ballot produce the turnout gap? In this chapter, I examine prominent contemporary forms of voting restrictions that are intended to reduce minority voting. I begin with a discussion of felon disenfranchisement, a restriction that predates the VRA and continues to remove an appreciable portion of minority voters from the electorate today. I then focus on the most salient, and most studied, contemporary restriction on voting: voter identification laws. Analyzing aggregate data and tracking individual participation before and after voter identification laws were implemented, I find small and inconsistent effects of these measures on the turnout gap. The retraction of favorable policies in the wake of the *Shelby County* v. *Holder* decision also does not *yet* provide a clear sign that methods making it significantly easier to vote influence the turnout gap. Again, all available evidence suggests that voting restrictions are implemented in places where there is an electoral incentive to exclude minority citizens from the electoral process. Yet when it comes to the turnout gap, countermobilization and the limited reach of these policies means that the impact is muted. I then briefly discuss election reforms that could ameliorate the turnout gap going forward, focusing on evidence regarding language assistance for Latinos and Asian Americans and automatic voter registration as a facilitator of mobilization efforts. While perhaps not as simple as the quote from then-President Obama opening this chapter, the overall conclusion is that modern barriers have less of an impact on turnout disparities than the empowerment and mobilization activities associated with heightened electoral influence.

FELON DISENFRANCHISEMENT

The practice of limiting political rights for individuals convicted of crimes has its origin in the earliest democracies (Manza and Uggen 2008: 22). Colonial America also featured voting restrictions for persons committing particular offenses, and before the Civil War, at least twelve states had laws that eliminated voting rights for persons convicted of perjury or bribery (Keyssar 2009: 50). After the Civil War, measures barring voting for certain crimes were championed by Southern and Western states, with substantial evidence that they were motivated by a desire to limit Black voting (Manza and Uggen 2008: 64). Offenses that were disproportionately charged against African Americans were intentionally designated as qualifying for disenfranchisement (Keyssar 2009: 131), and while states later codified that felonies alone could qualify for disenfranchisement, racial disparities in the criminal justice system ensure that felon disenfranchisement has an inordinate impact on African Americans (Burch 2013). A more extended history of felon disenfranchisement and associated racial differences may be found in Manza and Uggen (2008), but today, every state except for Maine and Vermont imposes at least temporary restrictions on voting for those convicted of felonies. Combining permanent and temporary disenfranchisement, in the 2016 election approximately 2.5 percent of citizen voting-age adults were ineligible to vote due to felon disenfranchisement laws, rising to 7.4 percent for African Americans nationwide.

In Chapter 5, I used information about the share of the population that was disenfranchised in order to provide the most accurate assessment possible of the turnout gap. Data on the total number of individuals who are ineligible to vote due to a felony conviction was based on state-level statistics from the Sentencing Project (Uggen, Shannon, and Manza 2012; Uggen, Larson, and Shannon 2016), specifically, their 2010 estimates of felon disenfranchisement rates. Uggen, Shannon, and Manza (2012) also provide rates of disenfranchisement for African Americans and non-African Americans, as they did for 2004 (Manza and Uggen 2008). However, more recent studies do not provide separate estimates of disenfranchisement for non-Hispanic Whites and Latinos. I estimate Latino disenfranchisement rates by extrapolating from a 2003 study by the Mexican American Legal Defense and

Education Fund (MALDEF), where Latino breakdowns of felon disenfranchisement are available for a subset of states composing about half of the Latino population (Demeo and Ochoa 2003).[1] The Latino rate was then compared to the total rate of disenfranchisement, and the Latino population-weighted average for all states was computed based on the observed differential in the states studied by Demeo and Ochoa (2003). Using contemporaneous data on Black and non-Black disenfranchisement, and assuming the rate of disenfranchisement for Asian Americans is similar to that of Whites, I am able to determine what share of non-Black disenfranchised felons are Latino for each state in 2004. Assuming no change in the Latino to non-Black ratio of disenfranchisement, conditional on population size, I extrapolate to the 2010 election and thus derive state-level estimates of disenfranchisement rates for Latinos and African-Americans.

Figure 7.1 indicates the relationship between state-level averages of the Black–White turnout gap and the rate of felon disenfranchisement for Black adults in the state. Averages are calculated for midterm and presidential elections in the event that such laws have a greater effect

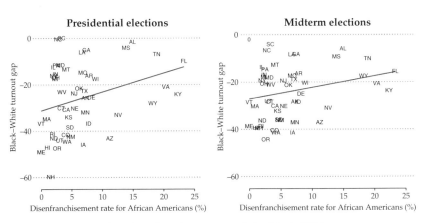

FIGURE 7.1 Felon disenfranchisement and the Black–White turnout gap
Note: State labels placed at the average Black–White turnout gap witnessed from 2006 to 2016, for presidential and midterm elections, respectively. Disenfranchisement rate is the estimated share of Black citizen adults who were unable to vote due to felon disenfranchisement laws in each state as of the 2010 election. Gray line indicates a least-squares fit.

---

[1] I thank Christoper Uggen for directing me to this study.

in lower-turnout midterms. Unlike the state and national-level data presented in Chapter 5, the Black–White turnout gap indicated here uses the Black citizen voting-age population (CVAP) as the denominator: disenfranchised felons are included as potential voters, and instead, the share of Black citizen adults who are disenfranchised is indicated on the *x*-axis. If more restrictive felon disenfranchisement laws exacerbate the turnout gap, we would see a negative relationship displayed in each of the panels of Figure 7.1. Instead, if anything, states where a greater share of African-Americans are disenfranchised see a *smaller* Black–White turnout gap, as Black turnout and White turnout are closer to each other in states where a sizable share of the Black population is not permitted to vote. Again, disenfranchised felons are *not* included in the denominator when calculating turnout rates for these figures, for either Whites or African Americans; even with as much as 25 percent of African Americans not permitted to vote, turnout among *eligible* African Americans is high enough to counter the effect of such laws.

As the above process of calculating disenfranchisement rates suggests, estimates of disenfranchisement for Latinos are somewhat more tentative than for African Americans. However, in Figure 7.2 we again see no evidence that felon disenfranchisement exacerbates the turnout gap. As the share of Latino citizen adults disenfranchised due to such laws increases, we do not see a growth of the turnout gap. There is essentially

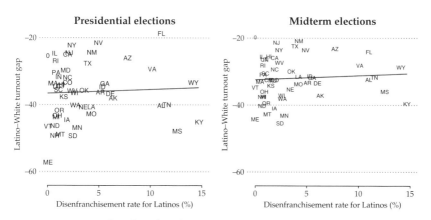

FIGURE 7.2 Felon disenfranchisement and the Latino–White turnout gap
Note: State labels placed at the average Latino–White turnout gap witnessed from 2006 to 2016, for presidential and midterm elections, respectively. Disenfranchisement rate is the estimated share of Latino citizen adults who were unable to vote due to felon disenfranchisement laws in each state as of the 2010 election. Gray line indicates a least-squares fit.

no relationship between the Latino–White turnout gap and the strictness of felon disenfranchisement provisions.

Why do rates of felon disenfranchisement not predict the turnout gap? One reason may be that individuals who would be disenfranchised would be unlikely to participate even if they were not explicitly barred from voting. Indeed, rates of turnout are lower for ex-felons who have the right to vote (Burch 2012), and notifications informing ex-felons that they could apply to restore their voting rights do not induce an increase in voting (Meredith and Morse 2014). Citizens who have contact with the criminal justice system in general are less likely to participate in politics (Burch 2013; Lerman and Weaver 2014), with those convicted of felonies perhaps even less likely to vote. Recent work by Gerber et al. (2017) challenges this perspective, indicating less clear effects of incarceration on political participation. It is beyond the scope of this section to investigate the behavior of those who were or are disenfranchised due to a prior felony conviction, but it is the very least plausible that many disenfranchised Latinos and African Americans would be non-voters regardless.

A second reason for this non-relationship may be that states with higher rates of felon disenfranchisement today also have relatively large shares of the population that is African American. We know that "racial threat" was one of the key reasons why felon disenfranchisement and related policies were reinforced in the post-Civil War era South (Manza and Uggen 2008). Pointing again to the theory of electoral influence outlined in Chapter 4, restricting the population eligible to vote could be one tactic of limiting the influence that racial/ethnic groups have in the political process. Yet, campaigns, candidates, and voters themselves can overcome this barrier when the incentives are present to do so. Felon disenfranchisement is one of the most racially disproportionate voting restrictions in place today, with consequences for both longstanding political inequalities and partisan outcomes (Keyssar 2009: 260; Burch 2012; Uggen, Larson, and Shannon 2016). Nothing in this analysis should be construed to indicate that felon disenfranchisement provisions have no substantive impact on potential minority voters. Indeed, the history of such laws should be enough to indicate that felon disenfranchisement is designed and implemented with an eye toward the disparate racial impact these laws continue to have (Manza and Uggen 2008). For instance, statistics indicating socioeconomic "progress" for the African American population are often biased as they do not take into account the relatively large felon population (Pettit 2012). However, when it comes to understanding the turnout gap, felon disenfranchisement laws are not a key source of variation.

VOTER IDENTIFICATION LAWS

Narratives of voter fraud in American elections stimulated the adoption of voter registration and the Australian ballot in the late 1800s and early 1900s (Keyssar 2009: 122–130). Opponents of these laws decried such measures as seeking to limit the voting power of immigrant groups in the North and African Americans in the South, and despite their ubiquitous presence today historians generally agree that, along with felon disenfranchisement, measures seeking to preserve the "sanctity" of the ballot were thinly veiled efforts to shape election outcomes. Yet today, and especially after close or contested elections, the specter of voter fraud makes an appearance. Such was the case after the 2000 election, where an exceptionally narrow victory in Florida for George W. Bush was followed by renewed claims of election fraud (Hasen 2012). The Republican answer to these claims was to put pressure on states to require individuals to present identification when voting (Keyssar 2009: 283–284). Most states began requiring first-time registrants to present photo identification at the polls if registering by mail as a result of the Help America Vote Act (HAVA) of 2002, but in 2005, Georgia and Indiana became the first states to require voters to present specific forms of photo identification every time they vote (NCSL 2018b). Upheld by the Supreme Court in *Crawford* v. *Marion County* in 2008, identification requirements like those in Georgia and Indiana have proliferated in recent years. Do these measures exacerbate racial/ethnic disparities in voter turnout?

Previous research indicates that minority citizens are less likely to have the kinds of photographic identification necessary to comply with these statutes. Even before the proposal of contemporary voter identification laws, the bipartisan National Commission on Federal Election Reform indicated that a nontrivial share of "poor and urban" adults do not have photo identification (NCFER 2001). Research conducted at the time of the *Crawford* v. *Marion County* (2008) case also made it clear that minority citizens are less likely to have identification (Barreto, Nuño, and Sanchez 2009), a finding that continues to be affirmed in later studies (Ansolabehere 2014). The turnout effects of voter identification laws, however, are far less clear (Ansolabehere 2009; Hershey 2009; Highton 2017). Among those who do not have or are less likely to have identification, turnout does appear to decrease slightly

(Erikson and Minnite 2009; Hood and Bullock 2012). Using voter file data provided by Catalist, Dropp (2013) finds a larger effect of approximately four percentage points, and analyzing the effect of the implementation of voter ID laws in Kansas and Tennessee, GAO (2014) did find a drop in overall turnout. Studies focusing on minority turnout are more rare, with Hajnal, Lajevardi, and Nielson (2017) providing the most thorough treatment to date. In their paper, Hajnal, Lajevardi, and Nielson (2017) investigate the relationship between the implementation of voter identification statutes and the Black–White and Latino–White turnout gaps. They find that the Latino–White turnout gap was 2.5 percentage points larger in states implementing voter identification laws in 2014, and the Black–White turnout gap was approximately 1.5 percentage points larger. That said, recent work has suggested that this effect is not robust to alternative specifications, highlighting a continuing need for research on the impact of voter identification laws on the turnout gap (Grimmer et al. 2018).

In reviewing the literature on voter identification laws and voter turnout, Highton (2017) indicates several challenges for those seeking to understand the causal impact of these identification mandates. These laws are implemented at the state level, and while the number of states implementing such provisions has grown, only eight states have ever imposed the strictest form of a voter identification law, all since 2008. In addition, the imposition of these laws is not random, and thus there is a need to account for state-level variation in turnout before implementation of a voter identification law (159–160). The analytical strategy favored in Highton's (2017) review is the difference-in-differences (DID) approach, where state-level variations in turnout for elections *before* ID implementation are compared to state-level variation in turnout *after* the law goes into effect. Relying on the parallel trends assumption, wherein there would be no systematic DID absent the factor of interest, DID methodologies are a common way of estimating causal effects with observational data (Morgan and Winship 2007) and may be superior to other methods relying on similarity across states in the same election (Keele and Minozzi 2013). The DID approach is used by Erikson and Minnite (2009) to study voter identification effects, though using self-reported survey data from the Current Population Survey. Dropp (2013) uses voter file data from Catalist, but this unpublished study only covers laws implemented up to the 2010 election. No published study integrates a DID approach, voter file data, and a robust comparison across racial/ethnic groups in contemporary elections.

Panel Data Spanning Voter ID Implementation

As noted above, previous efforts to establish the effect of voter identification laws on minority voter turnout have struggled to identify the *causal* impact of the implementation of such laws. Observational analyses using survey data to examine election reforms suffer from the same problem as any other study of voter turnout: individuals overstate participation (Ansolabehere and Hersh 2012). Validated studies of turnout do ensure actual participation is the dependent variable of interest (Hajnal, Lajevardi, and Nielson 2017), but still record behavior at only one point in time. A DID approach, comparing differences across states and before and after implementation of an election reform, may produce better estimates (Keele and Minozzi 2013). Yet, research using this approach has not examined the most recent expansion of voter identification laws (Dropp 2013; Highton 2017). Here I remedy these issues by using the same panel data used in Chapter 6, which was constructed from 1 percent samples of the Catalist voter file database and constitutes approximately 10 million individual registrants. As with redistricting, the samples can be used to track the behavior of individual registrants over multiple elections, in this case, before and after the implementation of voter identification laws.

Policies related to the presentation of identification at the polls fall into a number of categories. Alvarez, Bailey, and Katz (2008) identify no fewer than eight distinct categories of voter identification laws, ranging from requiring a voter to state her name to mandating photo identification to cast a regular ballot.[2] Here I focus on the effect of the two most stringent types of identification requirements: non-strict photo identification laws and strict photo identification laws (NCSL 2018b). Non-strict photo identification laws, sometimes characterized as "request" or "soft" photo identification provisions (Hasen 2016), allow voters to have their ballot counted under certain circumstances even without producing photo identification. For example, in the 2016 Michigan elections, a voter who did not present qualifying photo identification could sign an affidavit attesting to their identity and then cast a regular ballot. For some other states in this category, signature matching is used or poll workers may vouch for a voter's identity. In strict photo identification states, though, individuals who do not have qualifying identification

---

[2] States also vary in the types of photo identification that meet their requirements. Such variation is not examined here.

are forced to cast a provisional ballot *and* produce qualifying identification at a time after casting their ballot in order to have their vote counted. An instructive example is Indiana's voter identification law: a voter without qualifying identification who wishes to have their provisional vote counted must, within one week of the election, visit the county election board in person and either produce photo identification or sign an affidavit indicating that they are "indigent" or have religious objections to being photographed. Scholars interested in the effect of voter identification laws usually focus on these two types of measures (Dropp 2013; Hajnal, Lajevardi, and Nielson 2017; Highton 2017), and I do the same below.

The methodology I use largely accords with the strategies outlined by Highton (2017) and, in some respects, implemented by Dropp (2013). As I am using individual-level data, the DID design relies on matching to account for pre-implementation variation in voter turnout for two groups of states: those who implemented a voter identification law in election t (treated states), and those that did not (control states). I implement a similar matching technique as was used to study the impact of redistricting in Chapter 6, where registrants are exact matched on patterns of turnout for every election from 2004 to the implementation of the identification statute $(t-1)$. As turnout is the dependent variable of interest, this completes the first step of the DID process, setting pre-treatment differences across conditions are precisely zero (Athey and Imbens 2006: 448). Comparing turnout between treatment and control states in the election *after* implementation of the statute, we can then estimate the average effect of voter identification implementation with regard to deviations in turnout from zero. Unlike the redistricting analysis, the implementation of voter identification laws *does not* constitute an approximation of a natural experiment. Voter identification laws are enacted at the state level, thus it is not possible to exact match individuals across conditions who lived in the same state or to hold other electoral factors constant. Many other state-level factors also shift with voter identification laws (GAO 2014; Highton 2017), and given the research design, these may not be accounted for in the analysis. Furthermore, the method I use only provides credible estimates for elections proximate to the implementation of the ID statute.[3] At a minimum, however, these results indicate the

---

[3] As suggested by Vercellotti and Anderson (2009), and modeled by Hajnal, Lajevardi, and Nielson (2017), effects of these laws should be strongest when first implemented as voters may not be aware of the new rules. Thus, while I cannot estimate the long-run impact of these laws on turnout, I can provide estimates of the initial effect.

impact of state-level differences in voter identification provisions after removing pre-ID law variation in turnout.

The Inconsistent Effects of Voter ID Laws

I present results for strict photo voter identification laws (Figure 7.3) and either strict or non-strict photo identification laws (Figure 7.4), with separate results for Whites, African Americans, Latinos, and Asian Americans. Matching is conducted at the level of the racial/ethnic group, and includes variables covering matching on previous turnout, age group, and gender. A comparison of point estimates and uncertainty in the effect of voter identification laws helps us understand the immediate impact of these policies on the turnout gap.[4]

Figure 7.3 presents point estimates and 95 percent confidence intervals for the estimated difference in turnout associated with strict photo voter identification laws on turnout rates for White, Black, Latino, and Asian registered voters. Examining elections from 2008 to 2016, the estimates compare states that never implemented a strict photo identification law to states that had the law in force in the year indicated. Turnout is matched in elections prior to the imposition of the law. For 2008, 2012, and 2014, this means that turnout in all elections previous to the election in question was matched across voter identification states and non-voter identification states. For 2010 and 2016, elections two cycles prior are used as only one state gained a voter identification law in these years. As noted previously, this analysis focuses on the immediate impact of voter identification laws on turnout. After a state implements a law and turnout impacts are estimated for the indicated election, registrants from that state no longer form an appropriate treatment or control case and are thus removed from the analysis. For example, Georgia and Indiana registrants are not included in the analysis of 2012 through 2016 turnout, as Georgia and Indiana had voter identification laws for multiple election cycles by 2012.[5]

---

[4] Some may consider the comparison of voter ID effects across racial/ethnic groups to constitute a "difference-in-difference-in-differences" estimation strategy (Dropp 2013). However, matching takes place within racial/ethnic groups in order to ensure that the matched comparison is among samples that provide a realistic approximation of each racial/ethnic group's registrants (see Sen and Wasow (2016) for more information about making causal claims regarding race), and thus we must be cautious in not overstating the power of the research design to account for all pre-treatment differences in turnout across racial/ethnic groups.

[5] Texas implemented a strict photo identification law in 2014, but due to a court order reverted to a non-strict identification law for the 2016 election. Texas is therefore removed from the analysis of 2016 turnout.

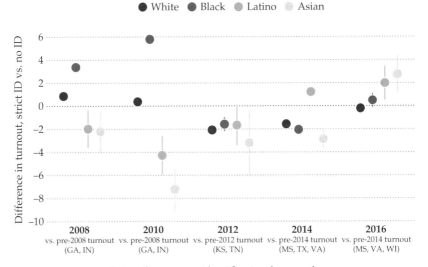

FIGURE 7.3 Strict photo voter identification laws and voter turnout
Note: Points represent difference in voter turnout for registered voters from the
indicated racial/ethnic group in states with strict voter identification laws versus
those in states without such laws, after exact matching on turnout in the indicated
previous elections, age group, and gender. State abbreviations indicate states with
strict ID laws where comparison is made to states that never had strict ID laws;
95 percent confidence intervals extend outward when larger than the marker used
for the point estimate.

Measuring differences in turnout plausibly attributable to strict voter
identification laws, we see clear heterogeneity across years and across
groups. Some heterogeneity is not surprising, as Dropp (2013) found that
midterm elections saw larger impacts than presidential election years.
Yet, comparing across racial/ethnic groups we see variation in effects that
challenges the notion that these laws have a clear impact on the turnout
gap. In 2008 and 2010, White voter turnout was 0–1 percentage points
higher with an identification law, but approximately two percentage
points *lower* for 2012 and 2014. Turnout for African American registrants in 2008 and 2010 was much *higher* in voter identification states,
approaching six percentage points in the 2010 election even after matching on previous turnout. For 2012 and 2014 Black turnout was lower,
though not consistently lower than White voter turnout in those years.
Latino and Asian American turnout is estimated with greater uncertainty,
but it appears that the implementation of voter identification requirements is related to lower Latino and Asian turnout from 2008 to 2012,

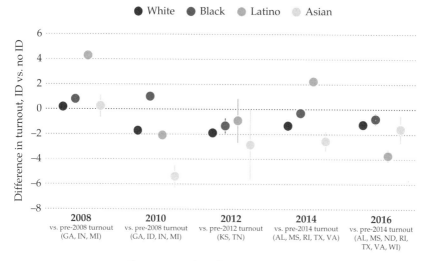

FIGURE 7.4 Photo voter identification laws and voter turnout
Note: Points represent difference in voter turnout for registered voters from the
indicated racial/ethnic group in states with strict or non-strict photo voter identification laws versus those in states without such laws, after exact matching on
turnout in the indicated previous elections, age group, and gender. State abbreviations indicate states with strict or non-strict ID laws where comparison is made to
states that never had strict or non-strict ID laws; 95 percent confidence intervals
extend outward when larger than the marker used for the point estimate.

but may be associated with an *increase* in Latino turnout for 2014 and
both Latino and Asian turnout for 2016.

Figure 7.4 instead groups states based on whether they at a minimum
request photographic identification or not. This threshold for identification laws means that they are more common,[6] meaning that state-level
variation coinciding with implementation may be better accounted for.
Yet here the story is similar to what Figure 7.3 suggests about the effect
of strict photo identification laws, though more muted. A decrease in
White turnout is more evident for laws taking effect from 2010 to 2016,
on the order of 1–2 percentage points. As with strict photo identification policies, Black turnout is sometimes higher (2008 and 2010) and
sometimes lower (2012–2016) in states where less strict types of identification laws were implemented, but importantly, in no election do we

---

[6] Florida, Louisiana, and South Dakota had non-strict photo identification laws before
the 2008 election (Alvarez, Bailey, and Katz 2008; Dropp 2013), and thus registrants
from these states are removed from the analysis as no comparison can be made to pre-ID
patterns of turnout.

see evidence that identification laws reduce Black voter turnout more than they reduce White voter turnout. Latino turnout impacts are more mixed than when using the stricter law threshold, but also do not indicate a greater drop for Latinos than Whites except in the 2016 election. Once again, the largest negative effects manifest for Asian Americans, where turnout is 1 to 5 percentage points lower in the 2010, 2012, 2014, and 2016 elections for Asian American registrants in states with voter identification requirements.

The heterogeneity we see in the impact of voter identification mandates across years indicates that studies selecting only a narrow timeframe of study may produce incorrect inferences (Highton 2017). Significant effects of voter identification laws *in either direction* can be found depending on which year we choose, suggesting that state-by-state and election-to-election variation in voter turnout rates is a more plausible source of these differences than ID laws.[7] As it pertains to this book, however, the clearer implication of Figures 7.3 and 7.4 is that we do not yet have consistent evidence of a differential, negative effect of voter identification laws on minority turnout as compared to non-Hispanic White voter turnout.

The analysis above should not be seen as conclusive evidence regarding the impact of voter identification laws on minority voters. Several studies indicate that, after implementation, minority voters face additional hurdles or have their credentials questioned to a greater degree than Whites (Ansolabehere 2009; Atkeson et al. 2010, 2014; White, Nathan, and Faller 2015). State legislators advocate for voter identification laws in circumstances where a disproportionate impact would disadvantage a sizable minority population (Bentele and O'Brien 2013; Biggers and Hanmer 2017), where legislators are less concerned about alienating minority constituents (McKee 2015), or where partisan considerations indicate gain for Republicans if these laws demobilize Democrats (Rocha and Matsubayashi 2014; Hicks et al. 2015; Biggers and Hanmer 2017; Highton 2017). If the above advocacy strategies are indeed motivated by in a real-world result that I am unable to detect, why might that be? Recall that the analysis conducted above relies on the parallel trends assumption, wherein voters in states where voter identification laws were

---

[7] It may be attractive to condition the analysis on changes in election results, as, for instance, voter identification laws may be passed in states that are trending in a particular direction (Highton 2017: 159). However, it is important to remember that many of the electoral *outcomes* that we might use to judge other types of electoral context could be the result of such laws, and are post-treatment from the perspective of making causal claims.

implemented should have followed the same path as their neighbors in the absence of implementation of the law. Many other factors may have changed at the same time that identification laws did, perhaps even extending to a countermobilization against such laws that boosts turnout by those otherwise disadvantaged (Valentino and Neuner 2017). Future research should continue to evaluate the impact of voter identification laws on minority turnout, but here we do not see evidence that they explain the large and persistent turnout gaps we witness in contemporary elections.

NEW RESTRICTIONS ON CONVENIENCE VOTING

Voter identification laws are not the only administrative tactic that could reduce minority voting. After the *Shelby County* v. *Holder* decision, a handful of states *reversed* previous reforms that were implemented to expand access to the ballot. As discussed by Keyssar (2009), the expansion of voting rights is often followed by episodes of retrenchment by those whose political interests are not favored by an expanded electorate. Of course, the "Redeemer" era coinciding with the end of Reconstruction provides one such example: as discussed in Chapter 2, *de facto* and then later *de jure* voting rights were effectively taken from African Americans in the late 1800s and early 1900s. Many point to the deactivation of federal preclearance through the *Shelby* decision as echoing this prior period (Hasen 2014; Berman 2015a), and of course, such a comparison is made all the more apt as states notorious for restricting African American and Latino voting now appeared able to do so again. The same day that the *Shelby* decision was handed down, Texas moved forward with a strict photo identification law that had previously been denied preclearance (Lopez 2014). Yet the narrative of North Carolina is particularly instructive for the breadth of election access provisions that could now be modified: three weeks after the *Shelby* decision, in late 2013, Republican members of the North Carolina state legislature introduced and passed a bill reducing early voting, restricting same-day registration, and eliminating a set of voter registration initiatives (Lopez 2014; Berman 2015a: 294). Beyond the South, states from Arizona to Nebraska to Ohio also restricted early and absentee voting (Brennan Center for Justice 2017). Might these new limits on voting impact the turnout gap?

First, we must ask whether the kinds of policies targeted by these new restrictions are more likely to be used by minority voters. Historically, minority voters were *not* more likely to use methods like absentee-by-mail or early voting (Oliver 1996; Stein 1998). Yet, Alvarez, Levin, and Sinclair (2012) indicate that African American and Hispanic voters were more likely to report using early voting in the 2008 election than non-Hispanic Whites. An analysis of Florida voter file data also indicated that Black and Latino registrants were disproportionately likely to vote early in 2008 and to visit the polls at the very same times targeted by a 2012 bill restricting early voting (Herron and Smith 2012). In Ohio, African Americans were again more likely to use early voting than Whites in 2008 and 2012 (Weaver 2015), and 70 percent of African Americans voted early in North Carolina in 2012, versus approximately half of non-Hispanic White voters (Berman 2015a: 296). Note that at the same time that this shift toward early voting by minority populations became more evident, early voting was being limited in heavily-minority counties within states (Fullmer 2015a). Thus, for early voting at least, it is clear that new restrictions will have more of an impact on minority voters than Whites. Courts appear to agree, ruling that measures reducing early voting or generating ID requirements are, as in the era preceding implementation of the VRA, designed to target African American voters with "almost surgical precision."[8]

What effect do policies like early voting have on voter turnout? Here evidence is decidedly mixed. Leighley and Nagler (2013) find evidence that in states that had particularly limited voting opportunities same-day registration and a longer period for registration can increase turnout slightly. However, Burden et al. (2014) find that while same-day registration increases turnout, the availability of early voting *decreases* voter turnout. McDonald, Shino, and Smith (2015) replicate and refine their analysis and determine that the set of election reforms associated with increasing the convenience of voting in fact boost voter turnout, though a 2016 GAO report also seemed to present conflicting evidence on turnout and making it easier to vote. No study examines racial differences in voter turnout as a product of these reforms, and it may be too soon after the *repeal* of parts of early voting statutes to identify a clear impact on the turnout gap. That said, indirect evidence implies we may be overstating the effect of these laws on turnout disparities. For instance, Berinsky (2005) found that reforms making it easier to vote tend to be used by the most engaged of citizens, such that an unintended consequence may be to exacerbate participatory disparities. Implementation, again, likely has important consequences; the limited availability of early voting in heavily

---

[8] *North Carolina State Conference of the NAACP v. McCrory* 831 F.3rd 204, 215.

Black counties could moderate a turnout impact for African Americans (Fullmer 2015b). Given that minority voters tend to support Democrats for office, we could imagine that a partisan effect of these reforms is suggestive evidence regarding their impact on the turnout gap. Yet, Burden et al. (2017) find that *Republicans* do better when early voting is available, going as far as to state that Republican legislators are disadvantaging Republican voters by limiting early voting and "do not always know what is good for them" (573). Again, it is difficult to assess the impact of recent convenience voting retrenchment. However, if the implementation of these laws has a limited impact, it is possible that their removal does as well.

Based on the analyses in this chapter, the impact of modern election restrictions on the Minority–White turnout gap appears to be inconsistent and relatively small in magnitude when compared to the other forces structuring the turnout gap. This finding buttresses the core theoretical argument made in this book: when minority groups have the potential to shape election outcomes, they will be more likely to vote. As discussed in Chapter 4, we may imagine that electoral institutions, here taking the form of restrictions, limit the effective size of groups in the electorate and thus deter voters through indirect means, such as discouraging mobilization and disempowering individuals. Indeed, states that passed restrictions post-*Shelby* had higher minority populations and had witnessed a surge in participation in the mid 2000s. We would expect these states to have the smallest turnout gaps, and as turnout is a cyclical process it should not be surprising that high turnout continues even with election restrictions. Furthermore, Valentino and Neuner (2017) demonstrate that *counter*mobilization resulting from opposition to restrictions may be strong enough to surmount an otherwise turnout depressing effect of these measures. As in the earlier era of restrictions on voting, concerted efforts to empower and mobilize minority voters can overcome substantial impediments to political equality.

EXPANDING ACCESS

At the same time as states were implementing voter identification laws or new restrictions on convenience voting, other states continued with or implemented reforms that sought to expand access to voting. *Shelby County* v. *Holder* did not invalidate all parts of the VRA, with provisions remaining that seek to ensure minority citizens have equal access to the ballot. Some states have also tested new measures designed to boost participation in elections beyond the VRA. Based on the theory of electoral influence, and the empirical results presented in earlier chapters of this book, there are two sets of reforms that are particularly promising for ameliorating persistent gaps in voter turnout. The first consists of the language minority provisions of the VRA, which guarantees that Latino, Asian American, and Native American voters who seek to vote in a language other than English have the opportunity to do so in jurisdictions where they are concentrated. The second, automatic voter registration, gives some obligation to states to register citizens to vote, removing what is otherwise an individual responsibility and facilitating mobilization during campaign season. In reviewing each of these reforms, I will discuss why they may have a particularly important impact on the turnout gap as they help to link group size to perceptions of electoral influence.

Language Provisions of the VRA

In Chapter 2 I noted that the 1975 Amendments to the VRA extended federal voting rights protections to Latinos, Asian Americans, and Native Americans. The first part of these protections was similar to those granted to African Americans in 1965 (Keyssar 2009: 212). Section 4(f)4 of the expanded VRA targeted states that used English-only elections as a *de facto* literacy test against Latino, Asian American, and Native American voters, bringing these counties and states under the preclearance provisions in Section 5 if they also had low turnout and a 5 percent or greater population of a "single language minority group" (Tucker 2009: 65–66).[9] Texas, Arizona, Alaska, and a handful of counties across the country with large Latino or Native American populations gained preclearance protections under this provision, and were directed to provide voting assistance in Spanish or relevant American Indian or Alaska Native languages. However, the *Shelby County* v. *Holder* decision struck this section of the VRA, despite no discussion in the majority opinion of Latino or Asian American voting rates that, unlike for African Americans, have not increased since the 1970s. An alternative coverage mechanism, found in Section 203(c), is the main language-related

[9] Guidelines for interpretation of the 1975 Amendments defined a "single language minority group" as "American Indians, Alaskan Natives, persons of Spanish Heritage, Chinese Americans, Filipino Americans, Japanese Americans, and Korean Americans," notably excluding European-origin immigrants who would presumably have a higher illiteracy rate than the national average (41 F.R. 29997 (1976)). Other Asian American groups were able to gain coverage as a result of the 1992 Amendments to the VRA.

provision that is active today. The Section 203(c) coverage formula has changed over the years (Schmidt 2000: 21; Tucker and Espino 2007; Tucker 2009), but to qualify today a state, county, or county equivalent must have a limited English proficient voting-age citizen population from a single language minority group that is 5 percent or more of the total CVAP in the jurisdiction, or for counties/county equivalents, numbers more than 10,000.[10] Counties or states qualifying for coverage are required to provide "registration or voting notices, forms, instructions, assistance, or other materials relating to the electoral process, including ballots" in the primary non-English language of the covered group. In 2010, more than 25 million Americans indicated that they speak English less than "very well," and while most are not citizens, a considerable portion are native born or naturalized and thus the language provisions of the VRA have the potential to influence rates of political participation for these Americans.

Details regarding historical and contemporary implementation of the language provisions may be found in Schmidt (2000), Tucker (2009), and Fraga and Merseth (2016). However, substantial evidence indicates that states and counties comply with the language provisions when required to do so (GAO 1986, 1997; Jones-Correa and Waismel-Manor 2007; GAO 2008; Tucker 2009; Higgins 2015). Every five years the Census releases information about which jurisdictions meet the thresholds for coverage, and which languages the jurisdiction has to provide assistance in. Out of approximately 4,000 jurisdictions eligible for coverage, in the most recent round of determinations 263 jurisdictions qualified for coverage, composing 68.8 million adult citizens and 21.7 million adult citizens from language groups subject to coverage.[11] A full listing of covered jurisdictions is published in the Federal Register,[12] with California, Florida, and Texas mandated to provide statewide coverage in Spanish and twenty-six out of the other forty-six states having at least one county providing some sort of language assistance under the VRA.

What effect do the language provisions have on the turnout gap? A review of the literature may be found in Fraga and Merseth (2016),

---

[10] 42 U.S.C. 1973aa-1a(b)(1–2), Changes contained in H.R. 9, May 2, 2006. "Limited English Proficient" is defined as individuals indicating that they speak English less than "Very Well." Groups must also have a higher rate of "illiteracy" than the national average to qualify for coverage, but in practice, all groups eligible for coverage meet this threshold.

[11] www.census.gov/newsroom/press-releases/2016/cb16-205.html

[12] For December 2016 determinations, 81 FR 87532.

but survey-based and voter file-based analyses seem to agree that Asian American and Latino voter turnout and registration in recent elections appear to be higher as a result of language coverage (Jones-Correa and Ramakrishnan 2004; Jones-Correa 2005; Fraga and Merseth 2016), particularly for citizens who have low levels of English proficiency (Lien et al. 2001; Hopkins 2011).[13] Fraga and Merseth (2016) examine jurisdictions just above and just below the coverage threshold in a regression discontinuity design, allowing the estimation of a causal effect, and indeed find a substantial gain in Latino voter registration and Asian voter turnout resulting from jurisdictions gaining coverage in 2012. Recall that the coverage trigger is tied in part to group size. With these results, election assistance may also be an important mechanism by which electoral influence translates into higher rates of voter turnout.

These more recent findings contrast with past indications that the language provisions were largely "symbolic" or "welcoming," indicating the incorporation of immigrant-origin minority groups into the political sphere (de la Garza and DeSipio 1997; Parkin and Zlotnick 2014). Therein lies a second important potential impact of the language provisions: multilingual election assistance indicates a more inclusive electoral process is under way. Candidates seeking office may be more likely to think that Latino or Asian American constituents *could* participate when language assistance is available, interrupting a cycle of low turnout due to non-mobilization. We could also imagine that candidates consider using targeted, language-appropriate appeals (García Bedolla and Michelson and 2012; Ramírez 2013) when they know that the recipients of those appeals could vote in their heritage language. Community organizations may also be stimulated by the availability of multilingual election materials, signaling that a community could now play an important role in politics. Future work must clarify the magnitude of these effects and the specific mechanisms at work. Of course, these measures are not without controversy, and indeed, the last renewal of the VRA saw greater criticism of the multilingual voting mandate (Gaouette 2006) than the preclearance formula that was eventually struck down by the Supreme Court (Tucker 2009). It is entirely possible that changes to the coverage formula or elimination of the mandate altogether are in the near future (Fraga and Merseth 2016). For now, however, the language provisions of

---

[13] McCool, Olson, and Robinson (2007: 156) also find a positive impact of VRA coverage on Native American voter turnout in San Juan County, New Mexico.

the VRA may play a role in ensuring the Latino–White and Asian–White turnout gaps are not even larger.

Automatic Voter Registration

In 1993, President Bill Clinton signed the National Voter Registration Act (NVRA). Popularly known as "Motor Voter," and based on earlier efforts in Michigan to facilitate voter registration, the bipartisan compromise called for states to allow individuals to register to vote by mail, at public agencies, and when applying for a driver's license. This last opportunity to register is critical, as individuals can sign up to vote in the process of completing another transaction where necessary documentation is readily available (Keyssar 2009: 255). The effect of the NVRA was to cut the number of unregistered Americans by nearly 20 percent. As noted in Chapter 2, I do not use the number of registered voters as a dependent variable or denominator when studying the turnout gap, as there is tremendous variation across states in registration policies and the connection between registration and voting in recent elections is not as clear as it once was (Erikson 1981; Ansolabehere and Konisky 2006; Brown and Wedeking 2006). However, recent efforts that build on the NVRA may play a special role as they further transform voter registration from an administrative step preceding a participatory act to a fully-fledged tool for ensuring states and politicians know who their potential voters are.

These measures, variously called automatic or automated voter registration, were first introduced in Oregon for the 2016 election (McGhee et al. 2017). In effect, automatic voter registration extends the logic of the NVRA's driver licensing process, but instead of requiring potential registrants to *opt in* to registering to vote, the Oregon statute automatically generates a provisional registration record for all individuals who are unregistered and have completed a transaction with their license branch in recent years. Registrants are then sent a mailer where they can *opt out* of registration or indicate their preferred party registration, and if they decline to opt out, address updates are also automatically reflected in the registration record. By mid 2018, twelve states[14] and the District of Columbia enacted automatic voter registration systems (NCSL 2018a), meaning that 30 percent of the U.S. population will live in states that have automatic voter registration in place for the 2020 election.

---

[14] AK, CA, CO, CT, IL, MD, NJ, OR, RI, VT, WA, WV.

No peer-reviewed analyses of the effect of automatic voter registration have yet been published. As automatic voter registration was only in place for one state in the 2016 election, it may be too early to assess with any level of certainty the impact of this specific method on voter turnout. Initial analyses indicate that voter turnout as a share of eligible voters was 1 to 3 percentage points higher in Oregon in 2016 than it would have been in the absence of this law (McGhee et al. 2017). However, the share of *registered* voters who voted decreased, as many of the automatically registered individuals did not turn out to vote. This mirrors the effect of the 1993 NVRA and other measures designed to ease voter registration (Knack 1995; Highton and Wolfinger 1998; Highton 2004; Hershey 2009, but cf. Franklin and Grier 1997). With regard to the turnout gap, we can only depend on prior studies of easing registration requirements which sometimes indicate political inequality is exacerbated (Brians and Grofman 1999, 2001), and sometimes do not (Brown and Wedeking 2006; Rigby and Springer 2011). Future work should identify racial/ethnic differences in registration rates resulting from these changes, even if the effect on turnout is small.

The power of registration reform may not be in its capacity to stimulate voter turnout directly. Instead, what may make automatic voter registration most relevant from the perspective of the turnout gap (and broader political inequality) is the shift in electoral norms it may induce. The burden of re-registering to vote after moving addresses falls disproportionately on the highly mobile population, including young people, low income persons, and racial/ethnic minorities (Squire, Wolfinger, and Glass 1987; Ansolabehere and Hersh 2012). Furthermore, the hotly debated practice of "purging" registration rolls may also change with automatic voter registration, as states could better track movers and better avoid removing active voters (Ansolabehere 2014). If the notion that states should maintain accurate lists of who *could* vote instead of who *decided to register to vote* takes hold, there may be nontrivial consequences for turnout inequalities. Efforts by mobilizers to register voters, long popular for low-turnout-prone groups, may instead shift toward GOTV efforts closer to election day. Of course, doing away with the need to register to vote is another option: by 2016, 17 states allowed prospective voters to register to vote at the same time that they cast their ballot. Election day registration also appears to boost turnout more than other election reforms (Burden et al. 2014), and when combined with Automatic Voter Registration, by 2020 at least 40 percent of the U.S. population will live in states where advance voter registration is either automatic or unnecessary for voting. Automatic voter registration confers yet another advantage: expanding the list of potential voters, giving candidates and campaigns a better sense of the pool of potential supporters. Recall that partisan mobilization is a key mechanism linking perceived electoral influence to a diminution of the turnout gap. Registration lists are the primary source of information used by campaigns to determine who their constituents are in a campaign context (Hersh 2015), and thus efforts to produce a more representative voter registration list may ensure campaigns find the disproportionately poor and minority unregistered and "unlisted" population (Jackman and Spahn 2017).

SUPPRESSION AND INFLUENCE

Measures constituting "voter suppression" have long been pursued by political agents seeking to gain an electoral advantage (Overton 2007; Keyssar 2009; Wang 2012; Berman 2015a). Emerging understandings of the 2016 election also suggest disparate turnout impacts of these laws shaped outcomes, with Democratic presidential candidate Hillary Clinton blaming her narrow loss in Wisconsin on the state's newly implemented strict photo identification law (Clinton 2017). The political, and often racial, intent of felon disenfranchisement, voter identification, and other election restrictions is clear. Why wouldn't these measures exacerbate the turnout gap?

Drawing on the best evidence available, including original analyses of felon disenfranchisement laws and voter identification provisions, the conclusion I reach is that provisions associated with contemporary vote suppression have an inconsistent and often small impact on racial/ethnic disparities in voter turnout. How is this possible? While more work needs to be done to understand the full effect of these provisions on Black, Latino, and Asian voting, there are two broad lessons when considering the other analyses found in this book: first, states that implement the most restrictive voting provisions often have higher-than-average minority voter turnout. As Chapter 4 and the empirical analyses since make clear, minority voter turnout is higher when they comprise a sizable share of the potential electorate. The combination of high turnout and large group size almost certainly instigates the implementation of these restrictive policies, especially after the *Shelby County* v. *Holder* decision. Heightened turnout may indeed be a contributing factor to the introduction of these laws, reversing the causal arrow and indicating that a small turnout gap may be a *cause* of these laws, not a deviant finding to be explained. Second, countermobilization and efforts that make the electoral power of minority citizens more obvious, such as the language provisions of the VRA and automatic voter registration, may do more to ameliorate the turnout gap than the removal of restrictions on voting. Again, given the fact that we witnessed meaningful gains in Black voting in the Jim Crow era, we should not be surprised that even the most clearly discriminatory of efforts can be countered by the effective mobilization and empowerment of Black, Latino, and Asian American citizens. While the struggle for voting rights clearly continues, the political inequalities we witness today have their origin elsewhere.

The beginning of this chapter features a quote from then-President Barack Obama, taken from his speech at Howard University's 2016 commencement. Before imploring students to "just vote," he noted that while there are indeed persistent, unjust barriers to participation today, but that these barriers cannot fully account for what we see in contemporary elections:

> It is absolutely true that 50 years after the Voting Rights Act, there are still too many barriers in this country to vote. There are too many people trying to erect new barriers to voting. This is the only advanced democracy on Earth that goes out of its way to make it difficult for people to vote. And there's a reason for that. There's a legacy to that. But let me say this: Even if we dismantled every barrier to voting, that alone would not change the fact that America has some of the lowest voting rates in the free world.

Just as no near-term electoral policy would lead to dramatically higher rates of participation, those seeking to eliminate the turnout gap should not rely solely on dreams of squashing every form of vote suppression or implementing all of the favorable reforms we can imagine. As I have shown throughout this book, it is instead the demographic reality of minority electoral power that structures the racial/ethnic political inequalities we witness, and that reality presents a tremendous challenge to efforts to produce greater political equality today. In the next chapter, I conclude the book by evaluating the consequences of the turnout gap on contemporary American elections, and what our demographic destiny suggests about the future of minority voter turnout.

8

Demographic Change and the Future of Minority Voter Turnout

On January 20, 2017, Republican Donald J. Trump was inaugurated as the 45th President of the United States. Surprising nearly every pundit, academic, and perhaps all but his most ardent supporters as well, Trump defeated Democrat Hillary Clinton in the November 2016 election. While losing the popular vote, Trump secured his victory with narrow wins spread over three historically Democratic-learning states: Wisconsin, Michigan, and Pennsylvania. Pennsylvania and Michigan had not gone to the Republican since 1992; Wisconsin longer still. Defying predictions built on demographic change, Trump was elected despite the most racially diverse population in American history and the lowest level of support from Black and Latino voters in forty years (Eisler 2016). Polling designed to produce accurate estimates of Latino voting indicates that for America's largest minority racial/ethnic group, Trump received less support than any presidential candidate that came before (Barreto, Reny, and Wilcox-Archuleta 2017; Barreto and Segura 2017).

Trump's unexpected victory was followed by a half-month "USA Thank You Tour," where the president-elect visited nine southern and midwestern states key to his triumph (Mitchell 2016). At one such stop, in Hershey, Pennsylvania, Trump touted his success with various demographic groups, including women, evangelical Christians, and Latinos. When it came to African Americans, he stated the following:

> We did great with the African-American community, so good. *[applause]* Remember? Remember the famous line, because I'd talk about crime, I'd talk about lack of education, talk about no jobs, and I'd say, what the hell do you have to lose, right? It's true. They're smart, and they picked up on it like you wouldn't believe. And you know what else? They didn't come out to vote for Hillary, they didn't come out. *[applause]* And that was big, so, thank you to the African-American community.[1]

[1] Transcript of speech by Donald J. Trump, Hershey, PA, December 15, 2016.

Black voter turnout was indeed down in 2016 as compared to 2012, and when combined with low rates of Latino and Asian American voter turnout, reduced African American participation may indeed have been a "big" part of his success in Pennsylvania and elsewhere.

At the beginning of this book, I identified two competing perspectives on contemporary American politics: one focused on the increased racial/ethnic diversity of our country, and the other emphasizing a demographic dominance of White voters seemingly exemplified by Donald J. Trump's victory. In the pages since, I demonstrated the persistence of a Minority–White turnout gap that limits the ability of demographic change to translate into increased political equality. In this chapter, I begin by demonstrating that these turnout disparities lead to Whites being more overrepresented as voters than they were half a century ago, producing election outcomes that increasingly diverge from the wishes of the non-White electorate. The book also indicated the circumstances under which Black, Latino, and Asian American voting reaches parity with Whites, namely, when minority voters are perceived to hold significant electoral influence. Charting demographic trends at the state and national level, here I reveal that non-Hispanic Whites will continue to be a dominant force across the country for decades to come. Thus, the demographic reality suggests a perpetuation of political inequality as minority turnout remains low, at least in the absence of a substantial shift in the phenomena that perpetuate the turnout gap. However, the opportunity to change this dynamic coincides with the "demographics are destiny" perspective, reconciling the competing understandings of the future of American politics and indicating that the incentives for a political party to capitalize on demographic change and reduce the turnout gap are fast approaching.

REPRESENTATIVENESS OF THE VOTING POPULATION

Chapter 2 indicated the persistence of the turnout gap across racial/ethnic groups. Even in the historic 2008 and 2012 elections, voter file data suggests that Black turnout continued to lag White turnout by a large margin (see Table 5.3). How should we think about the impact of these differences on politics, both past and present? One way of considering the importance of the turnout gap is the degree to which the voting population "looks like" the population that could vote. With regard to race and ethnicity, we can calculate the degree of overrepresentation or underrepresentation of different groups in the voting population, serving as a marker for the disproportionate sway certain populations, in this case non-Hispanic Whites, hold in national elections.

Figure 8.1 uses self-reported voter turnout data from the Current Population Survey (CPS) to indicate the continuing, and perhaps growing impact of racial/ethnic turnout differences on political inequality from 1948 to 2016. Here I compare turnout statistics with data on the demographic composition of the eligible electorate. In order to estimate racial/ethnic groups' shares of the voting eligible population over nearly seven decades, I rely primarily on the CPS's own estimates of the CVAP. Non-citizens are excluded for all groups when comparing the voting to voting eligible population from 1978 to 2016. For elections from 1972 to 1976, non-citizen Latinos are removed based on the 1978 CPS estimate of the citizen to non-citizen ratio for voting-age adults.[2] For African Americans and Whites, where the number of non-citizens was

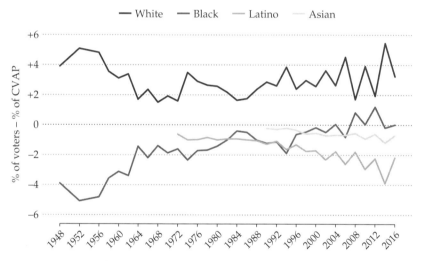

FIGURE 8.1 Share of voters versus share of eligible voters, 1948–2016
Note: Values represent percentage point difference between estimated voting eligible population for each racial/ethnic group and the population voting in the election. Positive values indicate the racial/ethnic group was overrepresented among voters, relative to the voting eligible population. "White" excludes Hispanic Whites from 1972 to 2016. For estimates prior to 1964, ANES data was used to calculate Black and White turnout rates, and interpolated Census estimates for the VAP. From 1964 onwards, CPS estimates of turnout and VAP or CVAP are used.

---

[2] The CPS estimates that 31 percent of voting-age Latino adults were non-citizens in 1978.

(and remains) relatively small, the voting-age population serves as an approximation for the CVAP from 1948 to 1976.[3]

Unlike the turnout gap statistics found in Figure 2.4, Figure 8.1 simultaneously accounts for turnout disparities and how much these disparities influence the overall impact of groups on national elections.[4] Each line on the plot corresponds to a different racial/ethnic group, and deviations from zero on the *y*-axis indicate that a group was over- (if > 0) or under- (if < 0) represented in the voting population relative to the *potential* voter population. In 2010, for instance, non-Hispanic Whites were 73.6 percent of the eligible to vote population, but 77.5 percent of the population that actually voted: a difference of 3.9 percentage points as indicated in Figure 8.1. Again, the figure accounts for both the size of the population and turnout disparities to measure the impact of these disparities on electoral outcomes. For instance, while Latinos had low rates of turnout in both the 1976 and 2016 elections, the far greater size of the Latino population in 2016 indicates that the gap between Latino turnout and non-Latino turnout will have more of an impact on the overall unrepresentativeness of the voting population.

Several patterns emerge in Figure 8.1, but perhaps the most important take-away regards the overrepresentation of Whites in the voting electorate. The CPS data used here is self-reported, so these results likely underestimate disparities in voting. Even so, the White population today is more overrepresented in elections than it was long before passage of the Voting Rights Act of 1965. In 2014, Whites made up nearly 6 percentage points more of the voting population than they did of the population eligible to vote, slightly more than the overrepresentation they had in the 1952 election when half of the African American population lived in the Jim Crow South. The source of this overrepresentation is not dramatically lower African American turnout, however. As the share of the population that is Latino or Asian has increased, the effect of rising African American turnout on reducing political inequality has been muted. Today, the persistent turnout gap, especially for Latinos and Asian Americans, means that Whites have substantially more of a say in elections than their population size would dictate.

---

[3] For years where ANES data is used to estimate turnout (1948–1962), I use a linear interpolation or extrapolation of the 1950 and 1960 Census estimates of the voting-age population for Whites and African Americans.

[4] In other words, as a low turnout population grows in size, the underrepresentation of the group in national elections also increases.

What If There Was No Turnout Gap?

Figure 8.1 also points to past elections where the overrepresentation of Whites in the electorate may have shaped outcomes. The 1994 "Republican Revolution," where Republicans gained fifty-four seats in the U.S. House and a majority for the first time since the 1950s, also saw Whites overrepresented by nearly 4 percentage points for the first time since the 1950s. Yet, President Reagan's reelection in 1984 also featured a relatively low level of White overrepresentation, but an 18 point victory for Reagan in the popular vote. It is difficult to identify an obvious pattern of minority underrepresentation and election outcomes. An estimated 83 percent of eligible voters were non-Hispanic White in 1984, only dropping to 81 percent ten years later. White voters clearly drove outcomes in previous decades no matter the specific turnout gap. The underrepresentation of minority voices in the electorate is, of course, accompanied by the underrepresentation of the young, low income, and other demographic characteristics associated with lower turnout (Leighley and Nagler 2013). Table 1.1 already indicated that who votes matters, but now we may shift the question to examine the particular impact of racial/ethnic disparities in participation: Would election outcomes change if there was no Minority–White turnout gap?

Below I use the same CCES data as in Chapter 1, but now present a scenario where the turnout of racial/ethnic minority citizens and White citizens is equal. To construct this counterfactual, I rely on CCES respondents' self-reported vote preference and validated voting data.[5] Gathering information on the vote preference of minority citizens who were not validated voters, I add vote share to the Democratic and Republican candidates for office that corresponds to the vote preferences of minority non-voters. I set the turnout *rate* for these minority non-voters equal to Whites, estimating how much support these non-voters would have contributed to each party's candidates had they turned out to vote.[6] Because the CCES does not necessarily provide a perfect measurement of state election outcomes, I compute the CCES-based additional percentage of the vote received by the Democratic candidate, and then combine

---

[5] YouGov, the polling firm that conducts the CCES, contracts with Catalist to verify whether each survey respondent voted. For more details regarding this validation process, see the CCES webpage at http://cces.harvard.edu

[6] As noted in Chapter 5, in some southern states African American turnout exceeds White turnout. In these states, I subtract a corresponding percentage of minority voters to equalize minority and White turnout.

TABLE 8.1 *Democratic Party electoral outcomes, actual results versus no turnout gap*

	U.S. House		U.S. Senate		President	
	Actual results (%)	*No turnout gap (%)*	*Actual results*	*No turnout gap*	*Actual results*	*No turnout gap*
2006	53.6	54.3	51	51		
2008	59.1	59.3	59	59	365	361
2010	44.4	46.9	53	54		
2012	46.2	47.1	55	57	332	332
2014	43.2	44.8	46	50		
2016	44.6	45.1	48	51	232	318

Note: Actual results represents the percentage of seats won (U.S. House), number of seats held (U.S. Senate) or number of Electoral College votes won (President) by the Democratic Party after the November election in each year. *No turnout gap* scenarios are counterfactual Democratic Party seats (U.S. House and U.S. Senate) or Electoral College votes awarded to the Democrat (President) based on equalizing minority turnout and White turnout and accounting for the vote preferences of minority respondents, as expressed in each year from 2006 to 2016.

this additional percentage with the *actual* election outcome we witness.[7] The result is a counterfactual set of recent elections where minority citizens *who expressed vote preferences* turn out at the same rate as the non-Hispanic White population. Again, the share of the population that is minority in each state or district does not change; Whites are still the dominant force in most state election outcomes. The only thing that changes is the turnout rate of minority voters.

Both Table 8.1 above and Table 1.1 indicate that changes in who votes induce a shift in the 2016 presidential election outcome. Of course, in such a close election, any number of factors could have influenced the result. However, if Black, Latino, and Asian American voters had turned out to vote at the same rate that non-Hispanic Whites did, or the converse,[8] Democrat Hillary Clinton would have won not only the three pivotal states of Michigan, Wisconsin, and Pennsylvania, but also Florida and Arizona, giving her 318 earned Electoral College votes. In fact, had voter turnout rates by race simply been equivalent to what was

[7] Thus, to the extent that the CCES does not accurately reflect election outcomes, this does not impact my results except if it also provides a biased estimate of the vote preferences of non-voting minority voters. Some scholars indicate that most national surveys tend to underestimate minority preference for Democratic candidates, so the estimates of change I produce here are likely conservative.

[8] The process used to "add" minority voters is symmetrical, in that the result is the same if minority turnout increases to the level of Whites or White turnout decreases to the level of minority voters.

witnessed in 2012, Michigan, Wisconsin, and Pennsylvania would have swung to Clinton, enough to give the Democrats the presidency for the third election in a row. President Obama, on the other hand, was already the recipient of higher minority voter turnout and would only have won the additional state of Missouri in 2008 if minority turnout was equal to White turnout. In fact, his close victory in North Carolina in 2008 would have instead been a narrow loss had Black voter turnout not exceeded White turnout in the state that year.

With states shifting in the Electoral College tally, it is likely not surprising that U.S. Senate outcomes would have been substantially different if there was no turnout gap. Again, only equalizing turnout rates between Black, Latino, Asian Americans, and Whites such that each group has an impact proportional to its share of the potential voter pool, the middle columns of Table 8.1 indicate that the Democrats would have gained and then maintained a majority in the Senate from 2006 to 2016. The 2014 election is particularly instructive, as the large overrepresentation of Whites in the electorate indicated in Figure 8.1 produced Senate losses for Democrats in Georgia and North Carolina. Gaining these two seats, along with Illinois in 2010 and Arizona in 2012, would have produced Democratic control of both the Senate and Presidency for at least ten years (2009–2019). As in Table 1.1, U.S. House elections are harder to shift, and my estimates may be conservative due to the small number of respondents from most congressional districts. However, Democrats would have gained an average of five additional House seats in each election year if the turnout gap did not exist.

The election results presented in Table 8.1 may be conservative estimates of the broader representational impact of the turnout gap. As noted in Chapter 4, cyclical non-mobilization or repeated losses may engender a sense of disempowerment for voters. The scenario is simply a counterfactual where *expressed* minority preferences are given a proportional weight to their share of the population. These estimates do not include the non-trivial share of the eligible Latino and Asian American population that does not express a preference for who to vote for, such that inequalities due to lack of political knowledge, political interest, or simply ambivalence between the candidates are not factored in. As noted by Hajnal and Lee (2011), Latino, Asian American, and at times, African American citizens may be particularly likely to feel disengaged or detached from partisan politics. Furthermore, low minority turnout may have a much greater effect in local elections, which are not examined here (Hajnal and Trounstine 2005; Hajnal 2010). Despite these limitations, clear evidence emerges that links the turnout gap to the representation all Americans receive.

As noted at the beginning of this book, the non-representativeness of election outcomes presents a formidable challenge to representative government (Schattschneider 1960; Verba, Schlozman, and Brady 1995). Past work indicated that, while the preferences of non-voters may be *slightly* different from voters, they are not different enough to change the outcome of elections (Wolfinger and Rosenstone 1980; Highton and Wolfinger 2001; Citrin, Schickler, and Sides 2003; DeNardo 1980). Yet, a handful of scholars have found that representational outcomes favor voters (Hill 1995; Griffin and Newman 2005; Hill 2017), and with the turnout gap being as substantial as it is, we should perhaps reevaluate previous work to search for specific racial effects (Burch 2012). For example, Griffin and Newman (2008) show that minority voters are particularly likely to be on the losing end of elections. The turnout gap likely contributes to this underrepresentation, with dramatic consequences for recent elections.

Leighley and Nagler (2013) close their book with a simple assertion: yes, it matters who votes (188). As a result of the turnout gap, we can now confidently affirm that yes, it matters, and likely in a more consequential way than ever before.

DEMOGRAPHIC REALITY AND DEMOGRAPHIC CHANGE

The fact that the Minority–White turnout gap has an impact on contemporary elections in some ways reaffirms the narrative that minority voters are critical to election outcomes. Yet, the usual framing of this assertion by analysts is that the growing *size* of the non-White population is what produces their impact on politics (Teixeira 2008; Bowler and Segura 2012; Frey 2015; Frey, Teixeira, and Griffin 2016; Phillips 2017). Some of this work was remarkably prescient, as for example, Judis and Teixeira (2002) assert that the Democratic Party could leverage demographic shifts to produce durable majorities in Congress and win the presidency, predictions that seemed to come true in 2008. Of course, demographers interested in charting the future of electoral politics also acknowledge low minority turnout. But across the six 2016 presidential election scenarios documented in Frey, Teixeira, and Griffin (2016), only one acknowledged the possibility that a combination of persistently low minority turnout and shifts among Whites in favor of the Republican Party could produce the election results we witnessed.

Despite demographic change, this "extreme" scenario is exactly what occurred.

As I have indicated throughout this book, there is a close connection between the demographic composition of the electorate and racial/ethnic disparities in voter turnout. In Chapter 5, I indicated that in nearly every state in the country, along with the vast majority of counties and congressional districts, White voters are the majority population and thus experience empowerment and mobilization to a far greater degree than minority citizens. Yet, it is undeniable that the United States is becoming more diverse. Chapter 1 indicated that the minority population has more than doubled since 1960, with a dramatic increase in the Latino and Asian American populations in particular. Here I examine what future trends we may see, before discussing implications for the turnout gap.

Consider the two charts that comprise Figure 8.2. The chart on the left displays data similar to that found in Figure 1.1, drawing on information from the U.S. Census about the total population. When individuals speak of a "majority–minority America," they often point to measures of the total population to assert that this demographic threshold will be reached by 2040, or earlier (Bowler and Segura 2012: 13–14). This is almost certainly the case, as in the most recent projections from the U.S. Census Bureau, we see the majority–minority threshold for the total population being reached by 2043. By 2060, the limit of the Census estimates, the

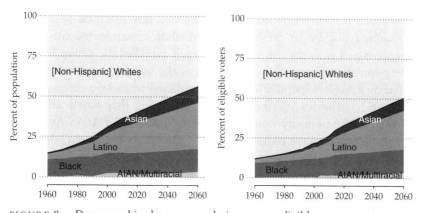

FIGURE 8.2 Demographic change, population versus eligible voters, 1960–2060
Note: Left panel indicates racial/ethnic group shares of the total U.S. population, right panel the racial/ethnic group shares of the CVAP. CPS and U.S. Census data used for 1960–2016. Projections for 2016 to 2060 based on U.S. Census Bureau estimates from December 2014, with citizenship rates for foreign-born voting age adults based on extrapolated 2016 estimates from ACS five-year data.

United States is predicted to be 43.6 percent non-Hispanic White and 56.4 percent minority. One hundred years before that, in 1960, I estimate the American population as 85 percent non-Hispanic White and only 15 percent minority. Using whichever metrics we choose, we are clearly a diversifying nation.

The rightmost panel of Figure 8.2, however, accounts for variation in age and citizenship across racial/ethnic groups. To do so, I use CPS and Census estimates of the CVAP for 1960 to 2016. The projections require a more complex process, as predictions of the citizen voting-age population are not available. Instead, I use the same Census projections as called upon for the leftmost figure, but include only adults of voting age and remove a portion of the projected foreign-born population based on citizenship rates drawn from the American Community Survey.[9] Here we see that the share of the *eligible* electorate that is minority lags fifteen to twenty years behind the estimates for the entire population. Though also resulting in a majority–minority voting eligible population within the timeframe of the analysis, this does not occur until 2059. While I also predict a growing similarity between the voting-age population and voting eligible population in the future, as indicated by Frey, Teixeira, and Griffin (2015), it is important to note that citizenship and age differences are substantial enough to produce a somewhat distinct picture of what the near-term demographic reality may imply for future elections.

Perhaps an even more important point is that while the United States will reach majority–minority status by 2050, non-Hispanic Whites will continue to be *by far* the largest racial/ethnic group in the country. In Figure 8.2, I indicate the share that each racial/ethnic group holds in the population through shading areas of the figure. As we can see, the African American population is not predicted to grow a large amount relative to other racial/ethnic groups, indicating that nearly all of the growth in the minority population will be Latino and Asian American. As these groups have particularly low rates of voter turnout, this indicates that the turnout gap will likely not only persist, but grow in the future. According to Census projections, Latino voting-age citizens will outnumber African American voting-age citizens by the 2020 election. That said, non-Hispanic Whites will still be a majority of citizens until 2058, and even after that point will still outnumber Latinos (the second largest group) 2:1 as Latinos compose less than a quarter of the CVAP.

9 Frey (2015) uses a multilevel modeling procedure to generate similar estimates.

At a national level, it is undeniable that minority citizens will make up an ever greater share of the population, but Whites will still be the largest racial/ethnic group in the nation. What about at the state level? The Census Bureau no longer publishes projections of state populations by race/ethnicity, and due to individuals moving across states it is difficult to predict demographic trends for states.[10] In order to construct an informed estimate of the impact of future demographic change on states I allocated the national Census-projected population growth by race to states based on their population growth by race from 2006 to 2016. Over the next decade, the only two states where Whites are not the plurality group are Hawaii and (by 2024) New Mexico. California, often cited as a majority–minority state, did indeed transition to majority–minority status in terms of the CVAP in the early 2010s. However, Whites still compose 47 percent of the CVAP and Latinos, at 30 percent, do not catch up to non-Hispanic Whites for at least a generation. Using a slightly different methodology, Frey, Teixeira, and Griffin (2015, 2016) produce similar results in the short term, and find California will become plurality Latino by 2036 and Texas by 2040 when using eligible voters as the indicator. The greater electoral influence gained in particular states may indeed yield dividends in the form of higher mobilization and empowerment in the long term.

As noted in Chapter 6, today congressional districts may be the most salient electoral jurisdictions where minority voters wield decisive influence on election outcomes. Historically, state governments have been compelled to create majority–minority districts to ensure electoral equity for Black and Latino voters. Reforms to the redistricting process, such as nonpartisan redistricting commissions or limits on partisan gerrymandering, may produce opportunities to grow the number of areas where racial/ethnic groups have influence in the electoral process. Beyond these possibilities, demographic growth at the state level will likely produce additional majority-Latino and (eventually) majority-Asian districts, perhaps helping to ameliorate the turnout gap for these groups. However, barring significant distributional changes of the African American population it is unlikely that additional areas of African American electoral influence will arise due to demographic change alone. A history of residential segregation still plays a major role in the contemporary racial/ethnic distribution of the population (Enos and Fowler 2017), but today, at least some of the residential patterns we witness may be

---

[10] See Frey, Teixeira, and Griffin (2015, 2016) for more comprehensive efforts to do so.

the result of individuals from *all* racial/ethnic groups preferring to live near a substantial co-ethnic population (Oliver 2010: 103). Demographic change is reshaping America, but its effects may be most concentrated in areas that are *already* quite diverse.

THE FUTURE OF THE TURNOUT GAP

When considering the future of racial/ethnic disparities in who turns out to vote, we may draw key lessons from the findings discussed in this book. I hypothesized that the perceived electoral influence groups hold in an electoral jurisdiction predicts the turnout gap. When this dynamic is changed, for example, by residing in a majority–minority district, we see a diminution of the turnout gap in both a correlational and causal sense. Operationalizing electoral influence as group size also has important implications for our interpretation of factors such as sociodemographic resources, as I did not find that disparities in SES explained away the turnout gap. Finally, examining both historical barriers and contemporary restrictions on voting, I found little evidence that anything but the most severe restrictions on participation by otherwise highly participatory adults has an appreciable impact on the turnout gap. The emerging narrative regarding modern "vote suppression," while important given the discriminatory intent of such laws, should be narrowed to intent instead of effect. Again, the theory of electoral influence helps us understand why this might be: heavily minority areas also tend to be in states with the greatest incentives to *suppress* minority turnout. Yet, these efforts are in response to mobilization, and that mobilization appears able to surmount contemporary barriers.

The analyses in this section also point to longer-term trends in minority turnout. Given the theoretical framework I use in this book, we should not be surprised that a gap between White turnout and non-White turnout persists: minority groups rarely have the kind of "representation and influence in political decisionmaking," (Bobo and Gilliam 1990) long thought to be a requisite to Black and Latino political participation, while non-Hispanic Whites almost always do. Based on previous understandings, it was not necessarily clear whether we should be trying to understand persistently *low* minority turnout, or persistently *high* White turnout. Now we see that the two are related, often inversely, as the group size-based electoral influence groups hold structures rates of political participation. However, future demographic trends clearly point to an increasingly large minority electorate, especially for Latinos and Asian Americans and even extending to the state level (Frey, Teixeira, and Griffin 2015). We may think that the response will be heightened turnout, at least in the very long run as politicians find it increasingly difficult to ignore these voices. The fact that electoral outcomes seem to be, in part, structured by rates of minority voter turnout may also encourage demographic influence to manifest in electoral influence, for voters and officeseekers alike.

The conclusions reached in this book also generate a number of questions for future research. Why do we see higher rates of turnout for African Americans than Latinos, despite the availability of majority-Latino districts and the fact that Latinos make up a larger share of more state populations? One major issue could be that groups like Latinos do not perceive their vote to matter. Promising experimental research on Latino voter mobilization strategies indicates that group targeted approaches are not only helpful, but may be necessary to ensure that Latinos feel incorporated into the political system (García Bedolla and Michelson 2012; Ramírez 2013; Valenzuela and Michelson 2016). Are campaigns actually adopting such strategies, perhaps Latino candidates in particular? In Chapter 6, I determined that dynamics in primary elections that limit incentives to mobilize Latinos may help explain why majority-Latino districts do not *always* stimulate turnout. The role of generation and acculturation here may be important as well (Logan, Oh, and Darrah 2009; Abrajano 2010). An investigation into the specific types of techniques used by campaigns to mobilize minority voters is an excellent next step.

We may also ask why we do not see a more considerable impact of electoral competition on minority voting rates. The notion that Black turnout might not be higher in majority-Black areas was often attributed to a lack of competition (Gay 2001), and models of Latino voting are often predicated on their importance in hotly contested elections (Barreto, Collingwood, and Manzano 2010). Perhaps voters are deciding to participate for less instrumental reasons. As Griffin and Newman (2008) indicate, incentives for African Americans to vote may be more obvious in heavily Black districts, as it is these places where representatives appear most responsive to the preferences of their Black constituents (194). Yet, Table 8.1 makes it clear that minority votes can make a difference, even in statewide elections. What will make parties and voters put in the work to mobilize and vote? Two cases are perhaps worth considering:

the Trump campaign and victory on the one hand, and the degree to which Democrats are, today, reliant on minority voters on the other.

2016: White Influence Matters?

First, we begin with the 2016 election. President-elect Trump himself noted that low African American turnout was an important part of his success in the 2016 election. Some academics, the author included, believed that African Americans would continue to be mobilized at a high rate when Barack Obama was no longer president. While evidence from both self-reports and voter file analyses indicate that Black turnout decreased in 2016, White turnout held steady or increased in key midwestern and southern states.

Why is White turnout so high? The simple answer is that White voters are determinative of election outcomes almost everywhere in the country. Yet, for 2016, we see another important reason related to the mobilization of a large group: a relatively small shift in White partisan preferences completely changes the electoral calculus as to which states matter and which states do not. For instance, post election, several media outlets questioned why Clinton visited Arizona and Florida close to election day, but not Wisconsin or Michigan. Yet, as Table 8.1 indicated, based on the demographic and partisan composition of Arizona and Florida she would have won these Sun Belt states with minority turnout equal to White turnout. Wisconsin and Michigan, on the other hand, were surprising shifts to the Republican column secured primarily through unexpectedly important changes in White partisan preferences. Again, we can reconcile the competing perspectives indicated above: demographic change is indeed our political destiny, but White voters still have dominant influence that exacerbates and is exacerbated by the turnout gap.

In the wake of Barack Obama's 2012 reelection, the Republican National Committee announced the creation of a project designed to review the election and how the Republican Party could move forward for 2016 and beyond (RNC 2013). The final report stemming from the project, known in many circles as the "Republican autopsy," in some ways mirrored previous efforts launched after the 1964 election to reshape the party. Several of the recommendations related to mobilizing and incorporating Hispanic, Asian American, and African American voters into the Republican Party, indicating that demographic change was inevitable and the party could not survive if alienating this growing voting block. Candidate Trump did not appear to accord with any of the report's guidelines, especially as they pertained to outreach to Latinos, yet he won anyway. After Trump's election win, the report was removed from the RNC website. Again, the demographic reality may be informative here. Since as far back as Key (1949), we have understood that the presence of a large minority population may incite a backlash by Whites. This backlash can be either psychological, in the form of prejudice (Enos 2017), or electoral, in the form of shifting allegiances to the competing party (Hood, Kidd, and Morris 2012) or shaping the agenda of one's own party to resist demographic change (Parker and Barreto 2013; Hajnal and Abrajano 2017). The 2018 and 2020 elections will be key tests of the campaign strategy waged by Trump,[11] but for now, the lesson of 2016 may be that the demographic reality in the contemporary United States can boost candidates that effectively shift a segment of the White electorate in their favor.

Democratic Party Reliance on Minority Voters

While the Republican Party may now rely on relatively high-turnout non-Hispanic White voters, the Democratic Party's base is increasingly non-White. According to the 2016 CCES, 35 percent of self-reported voters supporting Hillary Clinton were non-White, as were 42 percent of Democratic Party identifiers. Far smaller shares of Trump voters (11 percent) or Republican identifiers (12 percent) were non-White. This book is certainly not the first to indicate that the contemporary Democratic Party has become far more invested in minority support than Republicans (Bowler and Segura 2012; Phillips 2016), and after the 2016 election prominent voices continued to indicate that the easiest path forward for Democrats was to increase the mobilization of communities of color (Phillips 2017). The above data suggests that not addressing the turnout gap will continue to hamper prospects for Democrats: more than 40 percent of self-identified Democrats did not vote in the 2016 election, and half of the Democrats that did not vote were Black, Latino, or Asian American.

Though it is a fool's errand to project future party coalitions, under the current partisan configuration the Democratic Party will continue to

---

[11] The racial/ethnic makeup of the party coalitions has changed since the 2008 election, with Whites departing the Democratic Party even prior to Trump's candidacy (Sides, Tesler, and Vavreck 2017). However, much of this shift is attributable to racial attitudes and opinions regarding immigration, two key predictors of support for Trump among former Democrats in 2016 (Sides, Tesler, and Vavreck 2018).

be more reliant on non-White voters than Republicans are. However, comparing across racial/ethnic groups, we see that a plurality of *both* Democratic and Republican Party supporters are non-Hispanic White, with well over twice as many Democratic adherents identifying as non-Hispanic White versus African American (58 percent–24 percent). As I note in Chapter 4, strong partisanship for a group enhances the possibility that they will be seen as having electoral influence. African Americans are the best example here, with two-party identifiers choosing the Democratic party 9-to-1 in the 2016 CCES. Again, though, recall the discussion of state-level variation in electoral influence, both today (Chapter 5) and in the future (Frey, Teixeira, and Griffin 2015). According to recent predictions, only four states will have a non-White group forming a plurality of the citizenry by 2060, with the group holding the plurality being Latinos or Asians, not African Americans. Can the Democratic Party sustain itself with an increased number of votes from low-turnout groups, or should they instead attempt to persuade higher-turnout groups (specifically, White voters) back into the coalition?

Such debates come up frequently in discussions of Democrats' 2016 outreach strategies toward various demographic groups (Phillip and O'Keefe 2016; Allison 2017). Indeed, *two* paths forward have been suggested for the Democratic Party: regaining support from White former Democrats in Rust Belt states, or mobilizing minority voters in the Sun Belt and South. Only one of these strategies meets the challenge of demographic change, but it is not certain that the short-term gains outweigh the substantial cost of bringing hard-to-mobilize voters to the polls (Phillips 2017). In some states, such a tradeoff gives way to electoral necessity: the Democratic Party is highly dependent on African American voters in the South. The surprise victory of Democrat Doug Jones in the 2017 Alabama senate election, for instance, was attributed by many to redoubled efforts to mobilize African Americans who did not vote in 2016 (Marcotte 2017; Summers 2017). In other states, greater efficiency may be one way of balancing the tradeoff. Political science has increasingly been interested in which mobilization tactics are most effective, and future research should build on work by García Bedolla and Michelson (2012) and others that examines strategies for the mobilization of non-White citizens more directly. A key part of Jones's mobilization strategy was to engage with minority-led organizations (Eligon 2017; Newkirk II 2017), which exist outside of the South, of course. Furthermore, existing research states that, in a polarized electorate, it is difficult to persuade voters even with expensive canvassing operations (Kalla and

Broockman 2018). New strategies of mobilization may open opportunities for Democrats and make tradeoffs with persuasion less severe in future elections.

GOING FORWARD

In his introduction to *The Right To Vote*, Alexander Keyssar (2009) states "Americans no longer vote as much as they once did." While others have debunked the general conclusion that overall declines in turnout are severe (McDonald and Popkin 2001), there is still truth to this statement when considering racial/ethnic disparities in voter turnout. More than fifty years after passage of the Voting Rights Act of 1965, we witness a large, growing turnout gap between minority citizens and non-Hispanic Whites. For minority citizens, the exercise of the vote is still uncommon enough to have a substantial impact on contemporary American politics. When then-candidate Donald Trump asked African American voters "what do you have to lose?," the extended version of Representative John Lewis's quote that opened this book may serve as one possible response: "[t]here are forces in America that want to take us backwards ... We've come too far. We have made too much progress and we're not going back, we're going forward." Through the actions of Rep. Lewis, and so many others, the *right* to vote gained heightened protections. Now, to go forward, we must ask why many Americans do not *use* that right.

The answers I reach in this book tie together notions of electoral contestation and the political implications of demographic change. When racial/ethnic groups have meaningful influence in electoral outcomes, they will be more likely to vote. For at least eighty years after Reconstruction, efforts were made to restrict the influence minority groups have in the political process. Today, most barriers are gone and mobilization may be able to surmount those that remain (Valentino and Neuner 2017). Demographic change means that American electoral politics no longer features minority groups as minor players in a game where Whites are the key prize (Frymer 1999), but instead necessitates the acknowledgement of the interests and desires of a sizable minority electorate (Bowler and Segura 2012). Yet, continuing disparities in who turns out to vote defy conclusions that the outcomes we witness will necessarily reflect an increasingly diverse electorate.

The turnout gap thus presents a tremendous challenge to our democracy. The cyclical nature of turnout, mobilization, and voter empowerment makes it hard to break long-established dynamics of who has a say in politics and who does not. Is change on the horizon? As the United States continues to diversify, will minority groups be more likely to have their voices reflected in the democratic process? The continued underrepresentation of Black, Latino, and Asian American citizens is certainly a real possibility as long as they are not perceived to have influence in the electoral process. Shifting this dynamic will be difficult, but once again, demographic change could be a powerful ally. When parties, candidates, and voters themselves realize the tremendous potential of the minority electorate, the response is greater turnout and greater political equality for all Americans. Demography will indeed be our destiny. It might just take longer to get there than we thought.

APPENDICES

A.1 Aggregating Data on Race and Ethnicity

Definitions of race and ethnicity have changed substantially over time, reflecting the fact that race and ethnicity are sociopolitical constructs (Prewitt 2002; Hochschild and Powell 2008; Omi and Winant 2015). For the purposes of this book, I attempt to use racial/ethnic categories consistent with what Hollinger (1995) termed the contemporary "ethno-racial pentagon" of five categories: *Non-Hispanic White* (also referred to as *White* in the book), *African American* (also referred to as *Black*), *Latino* (also referred to as *Hispanic, Latina/o, or Latinx*), Asian American (also referred to as *Asian*), and *Native American* (also referred to as *American Indian and Alaska Native*).[1] This categorization follows guidelines provided by the Office of Management and Budget in 1997 (62 FR 58782), which combines what the U.S. Census Bureau defines as "race" and "ethnicity." While Hollinger (1995) himself challenges the ethno-racial pentagon as self-contradicting and not fully reflecting social scientific understandings of race, the five categories defined above have become reified in government policy and form a major part of the contemporary American "racial order" (Hochschild and Powell 2008).[2]

In this book, I combine data on the demographics and behavior of Americans over time and across sources. While the interest is in quantifying the demographics and behavior of individuals using the contemporary ethno-racial pentagon, aggregating such information required a series of decisions that readers should be aware of when interpreting

---

[1] As these sociopolitical constructs do not necessarily reflect (skin) colors and carry distinct historical and institutional weight, I capitalize these racial/ethnic categories throughout the book.

[2] See Denton (1997), Hollinger (2003), Omi and Winant (2015), and Davenport (2018) for further critiques of the ethno-racial pentagon.

my results. Below I document the main data sources that I use, indicating how I aggregate each source's information about race/ethnicity into groupings that are as consistent as possible.[3]

U.S. CENSUS

In Chapters 1 and 8, I use information from the decennial census to document the percent of the White and "minority" population over time. For estimates from 1960–1990, I estimate the minority population percentage as the inverse of the percent of the population that is "White, not of Hispanic Origin" according to the Census. Prior to the 1970s, it was common to include individuals of Latin American or Hispanic ancestry under the racial category of "White," without the ability to disaggregate by Hispanic ethnicity. Thus, for 1960 I extrapolate the Hispanic population based on estimates of the 1965 Hispanic population provided by Pew Research Center (2015) and the 1970 Census estimate of the "Spanish mother tongue" population, shifting these individuals to the minority totals. For 2000–2010, the minority population percentage also includes those who mark "White" plus another racial category in the Census. The 2020–2060 projections of the minority population also include individuals of mixed White and non-White ancestry. Native Hawaiians and Pacific Islanders were grouped with Asians prior to the 2000 Census, and indeed, contemporary research on Asian American politics still sees these distinct populations as linked (cf. Lien et al. 2001; Ong and Nakanishi 2003; Ramakrishnan et al. 2008). I follow this convention throughout my analysis, except for statistics regarding Hawaii where those classified as Native Hawaiian and Pacific Islander are grouped with the American Indian and Alaska Native population.

Chapter 8's estimated racial/ethnic breakdown of the minority population uses the single-race non-Hispanic White, Black (including Black Hispanics), and Asian (including Native Hawaiians, Pacific Islanders, and Hispanic Asians) populations, with AIAN/Multiracial including all individuals not falling into these categories. Unfortunately, the Census projections provided for 2020 to 2060 do not allow for me to distinguish between the Black Hispanic and Asian Hispanic populations, meaning that a small percentage of the Hispanic population is counted as both Black and Hispanic or Asian and Hispanic in the minority population

---

[3] Racial/ethnic definitions for estimates not using the below sources are described where they occur in the text.

breakdown. In order to provide an accurate estimate of the non-Hispanic White and minority shares of the population, I fix these percentages and then distribute the Asian, Latino, and Black populations based on their (potentially overlapping) percentages. As a result, the remainder labeled as "AIAN/Multiracial" is an underestimate of the Native American and multiracial population share's growth over time.

AMERICAN NATIONAL ELECTION STUDY AND CURRENT POPULATION SURVEY

Chapters 1–3 and 8 make use of survey data on race/ethnicity and voter turnout. The American National Election Study (ANES) is used to estimate rates of turnout for Whites and African Americans for years from 1948 to 1972. From 1948 to 1964, the race of respondents was determined by the (face-to-face) interviewer, with categories of "White," "Negro," and "Other" available. While a handful of interviewers coded their respondent as "Other" race (forty-two total respondents from 1948–1962), some of whom were likely Asian American, it is not as clear that interviewers would have classified Latino respondents as "Other." To identify and remove Hispanic and Asian respondents, I use questions regarding respondents' and respondents' parents' place of birth, determining that any individual with origins in Latin America or Asia is Latino or Asian, respectively; fifty-three Latino and 6 Asian respondents were identified in this fashion. For ANES data from 1966 to 1972, interviewer observation was again used to identify respondents' race, but the racial/ethnic categories available to interviewers expanded to include "Puerto Rican," "Mexican/Mexican American/Chicano," "Oriental," and "American Indian." Respondents' and respondents' parents place of birth was again used to identify additional Latino and Asian respondents, beyond interviewer classification. Thus, the ANES estimates of voter turnout for Whites and African Americans coincide as closely as possible to the contemporary understanding of these terms.

The Current Population Survey (CPS) is used to estimate rates of turnout for Whites and African Americans from 1964 to 2016, Latinos from 1972–2016, and Asian Americans from 1990 to 2016. Similar to the early ANES, early versions of the CPS used categories of "White," "Negro," or "Other." However, respondents self-reported their race in face-to-face interviews. The CPS began reporting an individual's "Spanish language or Spanish heritage" in 1972, and the 1974 survey asked an "Ethnicity" question regarding Hispanic ancestry. Estimates of White turnout in 1964, 1968, and 1970 may, therefore, include some Latino respondents, though Latinos made up less than 3 percent of the citizen voting-age population (CVAP) in the 1960s. Official CPS reports include Hispanic respondents in both the racial category denoted and the "Hispanic" category, so for Chapter 2 some Black and Asian Hispanics may be included in totals as "Black" or "Asian" and "Hispanic" to align with CPS practice. In Chapter 3, where the relationship between sociodemographic factors, race, and turnout necessitates clearer delineation of racial/ethnic categories, Black Hispanic and Asian Hispanic respondents are only counted as "Hispanic." "White" always indicates non-Hispanic Whites from 1972 to 2016. Categories of "White," "Negro," or "Other" were the only racial groups published in the Current Population Survey Voting and Registration Supplement until 1990, when "American Indian or Aleut" and "Asian or Pacific Islander" were included for the first time. Based on other Current Population Survey reports, it appears that Asian Americans were categorized as "Other" from the 1970s. However, I am only able to produce estimates of Asian American voter turnout with certainty from 1990 to 2016. After 2000, when respondents were able to select one or more racial/ethnic categories on the CPS, estimates for White, Black, Latino, and Asian turnout include the single race populations for these groups only.

AMERICAN COMMUNITY SURVEY

In order to estimate the CVAP by race/ethnicity for Chapters 5 and 6, I make use of American Community Survey (ACS) estimates of citizenship by race and age. However, the ACS only provides estimates of citizenship and age for single-race non-Hispanic Whites (Table B05003H), African Americans (Table B05003B), Hispanics (Table B05003I), Asians (Table B05003D), American Indian and Alaska Natives (Table B05003C), Native Hawaiians and Pacific Islanders (Table B05003E), "Some Other Race," and the "Two or More Race" Population. Thus, when using Census estimates of the population, the *White* and *Hispanic/Latino* categories are mutually exclusive, but for other racial groups a relatively small number of Hispanics may be included and are thus counted as both *Latino* and the corresponding single-race group. This has the most substantial impact on estimates for African Americans, as a nontrivial share of Caribbean-origin Latinos identify as Black. However, the vast majority (> 95%) of individuals identifying as single-race Black in the

United States are not of Hispanic descent, and an even smaller share of Asian Americans identify as Hispanic.

INTERCENSAL ESTIMATES AND POPULATION ESTIMATES PROGRAM

In Chapter 5, I estimate the voting age population by race/ethnicity from 2006 to 2016 by using a combination of Intercensal Estimates (for the period 2006–2010) and Population Estimates Program (PEP) estimates (2010–2016). The Intercensal and PEP estimates use similar categories to the ACS at a subnational level, again providing only single-race estimates. Here the *White* and *Hispanic/Latino* categories are mutually exclusive, but for other racial groups a relatively small number of Hispanics may be included.

COOPERATIVE CONGRESSIONAL ELECTION STUDY

In Chapters 1, 6, and 8 I use estimates of opinions, attitudes, and vote preferences by race/ethnicity from the Cooperative Congressional Election Study (CCES). More information about the CCES may be found in each chapter, and on the study website (http://cces.harvard.edu), but the categories available to CCES respondents changed slightly from the 2006–2008 waves of the survey to the 2010–2016 waves. Prior to 2010, I aggregate responses by race based on a question including "Hispanic or Latino" along with "White," "Black," "Asian," and other racial/ethnic categories. After 2010, a follow-up question was asked to respondents who did not initially indicate that they were Latino, asking if they were of Hispanic origin. After 2010, any respondents who indicated that they were Hispanic regardless of their initial response on the race question are counted as Latino.

CATALIST

A more detailed description of Catalist's procedure for estimating race/ethnicity of individual registrants may be found in Appendix A.3. However, the categories used by Catalist in their primary race model roughly align with the ethnoracial pentagon: "Caucasian," "Black," "Hispanic," "Asian," "Native American," "Other," or "Unknown." Classification into these groups is made via a combination of analyzing ACS data on the voting-age population within Census bloc groups, and comparison between the name of the respondent and Census lists of race/ethnicity. As a result, the Catalist categories of race are best understood as approximating the single-race, non-Hispanic groupings found in the decennial Census. In the nine states where individuals can indicate their race on the voter file, there is some variation as to the categories made available to registrants, but "Hispanic" includes any individual of Hispanic ancestry, regardless of race.

A.2 Accounting for Missing Data in the Current Population Survey

Chapters 2 and 3 rely on survey data to estimate voter turnout rates by race/ethnicity from 1948 to 2016. For the 1964–2016 period, the Current Population Survey (CPS) is used. However, a persistent issue with official reports from the CPS is their method of dealing with non-response. As noted by McDonald (2017b) and Hur and Achen (2013), by the 1990s it became clear that a substantial portion of the CPS sample either cannot be contacted or declines to participate. Differences by race/ethnicity in rates of "missingness" mean that our estimates of the turnout gap may be biased. As Figure A.1 demonstrates, non-response rates by voting-age citizens for all groups have grown over time. However, rates of non-response have increased more quickly and remained substantially higher for African Americans, Latinos, and Asian Americans than non-Hispanic Whites. To resolve this issue, I deviate from CPS practice and remove individuals who did not take any part of the Voting and Registration Supplement, refused to answer the vote question, or responded "Don't Know" to questions about voting and voter registration.[1] Such a procedure is commonly used in surveys like the American National Elections Study and Cooperative Congressional Election Study, and was the procedure used by Wolfinger and Rosenstone (1980) in their pioneering study of what factors influence voting (6).

Overall rates of missingness were far lower prior to the 1990s (Hur and Achen 2013). Indeed, fewer than 5 percent of CPS respondents

---

[1] Respondents who refused to answer or stated "Don't Know" for the voting question, but reported that they were not registered to vote, are counted as non-voters. Due to limitations in the data reported for early years of the CPS, totals from 1964 to 1970 also count as non-voters those who responded "Don't Know" to the voting question yet were registered to vote.

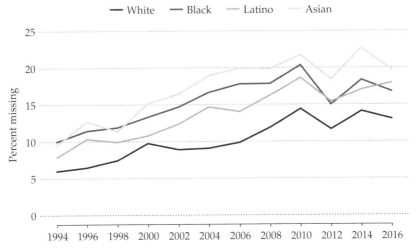

FIGURE A.1 Percent of adult citizens in the CPS with missing turnout information
Note: Data from the Current Population Survey (CPS) Voting and Registration Supplement, 1994–2014. Individuals counted as missing include those that did not take the Voting and Registration supplement, refused to answer the vote question, or responded "Don't Know" to the voting and registration questions.

declined to participate in the supplement's voting and registration questions in presidential election years between 1964 and 1972, stabilizing at approximately 6 percent from 1976 to 1992. Figure A.1 suggests similarity in missingness rates in 1994, indicating that racial/ethnic differences in non-response may have been less consequential for comparing rates of voter turnout prior to 1994. Yet, missing data creates a second problem when comparing rates of Latino and Asian turnout to Whites and African Americans. The CPS sampling frame was constructed using information about the adult population, regardless of citizenship status. Citizenship was not a question in the standard CPS questionnaire until 1994, and was instead included in the November supplement from 1966 to 1992. Thus, we do not have information as to the voting eligibility of those who did not take the supplement at all from 1964 to 1992. Estimates of Latino and Asian American turnout that count "missing" responses as potential voters are thus biased *downward* in these years when compared to Whites and African Americans who have higher rates of citizenship. From 1976 onward, therefore, an accurate measure of turnout among eligible Latinos and (starting in 1990) Asian Americans also necessitates the removal of those who refused or declined to take the supplement.

As a result, the CPS-derived estimates of voter turnout provided in Chapters 2 and 3 differ from both official reports produced by the Census Bureau (File 2013; Jennings 1993) and previous academic work quantifying rates of voter turnout by race (Teixeira 1992: 70; Leighley and Nagler 2013: 30). The results I provide generally indicate a slightly smaller difference between Black and White voter turnout than found in past work, and thus, my estimates should be seen as conservative when comparing these groups. With Latinos and Asian Americans, the situation changes as reporting norms shift for the Census Bureau. Pre-1994, calculations of Latino and Asian American voter turnout generally did not account for citizenship. Given that I account for citizenship throughout the analysis, the differences between White and Latino or White and Asian American voter turnout pre-1994 are smaller than what was reported previously. From 1994 onward, the CPS does account for citizenship, and estimates of the turnout gap approximate what is reported by the CPS.

A.3 Estimating Race/Ethnicity with Catalist Data

As noted in Chapter 5, the voter file database provided by Catalist, LLC contains information about the race/ethnicity of every registered voter in the country. In eight states,[1] Catalist simply uses the self-reported race of respondents as listed on the voter file. For the remaining forty-two states, Catalist models individual race using the name and geography of voters (see discussion in Chapter 5),[2] techniques that are rooted in a Bayesian estimation process where the existing literature indicates relatively high accuracy can be achieved with surname and basic demographic information about neighborhood composition (Elliott et al. 2008; Enos 2016; Imai and Khanna 2016). In particular, Imai and Khanna (2016) demonstrates that the Bayesian approach using name and geography outperforms ecological inference or ecological regression methods for estimating the racial/ethnic composition of a voting population. As of 2017, Catalist uses their model to provide an estimated probability that each individual belongs to each racial/ethnic group; campaigns use this information to determine who is highly likely to be from a given group, and then design their targeting strategies accordingly. As discussed in Hersh (2015), this information is critically important to campaigns. Thus while the exact formula and data used by Catalist are proprietary, their technique represents the cutting edge of efforts to determine the race/ethnicity of individuals as concordant with the incentives in place for Catalist to produce highly accurate information about every potential voter.

---

[1] These states are Alabama, Florida, Georgia, Louisiana, Mississippi, North Carolina, Tennessee, and South Carolina.

[2] See p. 105.

TABLE A.1 *Accuracy of Catalist race measures*

	Total (%)	Voter file (%)	Prediction (%)
All Voters	93.1	98.1	91.4
White	97.8	99.7	97.3
Black	77.1	98.1	66.7
Latino	79.8	79.8	75.7
Asian	72.8	88.1	68.9
N	15,562	3,115	12,447

Note: Estimates drawn from 2016 CCES respondents who were matched to Catalist registration records with 90% match confidence or greater. Cells indicate proportion of CCES respondents self-identifying with the indicated racial/ethnic group and having the same race/ethnicity listed in the Catalist database. *Voter File* isolates individuals whose race was listed in the state voter file. *Prediction* isolates individuals whose race is modeled by Catalist. **Total** represents the share whose race is predicted correctly by Catalist, or who have their race indicated in the Voter File.

ACCURACY OF CATALIST'S RACE PREDICTIONS

Just how accurate are Catalist's records of individual race/ethnicity? Based on the voter file and modeled race data that Catalist was using in early 2017, which was also used for the estimates in Chapter 5 and the observational analyses in Chapter 6, individuals who are non-Hispanic White, African American, Latino, or Asian American have their race/ethnicity correctly indicated in Catalist records approximately 93 percent of the time. This overall estimate was derived by comparing self-reported race/ethnicity in the Cooperative Congressional Election Study (CCES) 2016 survey to Catalist's measures of the race of these respondents. Table A.1 provides a detailed breakdown of these estimates, by source of race information and racial/ethnic group.

Combining respondents from any of the four indicated racial/ethnic groups, we see that even when Catalist is forced to model individual race, it corresponds with individual self-reports in the CCES 91.4 percent of the time. Accuracy is even higher for non-Hispanic Whites, with Catalist's predictions being nearly as accurate as Catalist's race information drawing directly from state voter files. For African Americans the correspondence rate is somewhat lower, though as a relatively large number of African Americans live in southern states with race on the file, overall accuracy is 77 percent. Latinos in the CCES have their Hispanic ethnicity predicted at almost the same rate as what is listed in the voter file, though the fact that 80 percent of Latinos have a different self-reported race in the voter file than self-reported race in the CCES should make us question the consistency of self-reported race altogether. Finally, for Asian Americans, we see prediction rates similar to African Americans, though once again a substantial share of Asians self-reported a different race on the voter file and the CCES. As indicated in the table, CCES respondents were only included here if Catalist's proprietary matching algorithm estimated a match confidence of 90 percent or greater; a substantial share of "inaccurate" race codings could be due to mismatched individuals. Given that I do not use Catalist–CCES matched data in this book, these may be downwardly biased estimates of the accuracy of Catalist's race predictions.

Independent analyses of the accuracy of voter file estimates of race confirm that the vast majority of race predictions are accurate. In a 2018 study comparing self-reported race of Pew Research Center panelists to five anonymous voter file vendors (Igielnik et al. 2018), Pew researchers found that, on average, 83 percent of panelists (min. = 74 percent, max. = 87 percent) with race predictions had the same race listed in the voter file. Correspondence rates were again lower for African Americans and Latinos than for Whites, and unlike the Catalist comparison in Table A.1, it is not clear what cutoffs Pew used to determine a successful "match," how many racial/ethnic categories were included in the comparison, or what the correspondence rate would be for voters versus the whole population. Even with these caveats, however, independent analysis of voter file information about individual race/ethnicity indicates the continued utility of voter file data for studying race and voter turnout.

The potential for bias in turnout estimates due to Catalist's misclassification of individual race is discussed in Fraga (2016a). There, I use the observed inaccuracy in Catalist's race coding as compared to CCES self-reports to generate estimates of error in turnout measurements at the district level. I find no evidence that the relative group size to turnout relationship changes in a regression context due to Catalist's mismeasurement of individual race. Thus, the regression-based analyses in Chapter 6 are unlikely to change if misclassification did not exist. Furthermore, nearly all misclassification is in the direction of incorrectly asserting that someone who is a racial/ethnic minority voter is instead non-Hispanic White, or what we might call *Type II error* from the perspective of predicting who is a minority voter. Thus, analyses that examine individual behavior over time, such as those in the second half of Chapter 6 (analyzing redistricting), would produce *conservative* estimates of racial/ethnic differences in voter turnout as influenced by factors that should, in theory, only impact minority group members.

AGGREGATING CATALIST'S RACE INFORMATION

As noted above, for each record in their database Catalist provides a probability that the individual belongs to each racial/ethnic group. One method of aggregating this information would be to average these probabilities. This is a viable solution when seeking to estimate the *share* of the voting population that each racial/ethnic group composes in a large jurisdiction, as the fact that a single individual contributes to totals for multiple racial/ethnic groups is relatively small and misclassification would likely be of little consequence overall. However, if we are interested in observing the behavior of individual members of different racial/ethnic groups, or desire to produce accurate estimates of voter turnout *rates* for each racial/ethnic group, especially at low levels of geography, such a technique may not be appropriate. While Catalist analysts recommend averaging probabilistic estimates of race for analysis of aggregate turnout, I instead acquired the *plurality* racial/ethnic prediction of each individual voter, and then assigned each voter the race/ethnicity corresponding to the plurality prediction. A primary reason for this modeling choice was to provide consistency with previous work. Of course, Census and survey self-reports of race/ethnicity are categorical, meaning that categorical classifications provide alignment with analytical techniques using self-reported race. In Fraga (2016a, 2016b) and Fraga and Merseth (2016), I relied on previous Catalist-provided models that only provided categorical race information. The Catalist sample data used in Chapters 6 and 7 also draw on this categorical data, as does the Catalist-CCES race prediction featured earlier in this Appendix. Yet, even outside of users of Catalist's proprietary model previous political science research also relies on categorical estimates of individual race. Both Enos (2016) and Imai and Khanna (2016) use Bayesian predictions of individual race similar to those produced more recently by Catalist, but also categorize each individual into a single racial/ethnic group in at least portions of their analyses.

In Chapter 5, I noted that the decision to use the plurality racial/ethnic prediction for each voter produces somewhat predictable consequences for raw estimates of the aggregate number of voters in some jurisdictions.[3] Specifically, the consequence of this modeling decision is a likely systematic overestimate of the Minority–White turnout gap a) in states, counties, or congressional districts where Whites are

---

[3] See p. 109.

both a large share of the electorate and levels of segregation are relatively low, and b) for racial/ethnic groups where geography plays a larger
role than last name in distinguishing individuals of different racial/ethnic
groups. The most obvious minority group facing this issue is African
Americans, and the most obvious place where the Black–White turnout
gap may be biased upward is in western states with small populations
of African Americans. States like Montana, which has fewer than 6,000
African American adults according to the Census Bureau, may have a
substantially larger or smaller Black–White turnout gap than what is
indicated in Chapter 5. Furthermore, the aggregate consequence of higher
turnout in areas with small, less segregated African American populations means that the Black–White turnout gap at the national level is also
larger than it would be if averaging probabilistic estimates of individual
race/ethnicity.

Two alternatives were considered, but rejected: First, survey data
could be used to supplement the Catalist estimates, perhaps using a
multilevel regression and poststratification (MRP) process that would
assume the turnout rate of e.g. Montana African Americans is similar
to that of better identified African Americans in other states with similar demographic characteristics. This option was rejected, as it is not
clear that the assumptions of MRP hold across geographies and survey samples of African Americans in these areas are so small that they
cannot be seen as providing an accurate demographic depiction of the
African American population. The second option would be to use instead
the aforementioned probabilistic values of voter race/ethnicity, averaging
these probabilities to the relevant geography and then multiplying the
average by the total number of voters to derive turnout estimates. However, as many last names associated with non-Hispanic Whites are also
associated with African Americans, the averages produce estimates of the
voting population that do not fit with known geographic distributions of
race from the Census enumeration, producing estimates of African American turnout well above 100 percent of the adult population in Montana,
Wyoming, and districts with very small minority populations. Making
this tradeoff, the plurality race coding that I use *may* overestimate the
turnout gap in areas where there are very few minority voters, impacting
the precise measurement of the national turnout gap and a handful of
state and county totals depicted in Chapter 5 and the first part of Chapter 6. Future work should delve deeper into rates of minority turnout
in these areas, seeking to understand whether the theory of electoral
influence holds in places with exceptionally small minority populations.

A.4 Details of the District-level Regression Analysis

In Chapter 6, I model the relationship between each racial/ethnic group's share of the CVAP and the group's turnout or turnout gap. To do so, I use a generalized estimating equation (GEE) regression framework (Nedler and Wedderburn 1972; Liang and Zeger 1986; Zorn 2006; Fraga 2016a). GEEs are a type of generalized linear models that allow the researcher to account for correlation in error terms across observations, or *heteroskedasticity*. For the analyses conducted in Chapter 6, where the unit of observation is a group's rate of turnout or the turnout gap (Y_{it}) for a district (i) in an election (t), we have strong reason to suspect that observations for the same district are correlated across elections. As the dependent variable (the group's turnout rate or the turnout gap) is continuous, I estimate the GEE with the same link function used in an ordinary least squares (OLS) regression. Expressed formally, for each group:

$$Y_{it} \sim f(y_{it}|\mu_{it}, V_{it}), \text{ where } \mu_{it} = x_{it}\beta \text{ and } V_{it} = 1$$

Similar to justifications for clustered standard errors, not accounting for these correlations would overstate our confidence as to the effect of our variable of interest, the racial/ethnic group's share of the population. Turnout is likely correlated over time; however, the precise nature of that correlation is difficult to determine: perhaps turnout in non-presidential years is strongly correlated for the same district over time, but less strongly correlated with presidential turnout. Instead of assuming that correlations between all observations for a district (i) are *exchangeable*, or have the same correlation, I specify an unstructured correlation matrix at the start, observe the correlations across districts and elections, and then correct the variance–covariance matrix generated by the regression model (which is used to generate standard errors) to compensate for the average correlation structure across units. The result allows me to compensate for the observed heteroskedasticity in district-level turnout, without assuming that turnout across districts follows a particular parametric distribution (as under a district random effects model) and without estimating the effect of within-district change in group size across elections (as under a district fixed effects model). Note that none of the effects that I find are dependent on the use of a GEE estimation procedure versus a traditional OLS approach, with or without clustered standard errors.

For Figures 6.4 and 6.5, along with Table 6.4, I include additional variables beyond year fixed effects and the group's percent of the district CVAP. Information about each of these variables may be found below.

- **Candidate Race/Ethnicity:** The race/ethnicity of members of Congress is provided each year by the Congressional Research Service (e.g., Manning 2017), but data on *candidates* for Congress is more difficult to acquire. Names of candidates were drawn from records of the Federal Elections Commission (FEC), which were then filtered to Democratic and Republican Party candidates who appeared on the ballot in the November general election. Well over 1,000 unique individuals appeared on the November ballot from 2006 to 2016, though most candidates ran more than once. For each candidate, I coded the race/ethnicity as either non-Hispanic White, African American, Latino, Asian American, or Native American, using statements made by candidates, membership in ethnic caucuses or organizations, affiliation with ethnic advocacy organizations, media reports, and/or archived candidate websites. Race/ethnicity could not be ascertained for fewer than ten general election candidates, none of whom received more than 10 percent of the vote in their respective elections. More details about the candidate data used here may be found in Fraga (2014).

- **Competitiveness:** To measure electoral competition, I use general election results from the Congressional Quarterly Voting and Elections database. Margin of victory is calculated as the percent of the total votes cast that separated the first-place candidate from the second-place candidate. Uncontested elections are coded as uncompetitive elections. A majority of studies examining electoral competition use measures based on the actual election result, which we may term *ex post* competitiveness (Geys 2006). The advantage of such a measure is its precision in accounting for the actual competition observed on election day. However, such competition may be a function of voter turnout: perhaps elections were close due to particularly high turnout. *Ex ante* measures of competitiveness would address this concern, as they are based on the *predicted* level of competition based on polling or expert analysis (Hill and McKee 2005; Lipsitz 2011; Shaw 2006). In Fraga and Hersh (2011), the difference between these measures is addressed in depth, and Fraga (2016a) demonstrates that the group size effect is robust to use of an *ex ante* measure of competition. Thus, I rely on a binary indicator of competition for the analysis, with districts having an actual election margin of 10 percentage points or less taking a value of 1, and 0 if not.

- **Income:** District-level income is measured for each racial/ethnic group based on the 2006–2010 American Community Survey (ACS) five-year estimates for pre-redistricting elections (2006, 2008, and 2010 elections) and the 2011–2016 ACS five-year estimates for post-redistricting elections (2012, 2014, and 2016 elections). I derive the percent of each racial/ethnic group's population that has a household income under $20,000 and over $75,000, then incorporate these two percentages into the regression models used for Table 6.4.

- **Education:** District-level education is measured for each racial/ethnic group based on the 2006–2010 American Community Survey (ACS) five-year estimates for pre-redistricting elections (2006, 2008, and 2010 elections) and the 2011–2016 ACS five-year estimates for post-redistricting elections (2012, 2014, and 2016 elections). I derive the percent of each racial/ethnic group's population over 25 years of age that has no high school diploma and the percent college graduate, then incorporate these two percentages into the regression models used for Table 6.4.

- **Age:** District-level age is measured for each racial/ethnic group based on the 2006–2010 American Community Survey (ACS) five-year estimates for pre-redistricting elections (2006, 2008, and 2010 elections) and the 2011–2016 ACS five-year estimates for post-redistricting elections (2012, 2014, and 2016 elections). I derive the percent of each racial/ethnic group's population over 18 years of age that is 18–35 years old, and the percent that is 55 years old or more, then incorporate these two percentages into the regression models used for Table 6.4.

Raw regression results used to construct Figures 6.4–6.5 and Table 6.4 may be found in the Online Appendix to this book.

A.5 Details of the Redistricting Analysis

The second set of analyses in Chapter 6 leverage the redistricting process in order to estimate the causal impact of assignment to a majority-Black, majority-Latino, or majority-White district. As described therein, redistricting has features that *approximate* a natural experiment, and thus I use the potential outcomes framework of Rubin (2005) (see also Morgan and Winship 2007) to estimate the effect of redistricting. Using this framework, to estimate the impact of a binary treatment D on an individual (i) for outcome Y, we would want to observe a specific individual's outcome (Y_i) when $D_i = 1$ (that is, when the individual is *treated*) and compare to Y_i when $D_i = 0$ (that is, when the individual is *not treated*): the estimation of $Y_i^1 - Y_i^0$. As we do not observe both conditions for a single person at the same time (known as the *counterfactual* for an individual i), we *estimate* the effect of treatment by comparing values of Y for individuals who received treatment to those who did not, formally: $E[Y_i \mid D_i = 1] - E[Y_i \mid D_i = 0]$. Thus, in the study I seek to estimate the average treatment effect of D on the treated (ATT^D), where $ATT^D \equiv E[Y_i^1 - Y_i^0 \mid D_i = 1]$, estimated via comparison of $E[Y_i \mid D_i = 1]$ to $E[Y_i \mid D_i = 0]$.

ESTIMATING THE AVERAGE TREATMENT EFFECT ON THE TREATED

I hypothesize that individuals are more likely to turn out to vote when assigned to congressional districts where their racial/ethnic group is a majority of the voting age population, *ceteris paribus*. Formalized, for individual i, $D_i = 1$ if the individual is assigned to majority-[group] district, and $D_i = 0$ if they are assigned to a district where their group is not in the majority. Formalized in terms of ATT, which is the average treatment effect for individuals assigned to majority-[group] districts:

$$ATT = E[Y_i^1 - Y_i^0 \mid D_i = 1] = E[Y_i \mid D_i = 1] - E[Y_i \mid D_i = 0]$$

Given that we are interested in the effect of assignment, we must ensure that the individuals did not receive treatment prior to assignment. This necessitates a time component, t to ensure that comparisons are only made for those where $D_{it-1} = 0$ (and remains 0 for the control group). Continuing from above:

$$ATT = E[Y_{it} \mid D_{it} = 1, D_{it-1} = 0] - E[Y_{it} \mid D_{it} = 0, D_{it-1} = 0]$$

In order to ensure that the assignment to a majority-[group] district is a meaningful change for the individual, I further restrict comparisons to individuals where their racial/ethnic group was less than 30 percent of the pre-redistricting district's population. This restriction is continued for the control group post-redistricting: to qualify, the post-redistricting district for control individuals must also be less than 30 percent group voting-age population. As such, any districts with a group VAP $\geq 30\%$ and $< 50\%$ are not eligible for inclusion in the analysis of said group's turnout.

MATCHING

Under the assumptions of random assignment, on average there should be no observable *or unobservable* differences between populations based on treatment status, such that $(Y^1, Y^0) \perp D$. Analyses making use of the redistricting process see redistricting as *approximating* random assignment. As Sekhon and Titiunik (2013) outline, individuals who resided in the same district pre-redistricting $(t-1)$, but were assigned into different districts for the election of interest (t), allow a researcher to plausibly estimate the effect on Y of the difference in treatment conditions $(D \in \{0, 1\})$ between the two districts in election t. Furthermore, the non-random nature of redistricting may mean that there are observable characteristics X that are correlated with treatment status D.[1]

To account for non-random assignment, I exact match (Ho et al. 2007) treated and control individuals in the same yearly sample based on their pre-redistricting district, race, age, gender, and turnout pattern for the 2006, 2008, and 2010 elections. Exact balance is thus achieved on all

---

[1] See Henderson, Sekhon, and Titiunik (2016) and Fraga (2016b) for examples.

of these variables pre-treatment. Then, I estimate the difference in Y between the treatment and control groups using a linear model with fixed effects for the pre-redistricting district, effectively using the population-weighted average difference in means across pre-redistricting districts as my estimate of the treatment effect (ATT). The process is repeated for each racial/ethnic group, and for each majority-[group] assignment. Estimates of the ATT are made for the 2012, 2014, and 2016 elections independently, but only pre-redistricting turnout is held constant via the matching procedure to avoid post-treatment bias.

The Online Appendix to this book provides the following robustness checks for the redistricting analysis:

- Effects when modifying the cutoff points for determining non-minority and majority–minority districts.
- Effects when using citizen voting-age population instead of voting-age population.
- Effects when accounting for electoral competition.

References

Abrajano, Marisa A. 2010. *Campaigning to the New American Electorate: Advertising to Latino Voters*. Stanford, CA: Stanford University Press.

Abramson, Paul R. and William Claggett. 1984. "Race-Related Differences in Self-Reported and Validated Turnout." *Journal of Politics* 46(2):719–738.

Acharya, Avidit, Matthew Blackwell, and Maya Sen. 2018. *Deep Roots: The Political Legacy of Southern Slavery*. Princeton, NJ: Princeton University Press.

Aldrich, John H. 1993. "Rational Choice and Turnout." *American Journal of Political Science* 37(1):246–278.

  1995. *Why Parties? The Origin and Transformation of Political Parties in America*. Chicago: University of Chicago Press.

Allison, Aimee. 2017. "Democrats' new 'Better Deal' comes up short for people of color." *The Hill*. August 2, 2017.

Alt, James E. 1994. "The Impact of the Voting Rights Act on Black and White Voter Registration in the South." In *Quiet Revolution in the South: The Impact of the Voting Rights Act, 1965–1990*, ed. Chandler Davidson and Bernard Grofman. Princeton, NJ: Princeton University Press, pp. 351–373.

Alvarez, R. Michael, Delia Bailey, and Jonathan N. Katz. 2008. "The Effect of Voter Identification Laws on Turnout." California Institute of Technology Social Science Working Paper 1267R.

Alvarez, R. Michael, Ines Levin, and J. Andrew Sinclair. 2012. "Making Voting Easier: Convenience Voting in the 2008 Presidential Election." *Political Research Quarterly* 65(2):248–262.

Anders, Evan. 1982. *Boss Rule in South Texas: The Progressive Era*. Austin, TX: University of Texas Press.

Andrews, William G. 1966. "American Voting Participation." *Western Political Quarterly* 19(4):639–652.

Anoll, Allison. 2015. "Race and the Resource–Participation Relationship." Draft book chapter, last updated March 2015.

Ansolabehere, Stephen. 2009. "Effects of Identification Requirements on Voting: Evidence from the Experiences of Voters on Election Day." *PS: Political Science and Politics* 42(1):127–130.

2014. "Corrected Supplemental Report." *Marc Veasey et al. v. Rick Perry et al.*: United States District Court, Southern District of Texas, Corpus Christi Division: 2:13-cv-193. Document 600–1, September 16, 2014.

Ansolabehere, Stephen and Bernard L. Fraga. 2016. "Do Americans Prefer Coethnic Representation? The Impact of Race on House Incumbent Evaluations." *Stanford Law Review* 68(6):1553–1594.

Ansolabehere, Stephen, David Brady, and Morris Fiorina. 1992. "The Vanishing Marginals and Electoral Responsiveness." *British Journal of Political Science* 22(1):21–38.

Ansolabehere, Stephen and David M. Konisky. 2006. "The Introduction of Voter Registration and Its Effect on Turnout." *Political Analysis* 14(1):83–100.

Ansolabehere, Stephen and Eitan Hersh. 2012. "Validation: What Big Data Reveal About Survey Misreporting and the Real Electorate." *Political Analysis* 20(4):437–459.

2014. "Voter Registration: The Process and Quality of Lists". In *The Measure of American Elections*, ed. Barry C. Burden and Charles Stewart, III. Cambridge: Cambridge University Press.

Ansolabehere, Stephen and James M. Snyder. 2008. *The End of Inequality: One Person, One Vote and the Transformation of American Politics.* New York: W. W. Norton.

Ansolabehere, Stephen, James M. Snyder, and Charles Stewart, III. 2000. "Old Voters, New Voters, and the Personal Vote: Using Redistricting to Measure the Incumbency Advantage." *American Journal of Political Science* 44(1):17–34.

Ansolabehere, Stephen and Philip Edward Jones. 2010. "Constituents' Responses to Congressional Roll-Call Voting." *American Journal of Political Science* 54(3, July):583–597.

Aoki, Andrew L. and Don T. Nakanishi. 2001. "Asian Pacific Americans and the New Minority Politics." *PS: Political Science and Politics* 34(3):605–610.

Arnold, R. Douglas. 1992. *The Logic of Congressional Action.* New Haven, CT: Yale University Press.

Arvizu, John R. and F. Chris Garcia. 1996. "Latino Voting Participation: Explaining and Differentiating Latino Voting Turnout." *Hispanic Journal of Behavioral Sciences* 18(2):104–128.

Athey, Susan and Guido W. Imbens. 2006. "Identification and Inference in Nonlinear Difference-in-Difference Models." *Econometrica* 74(2):431–497.

Atkeson, Lonna Rae, Lisa A. Bryant, Thad E. Hall, Kyle L. Saunders, and R. Michael Alvarez. 2010. "A New Barrier to Participation: Heterogeneous Application of Voter Identification Policies." *Electoral Studies* 29(1):66–73.

Atkeson, Lonna Rae, Yann P. Kerevel, R. Michael Alvarez, and Thad E. Hall. 2014. "Who Asks for Voter Identification? Explaining Poll Worker Discretion." *Journal of Politics* 76(4):944–957.

Banks, Jeffrey S. and D. Roderick Kiewiet. 1989. "Explaining Patterns of Candidate Competition in Congressional Elections." *American Journal of Political Science* 33(4):997–1015.

Barreto, Matt A. 2007. "¡Sí Se Puede! Latino Candidates and the Mobilization of Latino Voters." *American Political Science Review* 101(3):425–441.

2010. *Ethnic Cues: The Role of Shared Ethnicity in Latino Political Participation*. Ann Arbor, MI: University of Michigan Press.

Barreto, Matt A., Gary M. Segura, and Nathan D. Woods. 2004. "The Mobilizing Effect of Majority–Minority Districts on Latino Turnout." *American Political Science Review* 98(1):65–75.

Barreto, Matt A., Loren Collingwood, and Sylvia Manzano. 2010. "A New Measure of Group Influence in Presidential Elections: Assessing Latino Influence in 2008." *Political Research Quarterly* 20(10):1–14.

Barreto, Matt A., Stephen A. Nuño, and Gabriel R. Sanchez. 2009. "The Disproportionate Impact of Voter-ID Requirements on the Electorate – New Evidence from Indiana." *PS: Political Science and Politics* 42(1):111–116.

Barreto, Matt and Gary Segura. 2017. "Understanding Latino Voting Strength in 2016 and Beyond: Why Culturally Competent Research Matters." *Journal of Cultural Marketing Strategy* 2(2):190–201.

Barreto, Matt, Tyler Reny, and Bryan Wilcox-Archuleta. 2017. "A Debate about Survey Research Methodology and the Latina/o Vote: Why a Bilingual, Bicultural, Latino-centered Approach Matters to Accurate Data." *Aztlán: A Journal of Chicano Studies* 42(2).

Bartels, Larry M. 1998. "Where the Ducks Are: Voting Power in a Party System". In *Politicians and Party Politics*, ed. John Geer. Baltimore, MD: Johns Hopkins University Press, pp. 43–79.

Becker, David J. 2007. "Saving Section 5: Reflections on *Georgia v. Ashcroft* and Its Impact on the Reauthorization of the Voting Rights Act". In *Voting Rights Act Reauthorization of 2006: Perspectives on Democracy, Participation, and Power*, ed. Ana Henderson. Berkeley, CA: Institute for Governmental Studies Public Policy Press, pp. 223–256.

Belli, Robert F., Michael W. Traugott, and Matthew N. Beckmann. 2001. "What Leads to Voting Overreports? Contrasts of Overreporters to Validated Voters and Admitted Nonvoters in the American National Elections Studies." *Journal of Official Statistics* 17(4):479–498.

Bentele, Keith G. and Erin E. O'Brien. 2013. "Jim Crow 2.0? Why States Consider and Adopt Restrictive Voter Access Policies." *Perspectives on Politics* 11(4):1088–1116.

Berelson, Bernard, Paul Lazarsfeld, and William N. McPhee. 1954. *Voting*. Chicago: University of Chicago Press.

Berinsky, Adam. 2005. "The Perverse Consequences of Electoral Reform in the United States." *American Politics Research* 33(4):471–491.

Berman, Ari. 2015a. *Give Us The Ballot: The Modern Struggle for Voting Rights in America*. New York: Farrar, Straus, and Giroux.

2015b. "The Lost Promise of the Voting Rights Act." *The Atlantic*. August 5.

Bernstein, Robert, Anita Chadha, and Robert Montjoy. 2001. "Overreporting Voting: Why It Happens and Why It Matters." *Public Opinion Quarterly* 65(1):22–44.

Bertocchi, Graziella and Arcangelo Dimico. 2017. "De jure and de facto determinants of power: evidence from Mississippi." *Constitutional Political Economy* 28(4):321–345.

Biggers, Daniel R. and Michael J. Hanmer. 2017. "Understanding the Adoption of Voter Identification Laws in the American States." *American Politics Research* 45(4):560–588.

Bobo, Lawrence and Frank D. Gilliam. 1990. "Race, Sociopolitical Participation, and Black Empowerment." *American Political Science Review* 84(2): 377–393.

Bobo, Lawrence and Vincent L. Hutchings. 1996. "Perceptions of Racial Group Competition: Extending Blumer's Theory of Group Position to a Multiracial Social Context." *American Sociological Review* 61(6):951–972.

Bond, Jon R., Cary Covington, and Richard Fleisher. 1985. "Explaining Challenger Quality in Congressional Elections." *Journal of Politics* 47(2): 510–529.

Bond, Robert M., Christopher J. Fariss, Jason J. Jones, Adam D. I. Kramer, Cameron Marlow, Jaime E. Settle, and James H. Fowler. 2012. "A 61-Million-Person Experiment in Social Influence and Political Mobilization." *Nature* 489(7415):295–298.

Bositis, David A. 2006. "Impact of the 'Core' Voting Rights Act on Voting and Officeholding." In *The Voting Rights Act: Securing the Ballot*, ed. Richard M. Valelly. Washington, DC: CQ Press.

Boustan, Leah Platt. 2011. "Racial Residential Segregation in American Cities." In *Oxford Handbook of Urban Economics and Planning*, ed. Nancy Brooks, Kieran Donaghy, and Gerrit Knaap. New York: Oxford University Press.

Bowler, Shaun and Gary M. Segura. 2012. *The Future Is Ours: Minority Politics, Political Behavior, and the Multiracial Era of American Politics*. Washington, DC: CQ Press.

Bowler, Shaun, Stephen P. Nicholson, and Gary M. Segura. 2006. "Earthquakes and Aftershocks: Race, Direct Democracy, and Partisan Change." *American Journal of Political Science* 50(1):146–159.

Brace, Kimball, Lisa Handley, Richard G. Niemi, and Harold W. Stanley. 1995. "Minority Turnout and the Creation of Majority–Minority Districts." *American Politics Research* 23(2):190–203.

Branton, Regina P. 2009. "The Importance of Race and Ethnicity in Congressional Primary Elections." *Political Research Quarterly* 62(3, September):459–473.

Branton, Regina P., Erin C. Cassese, and Bradford S. Jones. 2012. "Race, Ethnicity, and U.S. House Incumbent Evaluations." *Legislative Studies Quarterly* 37(4):465–489.

Brennan Center for Justice. 2017. "New Voting Restrictions in America." Brennan Center for Justice at New York University School of Law. Version as of May 17, 2017. www.brennancenter.org/new-voting-restrictions-america

Brians, Craig Leonard and Bernard Grofman. 1999. "When Registration Barriers Fall, Who Votes? An Empirical Test of a Rational Choice Model." *Public Choice* 99:161–176.

Brians, Craig Leonard and Bernard Grofman. 2001. "Election Day Registration's Effect on U.S. Voter Turnout." *Social Science Quarterly* 82(1):170–183.

Brischetto, Robert, David R. Richards, Chandler Davidson, and Bernard Grofman. 1994. "Texas". In *Quiet Revolution in the South: The Impact of the Voting Rights Act, 1965–1990*, ed. Chandler Davidson and Bernard Grofman. Princeton, NJ: Princeton University Press, pp. 233–270.

Broockman, David E. and Christopher Skovron. 2017. "Conservative Bias in Perceptions of Public Opinion among American Political Elites." Working Paper, available at https://ssrn.com/abstract=2930362

Brown, Robert D. and Justin Wedeking. 2006. "People Who Have Their Tickets But Do Not Use Them: 'Motor Voter,' Registration, and Turnout Revisited." *American Politics Research* 34(4):479–504.

Browning, Rufus P., Dale Rogers Marshall, and David H. Tabb. 1984. *Protest Is Not Enough: The Struggle of Blacks and Hispanics for Equity in Urban Politics*. Berkeley, CA: University of California Press.

Browning, Rufus P., Dale Rogers Marshall, and David H. Tabb. 1986. "Protest Is Not Enough: A Theory of Political Incorporation." *PS* 19(3, summer): 576–581.

Bullock, Charles S. and Ronald K. Gaddie. 2009. *The Triumph of Voting Rights in the South*. Norman, OK: University of Oklahoma Press.

Burch, Traci. 2012. "Did Disfranchisement Laws Help Elect President Bush? New Evidence on the Turnout Rates and Candidate Preferences of Florida's Ex-Felons." *Political Behavior* 34(1):1–26.

2013. *Trading Democracy for Justice: Criminal Convictions and the Decline of Neighborhood Political Participation*. Chicago: University of Chicago Press.

Burden, Barry C., David T. Canon, Kenneth R. Mayer, and Donald P. Moynihan. 2014. "Election Laws, Mobilization, and Turnout: The Unanticipated Consequences of Election Reform." *American Journal of Political Science* 58(1):95–109.

Burden, Barry C., David T. Canon, Kenneth R. Mayer and Donald P. Moynihan. 2017. "The Complicated Partisan Effects of State Election Laws." *Political Research Quarterly* 70(3):564–576.

Burnham, Walter Dean. 1965. "The Changing Shape of the American Political Universe." *American Political Science Review* 59(2):7–28.

Burns, Nancy. 1994. *The Formation of American Local Governments: Private Values in Public Institutions*. New York: Oxford University Press.

Caldeira, Gregory A., Aage R. Clausen, and Samuel C. Patterson. 1990. "Partisan Mobilization and Electoral Participation." *Electoral Studies* 9(3):191–204.

Cameron, Charles, David Epstein, and Sharyn O'Halloran. 1996. "Do Majority–Minority Districts Maximize Substantive Black Representation in Congress?" *American Political Science Review* 90(4):794–812.

Campbell, Angus, Philip E. Converse, Warren E. Miller, and Donald E. Stokes. 1960. *The American Voter*. New York: Wiley.

Canon, David. 1999. *Race, Redistricting, and Representation: The Unintended Consequences of Black Majority Districts*. Chicago: University of Chicago Press.

Canon, David, Matthew M. Schousen, and Patrick J. Sellers. 1996. "The Supply Side of Congressional Redistricting: Race and Strategic Politicians, 1972–1992." *Journal of Politics* 58(3):846–862.

Cassel, Carol A. 2002. "Hispanic Turnout: Estimates from Validated Voting Data." *Political Research Quarterly* 55(2):391–408.
2004. "Voting Records and Validated Voting Studies." *Public Opinion Quarterly* 68:102–108.
Cho, Wendy K. Tam. 1999. "Naturalization, Socialization, Participation: Immigrants and (Non-) Voting." *Journal of Politics* 61(4):1140–1155.
Cillizza, Chris and Jon Cohen. 2012. "President Obama and the White Vote? No Problem." *Washington Post 'The Fix'* (blog). November 8, 2012, available at www.washingtonpost.com/news/the-fix/wp/2012/11/08/president-obama-and-the-white-vote-no-problem
Citrin, Jack, Eric Schickler, and John Sides. 2003. "What If Everyone Voted? Simulating the Impact of Increased Turnout in Senate Elections." *American Journal of Political Science* 47(1):75–90.
Clausen, Aage R. 1968–1969. "Response Validity: Vote Report." *Public Opinion Quarterly* 32(4):588–606.
Clifford, Scott. 2012. "Reassessing the Unequal Representation of Latinos and African Americans." *Journal of Politics* 74(3):903–916.
Clinton, Hillary Rodham. 2017. *What Happened*. New York: Simon & Schuster.
Cohn, Nate. 2016. "There Are More White Voters Than People Think. That's Good News for Trump." *New York Times 'The Upshot'* (blog). June 9, 2016, available at www.nytimes.com/2016/06/10/upshot/there-are-more-white-voters-than-people-think-thats-good-news-for-trump.html
Connelly, Gordon M. and Harry H. Field. 1944. "The Non-Voter – Who He Is, What He Thinks." *Public Opinion Quarterly* 8(2):175–187.
Conover, Pamela J. 1984. "The Influence of Group Identification on Political Participation and Evaluation." *Journal of Politics* 46:760–785.
Cox, Gary W. and Jonathan N. Katz. 2002. *Elbridge Gerry's Salamander: The Electoral Consequences of the Reapportionment Revolution*. New York: Cambridge University Press.
Cox, Gary W. and Michael C. Munger. 1989. "Closeness, Expenditures, and Turnout in the 1982 U.S. House Elections." *American Political Science Review* 83(1):217–231.
Davenport, Lauren D. 2018. *Politics Beyond Black and White: Biracial Identity and Attitudes in America*. New York: Cambridge University Press.
Davidson, Chandler. 1992. "The Voting Rights Act: A Brief History". In *Controversies in Minority Voting*, ed. Bernard Grofman and Chandler Davidson. Washington, DC: Brookings Institution, pp. 7–51.
Davidson, Chandler and Bernard Grofman. 1994. "The Voting Rights Act and the Second Reconstruction." In *Quiet Revolution in the South: The Impact of the Voting Rights Act, 1965–1990*, ed. Chandler Davidson and Bernard Grofman. Princeton, NJ: Princeton University Press, pp. 378–387.
Dawson, Michael C., Ronald E. Brown, and Richard L. Allen. 1990. "Racial Belief Systems, Religious Guidance, and African-American Political Participation." *National Political Science Review* 2(1):22–44.
de la Garza, Rodolfo O. and Louis DeSipio. 1993. "Save the Baby, Change the Bathwater, and Scrub the Tub: Latino Electoral Participation After Seventeen Years of Voting Rights Act Coverage." *Texas Law Review* 71(7):1479–1540.

de la Garza, Rodolfo O. and Louis DeSipio. 1997. "Save the Baby, Change the Bathwater, and Scrub the Tub: Latino Electoral Participation after Twenty Years of Voting Rights Act Coverage". In *Pursuing Power: Latinos and the Political System*, ed. F. Chris Garcia. Notre Dame, IN: University of Notre Dame Press, pp. 72–126.

De León, Arnoldo. 1979. *In Re Ricardo Rodriguez: An Attempt at Chicano Disenfranchisement in San Antonio: 1896–1897*. San Antonio, TX: Caravel Press.

Demeo, Marisa J. and Steven A. Ochoa. 2003. "Diminished Voting Power in the Latino Community: The Impact of Felony Disenfranchisement Laws in Ten Targeted States." MALDEF Report, Los Angeles, CA.

DeNardo, James. 1980. "Turnout and the Vote: The Joke's on the Democrats." *American Political Science Review* 74(2):406–420.

Denton, Nancy A. 1997. "Racial Identity and Census Categories: Can Incorrect Categories Yield Correct Information?" *Law & Inequality* 15:83–97.

Deufel, Benjamin J. and Orit Kedar. 2010. "Race and Turnout in U.S. Elections: Exposing Hidden Effects." *Public Opinion Quarterly* 74(2):286–318.

DOJ, United States Department of Justice. Officer of Justice Programs. Bureau of Justice Statistics. 2017. "National Prisoner Statistics, 1978–2015." Version 1. https://doi.org/10.3886/ICPSR36657.v1. Ann Arbor, MI: Inter-university Consortium for Political and Social Research [distributor].

Downs, Anthony. 1957. *An Economic Theory of Democracy*. New York: Harper.

Dropp, Kyle A. 2013. "Voter ID Laws and Voter Turnout." Working paper, draft as of September 21.

Du Bois, W. E. B. 1971 [1935]. *Black Reconstruction in America: An Essay Toward a History of the Part Which Black Folk Played in the Attempt to Reconstruct Democracy in America, 1860–1880*. New York: Atheneum [originally published by Harcourt Brace].

Dunning, Thad. 2012. *Natural Experiments in the Social Sciences: A Design-Based Approach*. Cambridge: Cambridge University Press.

Eisler, Peter. 2016. "Trump won with lowest minority vote in decades, fueling divisions." *Reuters*. November 23.

Eligon, John. 2017. "Win in Alabama Shows Muscle of Minority Voters." *New York Times*. December 14.

Elliott, Marc N., Allen Fremont, Peter A. Morrison, Philip Pantoja, and Nicole Lurie. 2008. "A New Method for Estimating Race/Ethnicity and Associated Disparities Where Administrative Records Lack Self-Reported Race/Ethnicity." *Health Services Research* 43(5):1722–1736.

Engstrom, Richard L. 2011. "Influence Districts – A Note of Caution and a Better Measure." Research Brief: Warren Institute on Law and Social Policy, University of California, Berkeley.

Enos, Ryan D. 2016. "What the Demolition of Public Housing Teaches Us about the Impact of Racial Threat on Political Behavior." *American Journal of Political Science* 60(1):123–142.

2017. *The Space Between Us: Social Geography and Politics*. New York: Cambridge University Press.

Enos, Ryan D. and Anthony Fowler. 2014. "Pivotality and Turnout: Evidence from a Field Experiment in the Aftermath of a Tied Election." *Political Science Research and Methods* 2(2):309–319.

2017. "Aggregate Effects of Large-Scale Campaigns on Voter Turnout." *Political Science Research and Methods* Forthcoming.

Enos, Ryan D., Anthony Fowler, and Lynn Vavreck. 2014. "Increasing Inequality: The Effect of GOTV Mobilization on the Composition of the Electorate." *Journal of Politics* 76(1):273–288.

Epstein, David and Sharyn O'Halloran. 1999. "Measuring the Electoral Impact of Majority–Minority Voting Districts." *American Journal of Political Science* 43(2):367–395.

Erikson, Robert S. 1981. "Why Do People Vote? Because They Are Registered." *American Politics Research* 9(3):259–276.

Erikson, Robert S. and Lorraine C. Minnite. 2009. "Modeling Problems in the Voter Identification – Voter Turnout Debate." *Election Law Journal* 8(2): 85–101.

Farris, Emily M. and Mirya R. Holman. 2017. "All Politics Is Local? County Sheriffs and Localized Policies of Immigration Enforcement." *Political Research Quarterly* 70(1):142–154.

Fenno, Richard F. Jr. 1978. *Home Style: House Members in their Districts*. New York: Little, Brown and Company.

File, Thom. 2013. "The Diversifying Electorate – Voting Rates by Race and Hispanic Origin in 2012 (and Other Recent Elections)." Current Population Survey Reports, P20-569. U.S. Census Bureau, Washington, DC.

2015. "Who Votes? Congressional Elections and the American Electorate: 1978–2014." Current Population Survey Reports, P20-577. U.S. Census Bureau, Washington, DC.

Fiorina, Morris P. 1976. "The Voting Decision: Instrumental and Expressive Aspects." *Journal of Politics* 38(2):390–413.

Foner, Eric. 1988. *Reconstruction: America's Unfinished Revolution, 1863–1877*. New York: Harper & Row.

Foner, Philip S. and Daniel Rosenberg, eds. 1993. *Racism, Dissent, and Asian Americans from 1850 to the Present: A Documentary History*. Westport, CT: Greenwood Press.

Fowler, Anthony and Andrew B. Hall. 2017. "Long-Term Consequences of Election Results." *British Journal of Political Science* 47(2):351–372.

Fraga, Bernard L. 2014. "Race, Party, and Candidate Prospects across the Multiple Stages of Congressional Elections." Working paper, draft as of March 12.

2016a. "Candidates or Districts? Reevaluating the Role of Race in Voter Turnout." *American Journal of Political Science* 60(1, January):97–122.

2016b. "Redistricting and the Causal Impact of Race on Voter Turnout." *Journal of Politics* 78(1, January):19–34.

Fraga, Bernard and Eitan Hersh. 2011. "Voting Costs and Voter Turnout in Competitive Elections." *Quarterly Journal of Political Science* 5(4): 339–356.

Fraga, Bernard L. and Julie Lee Merseth. 2016. "Examining the Causal Impact of the Voting Rights Act Language Minority Provisions." *Journal of Race, Ethnicity, and Politics* 1(1):31–59.

Fraga, Luis R., John A. Garcia, Rodney E. Hero, Michael Jones-Correa, Valerie Martinez-Ebers, and Gary M. Segura. 2012. *Latinos in the New Millennium: An Almanac of Opinion, Behavior, and Policy Preferences.* New York: Cambridge University Press.

Fraga, Luis R. and David L. Leal. 2004. "Playing the 'Latino Card': Race, Ethnicity, and National Party Politics." *Du Bois Review* 1(2):297–317.

Fraga, Luis R. and Ricardo Ramírez. 2003. "Latino Political Incorporation in California, 1990–2000". In *Latinos and Public Policy in California: An Agenda for Opportunity*, ed. David Lopez and Andres Jimenez. Berkeley, CA: Institute for Governmental Studies, University of California at Berkeley, pp. 301–335.

2004. "Demography and Political Influence: Disentangling the Latino Vote." *Harvard Journal of Hispanic Policy* 16(1):69–96.

Franklin, Daniel P. and Eric E. Grier. 1997. "Effects of Motor Voter Legislation: Voter Turnout, Registration, and Partisan Advantage in the 1992 Presidential Election." *American Politics Quarterly* 25(1):104–117.

Franklin, Mark N. 2004. *Voter Turnout and the Dynamics of Electoral Competition in Established Democracies since 1945.* Cambridge: Cambridge University Press.

Fresh, Adriane. 2018. "The Effect of the Voting Rights Act on Enfranchisement: A Natural Experiment in North Carolina." *Journal of Politics.* Forthcoming.

Frey, William H. 2015. *Diversity Explosion: How New Racial Demographics are Remaking America.* Washington, DC: Brookings Institution Press.

Frey, William H., Ruy Teixeira and Robert Griffin. 2015. "States of Change: The Demographic Evolution of the American Electorate, 1974–2060." Washington, DC: Center for American Progress, American Enterprise Institute, and the Brookings Institution.

2016. "America's Electoral Future: How Changing Demographics Could Impact Presidential Elections from 2016 to 2032." Washington, DC: Center for American Progress, American Enterprise Institute, and the Brookings Institution.

Friedman, John H. and Richard T. Holden. 2008. "Optimal Gerrymandering: Sometimes Pack, But Never Crack." *American Economic Review* 98(1): 113–144.

Frymer, Paul. 1999. *Uneasy Alliances: Race and Party Competition in America.* Princeton, NJ: Princeton University Press.

Fullerton, Andrew S., Jeffrey C. Dixon, and Casey Borch. 2007. "Bringing Registration into Models of Vote Overreporting." *Public Opinion Quarterly* 71(4):649–660.

Fullmer, Elliot B. 2015a. "Early Voting: Do More Sites Lead to Higher Turnout?" *Election Law Journal* 14(2):81–96.

2015b. "The Site Gap: Racial Inequalities in Early Voting Access." *American Politics Research* 43(2):283–303.

GAO, U.S. Government Accountability Office. 1986. "Bilingual Voting Assistance: Costs of and Use During the November 1984 General Election." September 15. Publication No. GGD-86-143BR.

1997. "Bilingual Voting Assistance: Assistance Provided and Costs." May 9. Publication No. GGD-97-81.

2008. "Bilingual Voting Assistance: Selected Jurisdictions' Strategies for Identifying Needs and Providing Assistance." January 18. Publication No. GAO-08-182.

2014. "Elections: Issues Related to State Voter Identification Laws." September, Publication No. GAO-14-634.

2016. "Elections: Issues Related to Registering Voters and Administering Elections." June, Publication No. GAO-16-630.

Gaouette, Nicole. 2006. "House GOP Group Targets Bilingual Ballots." *Los Angeles Times*. May 6.

García Bedolla, Lisa and Melissa R. Michelson. 2012. *Mobilizing Inclusion: Transforming the Electorate through Get-Out-the-Vote Campaigns*. New Haven, CT: Yale University Press.

Garcia-Rios, Sergio I. and Matt A. Barreto. 2016. "Politicized Immigrant Identity, Spanish-Language Media, and Political Mobilization in 2012." *RSF: Russell Sage Foundation Journal of the Social Sciences* 2(3):78–96.

Gardiner, Joseph C., Zhehui Luo and Lee Ann Roman. 2009. "Fixed Effects, Random Effects and GEE: What Are the Differences?" *Statistics In Medicine* 28(2):221–239.

Gay, Claudine. 2001. "The Effect of Black Congressional Representation on Political Participation." *American Political Science Review* 95(3):589–602.

Gelman, Andrew and Gary King. 1994. "A Unified Method of Evaluating Electoral Systems and Redistricting Plans." *American Journal of Political Science* 38(2):514–554.

Gerber, Alan, Donald P. Green and Christopher Larimer. 2008. "Social Pressure and Voter Turnout: Evidence from a Large-Scale Field Experiment." *American Political Science Review* 102(1):33–48.

Gerber, Alan S., Gregory A. Huber, Marc Meredith, Daniel R. Biggers, and David J. Hendry. 2017. "Does Incarceration Reduce Voting? Evidence about the Political Consequences of Spending Time in Prison." *Journal of Politics* 79(4):1130–1146.

Gerken, Heather K. 2001. "Understanding the Right to an Undiluted Vote." *Harvard Law Review* 114(6):1663–1743.

Geys, Benny. 2006. "Explaining Voter Turnout: A Review of Aggregate-Level Research." *Electoral Studies* 25(4):637–663.

Ghitza, Yair and Andrew Gelman. 2013. "Deep Interactions with MRP: Election Turnout and Voting Patterns Among Small Electoral Subgroups." *American Journal of Political Science* 57(3):762–776.

Gibson, Campbell and Kay Jung. 2006. "Historical Census Statistics on the Foreign-Born Population of the United States: 1850–2000." Population Division, Working Paper 81. U.S. Census Bureau, Washington, DC.

Gilens, Martin. 2014. *Affluence and Influence: Economic Inequality and Political Power in America*. Princeton, NJ: Princeton University Press.

Gimpel, James G., Joshua J. Dyck, and Daron R. Shaw. 2004. "Registrants, Voters, and Turnout Variability across Neighborhoods." *Political Behavior* 26(4):343–375.

Glaser, James M. 1996. *Race, Campaign Politics, and the Realignment in the South*. New Haven, CT: Yale University Press.

Goldman, Robert M. 2001. *Reconstruction and Black Suffrage: Losing the Vote in Reese and Cruikshank*. Lawrence, KS: University of Kansas Press.

Gonzales, Nathan L. 2013. "Analysis: Hispanics Fail to Win Hispanic Congressional Districts." *NBCLatino*. February 13.

Gosnell, Harold F. 1948. "Mobilizing the Electorate." *Annals of the American Academy of Political and Social Science* 259:98–103.

Green, Donald P. and Alan S. Gerber. 2008. *Get Out the Vote: How to Increase Voter Turnout*. 2nd edn. Washington, DC: Brookings Institution Press.

　　2010. "Introduction to Social Pressure and Voting: New Experimental Evidence." *Political Behavior* 32(3): 331–336.

Green, Donald P., Mary C. McGrath, and Peter M. Aronow. 2013. "Field Experiments and the Study of Voter Turnout." *Journal of Elections, Public Opinion, and Parties* 23(1):27–48.

Gregory, James N. 2009. "The Second Great Migration: A Historical Overview". In *African American Urban History Since World War II*, ed. Kenneth L. Kusmer and Joe W. Trotter. Chicago: University of Chicago Press.

Griffin, John D. and Brian Newman. 2005. "Are Voters Better Represented?" *Journal of Politics* 67(4):1206–1227.

　　2008. *Minority Report: Evaluating Political Equality in America*. Chicago: University of Chicago Press.

Griffin, John D. and Michael Keane. 2006. "Descriptive Representation and the Composition of African-American Turnout." *American Journal of Political Science* 50(4):998–1012.

Grimmer, Justin, Eitan Hersh, Marc Meredith, Jonathan Mummolo, and Clayton Nall. 2018. "Obstacles to Estimating Voter ID Laws' Effect on Turnout." *Journal of Politics*.

Griswold del Castillo, Richard. 1990. *The Treaty of Guadalupe Hidalgo: A Legacy of Conflict*. Norman, OK: University of Oklahoma Press.

Grofman, Bernard, Lisa Handley, and David Lublin. 2001. "Drawing Effective Minority Districts: A Conceptual Framework and Some Evidence." *North Carolina Law Review* 79:1383–1430.

Grofman, Bernard, Lisa Handley, and Richard G. Niemi. 1992. *Minority Representation and the Quest for Voting Equality*. Cambridge: Cambridge University Press.

Grose, Christian R. 2007. "Black-Majority Districts or Black Influence Districts? Evaluating the Representation of African Americans in the Wake of Georgia v. Ashcroft". In *Voting Rights Act Reauthorization of 2006: Perspectives on Democracy, Participation, and Power*, ed. Ana Henderson. Berkeley, CA: Institute for Governmental Studies Public Policy Press, pp. 3–25.

　　2011. *Congress in Black and White: Race and Representation in Washington and at Home*. Cambridge: Cambridge University Press.

Guinier, Lani. 1993. *The Tyranny of the Majority: Fundamental Fairness in Representative Democracy*. New York: Free Press.

Gutiérrez, José Angel. 1999. *The Making of a Chicano Militant: Lessons from Cristal*. Madison, WI: University of Wisconsin Press.

Gyory, Andrew. 1998. *Closing the Gate: Race, Politics, and the Chinese Exclusion Act*. Chapel Hill, NC: University of North Carolina Press.

Hajnal, Zoltan L. 2010. *America's Uneven Democracy: Race, Turnout, and Representation in City Politics*. New York: Cambridge University Press.

Hajnal, Zoltan L. and Marisa Abrajano. 2017. *White Backlash: Immigration, Race, and American Politics*. Princeton, NJ: Princeton University Press.

Hajnal, Zoltan, Nazita Lajevardi, and Lindsay Nielson. 2017. "Voter Identification Laws and the Suppression of Minority Votes." *Journal of Politics*.

Hajnal, Zoltan L. and Taeku Lee. 2011. *Why Americans Don't Join the Party: Race, Immigration, and the Failure (of Political Parties) to Engage the Electorate*. Princeton, NJ: Princeton University Press.

Hajnal, Zoltan and Jessica Trounstine. 2005. "Where Turnout Matters: The Consequences of Uneven Turnout in City Politics." *Journal of Politics* 67(2):515–535.

Haney López, Ian. 2006. *White By Law: The Legal Construction of Race*. 10th anniv. ed. New York: New York University Press.

Harris, Frederick. 1999. *Something Within: Religion in African-American Political Activism*. New York: Oxford University Press.

Harris, Joseph P. 1929. *Registration of Voters in the United States*. Washington, DC: Brookings Institution Press.

Harvey, Anna L. 1996. "The Political Consequences of Suffrage Exclusion: Organizations, Institutions, and the Electoral Mobilization of Women." *Social Science History* 20(1):97–132.

Hasen, Richard L. 2012. *The Voting Wars: From Florida 2000 to the Next Election Meltdown*. New Haven, CT: Yale University Press.

  2014. "Essay: Race or Party?: How Courts Should Think about Republican Efforts to Make It Harder to Vote in North Carolina and Elsewhere." *Harvard Law Review* 127(1):58–75.

  2015. "Essay: Racial Gerrymandering's Questionable Revival." *Alabama Law Review* 67(2):365–385.

  2016. "The Hard Power of 'Soft' Voter-ID Laws." *The Atlantic*. March 14.

Hayduk, Ron. 2006. *Democracy for All: Restoring Immigrant Voting Rights in the United States*. New York: Routledge.

Heinicke, Craig. 1994. "African-American Migration and Urban Labor Skills: 1950 and 1960." *Agricultural History* 68(2):185–198.

Henderson, John A., Jasjeet S. Sekhon, and Rocío Titiunik. 2016. "Cause or Effect? Turnout in Hispanic Majority-Minority Districts." *Political Analysis* 24(3):404–412.

Hero, Rodney E. and Robert R. Preuhs. 2013. *Black-Latino Relations in U.S. National Politics: Beyond Conflict or Cooperation*. New York: Cambridge University Press.

Herron, Michael C. and Daniel A. Smith. 2012. "Souls to the Polls: Early Voting in Florida in the Shadow of House Bill 1355." *Election Law Journal* 11(3):331–347.

Hersh, Eitan. 2015. *Hacking the Electorate: How Campaigns Perceive Voters.* Cambridge: Cambridge University Press, Ch. 6.

Hershey, Marjorie Randon. 2009. "What We Know about Voter-ID Laws, Registration, and Turnout." *PS: Political Science and Politics* 42(1):87–91.

Hicks, William D., Seth C. McKee, Patrick J. Sellers, and Daniel A. Smith. 2015. "A Principle or a Strategy? Voter Identification Laws and Partisan Competition in the American States." *Political Research Quarterly* 68(1):18–33.

Higgins, Matthew. 2015. "Language Accommodations and Section 203 of the Voting Rights Act: Reporting Requirements as a Potential Solution to the Compliance Gap." *Stanford Law Review* 67(4):917–960.

Highton, Benjamin. 2004. "White Voters and African American Candidates for Congress." *Political Behavior* 26(1):1–25.

2005. "Self-Reported versus Proxy-Reported voter Turnout in the Current Population Survey." *Public Opinion Quarterly* 69(1): 113–123.

2017. "Voter Identification Laws and Turnout in the United States." *Annual Review of Political Science* 20(1):149–167.

Highton, Benjamin and Raymond E. Wolfinger. 1998. "Estimating the Effects of the National Voter Registration Act of 1993." *Political Behavior* 20(2): 79–104.

2001. "The Political Implications of Higher Turnout." *British Journal of Political Science* 31:179–223.

Hill, David and Seth C. McKee. 2005. "The Electoral College, Mobilization, and Turnout in the 2000 Presidential Election." *American Politics Research* 33(5, September):700–725.

Hill, Kevin. 1995. "Does the Creation of Majority Black Districts Aid Republicans?" *Journal of Politics* 57(2):384–401.

Hill, Kim Quaile, Jan E. Leighley and Angela Hinton-Andersson. 1995. "Lower-Class Mobilization and Policy Linkage in the U.S. States." *American Journal of Political Science* 39(1):75–86.

Hill, Kim Quaile and Patricia A. Hurley. 1984. "Nonvoters in Voters' Clothing: The Impact of Voting Behavior Misreporting on Voting Behavior Research." *Social Science Quarterly* 65(1):199–206.

Hill, Seth J. 2017. "Changing Votes or Changing Voters? How Candidates and Election Context Swing Voters and Mobilize the Base." *Electoral Studies* 48:131–148.

Ho, Daniel, Kosuke Imai, Gary King, and Elizabeth Stuart. 2007. "Matching as Nonparametric Preprocessing for Reducing Model Dependence in Parametric Causal Inference." *Political Analysis* 15:199–236.

Hochschild, Jennifer L. and Brenna Marea Powell. 2008. "Racial Reorganization and the United States Census 1850–1930: Mulattoes, Half-Breeds, Mixed Parentage, Hindoos, and the Mexican Race." *Studies in American Political Development* 22(1):59–96.

Holbrook, Thomas and Brianne Heidbreder. 2010. "Does Measurement Matter? The Case of VAP and VEP in Models of Voter Turnout in the United States." *State Politics and Policy Quarterly* 10(2):157–179.

Hollinger, David A. 1995. *Postethnic America: Beyond Multiculturalism*. New York: Basic Books.

2003. "Amalgamation and Hypodescent: The Question of Ethnoracial Mixture in the History of the United States." *American Historical Review* 108(5):1363–1390.

Holtby, David V. 2012. *Forty-Seventh Star: New Mexico's Struggle for Statehood*. Norman, OK: University of Oklahoma Press.

Honda, Harry K. (ed). 1975. "Congress Passes 7-Yr. Extension of Voting Act." *Pacific Citizen* 81(6):1.

Hood, M.V. III and Charles S. III Bullock. 2012. "Much Ado About Nothing? An Empirical Assessment of the Georgia Voter Identification Statute." *State Politics and Policy Quarterly* 12(4):394–414.

Hood, M.V. III, Quentin Kidd and Irwin L. Morris. 2012. *The Rational Southerner: Black Mobilization, Republican Growth, and the Partisan Transformation of the American South*. New York: Oxford University Press.

Hopkins, Daniel J. 2010. "Politicized Places: Explaining Where and When Immigrants Provoke Local Opposition." *American Political Science Review* 104(1):40–60.

2011. "Translating into Votes: The Electoral Impacts of Spanish-Language Ballots." *American Journal of Political Science* 55(4):813–829.

Hur, Aram and Christopher H. Achen. 2013. "Coding Voter Turnout Responses in the Current Population Survey." *Public Opinion Quarterly* 77(4):985–993.

Hutchings, Vincent L. and Nicholas A. Valentino. 2004. "The Centrality of Race in American Politics." *Annual Review of Political Science* 7:383–408.

Igielnik, Ruth, Scott Keeter, Courtney Kennedy, and Bradley Spahn. 2018. "Commercial Voter Files and the Study of U.S. Politics." Pew Research Center Report, Washington, DC, available at www.pewresearch.org/2018/02/15/commercial-voter-files-and-the-study-of-u-s-politics

Imai, Kosuke, Gary King, and Olivia Lau. 2007. *Zelig: Everyone's Statistical Software*, available at http://gking.harvard.edu/zelig

Imai, Kosuke and Kabir Khanna. 2016. "Improving Ecological Inference by Predicting Individual Ethnicity from Voter Registration Records." *Political Analysis* 24(2):263–272.

Jackman, Simon and Bradley Spahn. 2016. "Why Does the American National Election Study Overestimate Voter Turnout?" Working paper, draft as of August 25.

2017. "Politically Invisible in America." Working paper, version as of July 10.

Jacobson, Gary C. 1987. "The Marginals Never Vanished: Incumbency and Competition in Elections to the U.S. House of Representatives, 1952–82." *American Journal of Political Science* 31(1):126–141.

Jacobson, Gary C. and Samuel Kernell. 1983. *Strategy and Choice in Congressional Elections*. New Haven, CT: Yale University Press.

Jang, Seung-Jin. 2009. "Get Out on Behalf of Your Group: Electoral Participation of Latinos and Asian Americans." *Political Behavior* 31(4):511–535.

Jennings, Jerry T. 1993. "Voting and Registration in the Election of November 1992." Current Population Reports, P20-466. U.S. Census Bureau, Washington, DC.

Jones-Correa, Michael. 2005. "Language Provisions Under the Voting Rights Act: How Effective Are They?" *Social Science Quarterly* 86(3):549–564.

Jones-Correa, Michael A. and David L. Leal. 2001. "Political Participation: Does Religion Matter?" *Political Research Quarterly* 54(4):751–770.

Jones-Correa, Michael and Karthick Ramakrishnan. 2004. "Studying the Effects of Language Provisions Under the Voting Rights Act." Presented at the 2004 Western Political Science Association Annual Meeting, Portland, OR.

Jones-Correa, Michael and Israel Waismel-Manor. 2007. "Verifying Implementation of Language Provisions in the Voting Rights Act". In *Voting Rights Act Reauthorization of 2006: Perspectives on Democracy, Participation, and Power*, ed. Ana Henderson. Berkeley, CA: Institute for Governmental Studies Public Policy Press, pp. 161–180.

Judis, John B. and Ruy Teixeira. 2002. *The Emerging Democratic Majority*. New York: Lisa Drew Books.

Jusko, Karen Long. 2017. *Who Speaks for the Poor? Electoral Geography, Party Entry, and Representation*. New York: Cambridge University Press.

Kalla, Joshua L. and David E. Broockman. 2018. "The Minimal Persuasive Effects of Campaign Contact in General Elections: Evidence from 49 Field Experiments." *American Political Science Review* 112(1):148–166.

Kaufmann, Karen M. 2004. *The Urban Voter: Group Conflict and Mayoral Voting Behavior in American Cities*. Ann Arbor, MI: University of Michigan Press.

Keele, Luke and William Minozzi. 2013. "How Much Is Minnesota Like Wisconsin? Assumptions and Counterfactuals in Causal Inference with Observational Data." *Political Analysis* 21(2):193–216.

Keele, Luke and Ismail White. 2011. "African-American Turnout in Majority-Minority Districts." Paper presented at the American Political Science Association Annual Meeting, Seattle, WA.

Keele, Luke, Paru Shah, Ismail White and Kristine Kay. 2014. "Black Candidates and Black Turnout: A Study of Mayoral Elections in the New South." Presented at the 2014 Midwest Political Science Association Annual Meeting, Chicago, IL.

Key, V. O. 1949. *Southern Politics in State and Nation*. New York: Knopf.

Keyssar, Alexander. 2009. *The Right To Vote: The Contested History of Democracy in the United States*, rev. edn. New York: Basic Books.

Kimball, David C. and Martha Kropf. 2006. "The Street-Level Bureaucrats of Elections: Selection Methods for Local Election Officials." *Review of Policy Research* 23(6):1257–1268.

King, Roland F. 2000. "Hayes Wins: A Revisionist Account of the Presidential Vote in 1876." *PRG Report: Newsletter of the Presidency Research Group* 23(1):20–25.

Klarman, Michael J. 2001. "The White Primary Rulings: A Case Study in the Consequences of Supreme Court Decisionmaking." *Florida State University Law Review* 29(1):55–107.

Klinkner, Philip A. and Rogers M. Smith. 1999. *The Unsteady March: The Rise and Decline of Racial Equality in America*. Chicago: University of Chicago Press.

Knack, Stephen. 1995. "Does Motor Voter Work? Evidence from State-Level Data." *Journal of Politics* 57(3):796–811.

Kousser, J. Morgan. 1974. *The Shaping of Southern Politics: Suffrage Restriction and the Establishment of the One-Party South, 1880–1910*. New Haven, CT: Yale University Press.

1996. "Estimating the Partisan Consequences of Redistricting Plans – Simply." *Legislative Studies Quarterly* 21(4):521–541.

1999. *Colorblind Injustice: Minority Voting Rights and the Undoing of the Second Reconstruction*. Chapel Hill, NC: University of North Carolina Press.

Kreiss, Daniel. 2012. *Taking Our Country Back*. New York: Oxford University Press.

Lam, Patrick. 2007. "normal.gee: General Estimating Equation for Normal Regression." In *Zelig: Everyone's Statistical Software*, ed. Kosuke Imai, Gary King, and Olivia Lau, available at http://gking.harvard.edu/zelig

Landy, David, Tyler Marghetis, and Brian Guay. 2017. "Bias and Ignorance in Demographic Perception." *Psychonomic Bulletin and Review*.

Lane, Robert E. 1959. *Political Life: Why People Get Involved in Politics*. Glencoe, IL: Free Press.

Lawrence, Eric D. and John Sides. 2014. "The Consequences of Political Innumeracy." *Research and Politics* 1(2):1–8.

Lawson, Steven F. 1976. *Black Ballots: Voting Rights in the South, 1944–1969*. New York: Columbia University Press.

Leighley, Jan. 2001. *Strength in Numbers? The Political Mobilization of Racial and Ethnic Minorities*. Princeton, NJ: Princeton University Press.

Leighley, Jan and Arnold Vedlitz. 1999. "Race, Ethnicity, and Political Participation: Competing Models and Contrasting Explanations." *Journal of Politics* 61(4):1092–1114.

Leighley, Jan E. 1995. "Attitudes, Opportunities and Incentives: A Field Essay on Political Participation." *Political Research Quarterly* 48(1):181–209.

Leighley, Jan E. and Jonathan Nagler. 2013. *Who Votes Now? Demographics, Issues, Inequality, and Turnout in the United States*. Princeton, NJ: Princeton University Press.

2016. "Latino Electoral Participation: Variations on Demographics and Ethnicity." *RSF: Russell Sage Foundation Journal of the Social Sciences* 2(3):148–164.

Lerman, Amy E. and Vesla M. Weaver. 2014. *Arresting Citizenship*. Chicago: University of Chicago Press.

Levitt, Justin. 2010. *A Citizen's Guide to Redistricting*. New York: Brennan Center for Justice at New York University School of Law.

Lewinson, Paul. 1932. *Race, Class, and Party: A History of Negro Suffrage and White Politics in the South.* New York: Oxford University Press.

Li, Michael. 2012. "OHRVS? It Stands for 'Optimal Hispanic Republican Voting Strength,'" In *Texas Redistricting and Election Law* (Blog). Post dated January 19, 2012. Last accessed July 1, 2014: http://txredistricting.org/post/16132607835/ohrvs-it-stands-for-optimal -hispanic-republican

Liang, Kung-Yee and Scott L. Zeger. 1986. "Longitudinal Data Analysis Using Generalized Linear Models." *Biometrika* 73(1):13–22.

Lien, Pei-Te. 1994. "Ethnicity and Political Participation: A Comparison between Asian and Mexican Americans." *Political Behavior* 16(2):237–264.

2004. "Asian Americans and Voting Participation: Comparing Racial and Ethnic Differences in Recent U.S. Elections." *International Migration Review* 38(2):493–517.

Lien, Pei-Te, Christian Collet, Janelle Wong, and S. Karthick Ramakrishnan. 2001. "Asian Pacific-American Public Opinion and Political Participation." *PS: Political Science and Politics* 34:625–630.

Lijphart, Arend. 1997. "Unequal Participation: Democracy's Unresolved Dilemma." *American Political Science Review* 91(1):1–14.

2012. *Patterns of Democracy: Government Forms and Performance in Thirty-Six Countries,* 2nd edn. New Haven, CT: Yale University Press.

Lipset, Seymour Martin. 1960. *Political Man: The Social Bases of Politics.* Garden City, NY: Doubleday.

Lipsitz, Keena. 2011. *Competitive Elections and the American Voter.* Philadelphia, PA: University of Pennsylvania Press.

Logan, John R., Sookhee Oh, and Jennifer Darrah. 2009. "The Political Impact of the New Hispanic Second Generation." *Journal of Ethnic and Migration Studies* 35(7):1201–1223.

Lopez, Tomas. 2014. "'Shelby County': One Year Later." Brennan Center for Justice at New York University School of Law, June 24.

Lublin, David. 1997. *The Paradox of Representation: Racial Gerrymandering and Minority Interests in Congress.* Princeton, NJ: Princeton University Press.

1999. "Racial Redistricting and African-American Representation: A Critique of 'Do Majority-Minority Districts Maximize Substantive Black Representation in Congress?'" *American Political Science Review* 93(1):183–186.

McCarty, Nolan, Keith T. Poole, and Howard Rosenthal. 2006. *Polarized America: The Dance of Ideology and Unequal Riches.* Cambridge, MA: MIT Press.

McCain, Sen. John and Sen. Sheldon Whitehouse. 2017. "Statement by Senators McCain and Whitehouse on *Gill* v. *Whitford.*" Washington, DC., October 3.

McClain, Paula D. and Albert K. Karnig. 1990. "Black and Hispanic Socioeconomic and Political Competition." *American Political Science Review* 84(2):535–545.

McClain, Paula D., Michael C. Brady, Niambi M. Carter, Efrén O. Pérez, and Victoria M. DeFranceso Soto. 2006. "Rebuilding Black Voting Rights before the Voting Rights Act." In *The Voting Rights Act: Securing the Ballot*, ed. Richard M. Valelly. Washington, DC: CQ Press.

McClerking, Harwood K. and Ray Block Jr. 2016. "Say Our Name (and Say it Right)! Extending Walton et al. on the Evolution of Race in Political Science Scholarship." *Research and Politics* 3(2):1–8.

McConnaughy, Corrine M. 2013. *The Woman Suffrage Movement in America: A Reassessment*. New York: Cambridge University Press.

McConnaughy, Corrine M., Ismail K. White, David L. Leal, and Jason P. Casellas. 2010. "A Latino on the Ballot: Explaining Coethnic Voting Among Latinos and the Response of White Americans." *Journal of Politics* 72(4, October):1199–1211.

McCool, Daniel, Susan M. Olson, and Jennifer Lynn Robinson. 2007. *Native Vote: American Indians, the Voting Rights Act, and the Right to Vote.* Cambridge: Cambridge University Press.

McDonald, Michael P. 2002. "The Turnout Rate among Eligible Voters in the States, 1980–2000." *State Politics and Policy Quarterly* 2(2):199–212.

2007. "The True Electorate: A Cross-Validation of Voter Registration Files and Election Survey Demographics." *Public Opinion Quarterly* 71(4): 588–602.

2010. "American Voter Turnout in Historical Perspective." In *Oxford Handbook of American Elections and Political Behavior*, ed. Jan E. Leighley. New York: Oxford University Press.

2017a. "Voter List Information." *United States Elections Project.* voterlist .electproject.org. Last accessed on April 18, 2017.

2017b. "Voter Turnout." *United States Elections Project.* www.electproject .org/home/voter-turnout/voter-turnout-data. Last accessed on March 7, 2017.

2017c. "Voter Turnout Demographics." *United States Elections Project.* www .electproject.org/home/voter-turnout/demographics. Last accessed on March 7, 2017.

McDonald, Michael P. and Samuel L. Popkin. 2001. "The Myth of the Vanishing Voter." *American Political Science Review* 95(4):963–974.

McDonald, Michael P., Enrijeta Shino, and Daniel A. Smith. 2015. "Convenience Voting and Turnout: Reassessing the Effects of Election Reforms." Presented at the 2015 New Research on Election Administration and Reform Conference at MIT, Cambridge, MA.

McGhee, Eric. 2014. "Measuring Partisan Bias in Single-Member District Electoral Systems." *Legislative Studies Quarterly* 39(1):55–85.

McGhee, Eric, Paul Gronke, Mindy Romero, and Rob Griffin. 2017. "Voter Registration and Turnout under 'Oregon Motor Voter': A Second Look." Presented at the 2017 American Political Science Association Annual Meeting, San Francisco, CA.

McKee, Seth C. 2015. "Politics Is Local: State Legislator Voting on Restricting Voter Identification Legislation." *Research and Politics* 2(3):1–7.

McKee, Seth C., M. V. Hood III, and David Hill. 2012. "Achieving Validation: Barack Obama and Black Turnout in 2008." *State Politics and Policy Quarterly* 12(1):3–22.

Malhotra, Neil, Melissa R. Michelson, Todd Rogers, and Ali Adam Valenzuela. 2011. "Text Messages as Mobilization Tools: The Conditional Effect of Habitual Voting and Election Salience." *American Politics Research* 39(4):664–681.

Manning, Jennifer E. 2017. "Membership of the 115th Congress: A Profile." Congressional Research Service, Report R44762. Washington, DC.

Manza, Jeff and Christopher Uggen. 2008. *Locked Out: Felon Disenfranchisement and American Democracy*. New York: Oxford University Press.

Marcotte, Amanda. 2017. "Doug Jones' Alabama miracle: It all came down to turnout." *Salon*. December 13, available at www.salon.com/2017/12/13/doug-jones-alabama-miracle-it-all-came-down-to-turnout

Massey, Douglas S. and Nancy A. Denton. 1998. *American Apartheid: Segregation and the Making of the Underclass*. Cambridge, MA: Harvard University Press.

Matthews, Donald R. and James W. Prothro. 1963. "Social and Economic Factors and Negro Voter Registration in the South." *American Political Science Review* 57(1):24–44.

1966. *Negroes and the New Southern Politics*. New York: Harcourt, Brace and World.

May, Gary. 2013. *Bending Toward Justice: The Voting Rights Act and the Transformation of American Democracy*. New York: Basic Books.

Mayhew, David R. 1975. *Congress: The Electoral Connection*. New Haven, CT: Yale University Press.

Meredith, Marc and Michael Morse. 2014. "Do Voting Rights Notification Laws Increase Ex-Felon Turnout?" *Annals of the American Academy of Political and Social Science* 651(1):220–248.

Merriam, Charles Edward and Harold Foote Gosnell. 1924. *Non-Voting: Causes and Methods of Control*. Chicago: University of Chicago Press.

Mickey, Robert. 2015. *Paths Out of Dixie: The Democratization of Authoritarian Enclaves in America's Deep South, 1944–1972*. Princeton, NJ: Princeton University Press.

Mitchell, Rich. 2016. "Donald Trump and Mike Pence USA Thank You Tour Schedule and Links." *Conservative Daily News*. December 2, available at www.conservativedailynews.com/2016/12/donald-trump-mike-pence-usa-thank-you-tour-schedule-and-links

Montejano, David. 1987. *Anglos and Mexicans in the Making of Texas: 1836–1986*. Austin, TX: University of Texas Press.

Morgan, Stephen L. and Christopher Winship. 2007. *Counterfactuals and Causal Inference: Methods and Principles for Social Research*. Cambridge: Cambridge University Press.

Morrison, Minion K. C. 1987. *Black Political Mobilization: Leadership, Power and Mass Behavior*. Albany, NY: State University of New York Press.

Morrison, Peter A. 2014. "Quantifying the Effect of Age Structure on Voter Registration." *Social Science Quarterly* 95(1):286–294.

Morton, Rebecca B. 1991. "Groups in Rational Turnout Models." *American Journal of Political Science* 35(3):758–776.

Mummolo, Jonathan and Clayton Nall. 2016. "Why Partisans Do Not Sort: The Constraints on Political Segregation." *Journal of Politics* 79(1):45–59.

Nadeau, Richard, Richard G. Niemi, and Jeffrey Levine. 1993. "Innumeracy about Minority Populations." *Public Opinion Quarterly* 57(3):332–347.

Nagler, Jonathan. 1991. "The Effect of Registration Laws and Education on U.S. Voter Turnout." *American Political Science Review* 85:1393–1405.

National Election Pool. 2008. "National Election Pool Poll #2008-NATELEC: National Election Day Exit Poll." Edison Media Research (producer). Ithaca, NY: Roper Center for Public Opinion Research, Cornell University (distributor).

Navarro, Armando. 2000. *La Raza Unida Party: A Chicano Challenge to the U.S. Two-Party Dictatorship*. Philadelphia: Temple University Press.

NCFER, National Commission on Federal Election Reform. 2001. *To Assure Pride and Confidence in the Electoral Process*. Report, August 2001. Charlottesville, VA and New York, NY: Miller Center of Public Affairs and The Century Foundation.

NCSL, National Council of State Legislators. 2018a. "Automatic Voter Registration." www.ncsl.org/research/elections-and-campaigns/automatic-voter-regi stration.aspx

2018b. "Voter Identification Requirements | Voter ID Laws." www.ncsl.org/ research/elections-and-campaigns/voter-id.aspx

Nedler, John A. and Robert W. M. Wedderburn. 1972. "Generalized Linear Models." *Journal of the Royal Statistical Society* 135(3):370–384.

Newkirk II, Vann R. 2017. "How Grassroots Organizers Got Black Voters to the Polls in Alabama." *Salon*. December 19, available at www.theatlantic.com /politics/archive/2017/12/sparking-an-electoral-revival-in-alabama/548504

Nostrand, Richard L. 1975. "Mexican Americans Circa 1850." *Annals of the Association of American Geographers* 65(3):378–390.

Nyhan, Brendan, Christopher Skovron and Rocío Titiunik. 2017. "Differential Registration Bias in Voter File Data: A Sensitivity Analysis Approach." *American Journal of Political Science* 61(3):744–760.

Oberholzer-Gee, Felix and Joel Waldfogel. 2005. "Strength in Numbers: Group Size and Political Mobilization." *Journal of Law and Economics* 48(1): 73–91.

Oliver, J. Eric. 1996. "The Effects of Eligibility Restrictions and Party Activity on Absentee Voting and Overall Turnout." *American Journal of Political Science* 40(2):498–513.

Oliver, J. Eric. 2010. *The Paradoxes of Integration: Race, Neighborhood, and Civic Life in Multiethnic America*. Chicago: University of Chicago Press.

Oliver, J. Eric and Janelle Wong. 2003. "Intergroup Prejudice in Multiethnic Settings." *American Journal of Political Science* 47(4):567–582.

Omi, Michael and Howard Winant. 2015. *Racial Formation in the United States*, 3rd edn. New York: Routledge.

Ong, Paul M. and Don T. Nakanishi. 2003. "Becoming Citizens, Becoming Voters: The Naturalization and Political Participation of Asian Pacific Immigrants." In *Asian American Politics, Law, Participation and Policy.*, ed.

Don T. Nakanishi and James S. Lai. Boulder, CO: Rowman & Littlefield, pp. 113–133.

Osborn, Tracy, Scott D. McClurg and Benjamin Knoll. 2010. "Voter Mobilization and the Obama Victory." *American Politics Research* 2:211–232.

Overton, Spencer. 2007. *Stealing Democracy: The New Politics of Voter Suppression*. New York: W. W. Norton.

Padilla, Fernando V. 1980. "Early Chicano Legal Recognition: 1846–1897." *Journal of Popular Culture* 13(3):564–574.

Panagopoulos, Costas. 2016. "All About that Base: Changing Campaign Strategies in U.S. Presidential Elections." *Party Politics* 22(2):179–190.

Pantoja, Adrian D. and Sarah Allen Gershon. 2006. "Political Orientations and Naturalization Among Latino and Latina Immigrants." *Social Science Quarterly* 87(5):1171–1187.

Pantoja, Adrian D., Ricardo Ramirez and Gary M. Segura. 2001. "Citizens by Choice, Voters by Necessity: Patterns in Political Mobilization by Naturalized Latinos." *Political Research Quarterly* 54(4):729–750.

Parker, Christopher S. 2009. *Fighting for Democracy: Black Veterans and the Struggle Against White Supremacy in the Postwar South*. Princeton, NJ: Princeton University Press.

Parker, Christopher S. and Matt A. Barreto. 2013. *Change They Can't Believe In: The Tea Party and Reactionary Politics in America*. Princeton, NJ: Princeton University Press.

Parkin, Michael and Frances Zlotnick. 2014. "The Voting Rights Act and Latino Voter Registration: Symbolic Assistance for English-Speaking Latinos." *Hispanic Journal of Behavioral Sciences* 36(1):48–63.

Perman, Michael. 2001. *Struggle for Mastery: Disenfranchisement in the South, 1888–1908*. Chapel Hill, NC: University of North Carolina Press.

Persily, Nathaniel. 2007. "The Promise and Pitfalls of the New Voting Rights Act." *Yale Law Journal* 117.

Pettigrew, Stephen. 2017. "The Racial Gap in Wait Times: Why Minority Precincts are Underserved by Local Election Officials." *Political Science Quarterly* 132(3):527–547.

Pettit, Becky. 2012. *Invisible Men: Mass Incarceration and the Myth of Black Progress*. New York: Russell Sage Foundation.

Pew Research Center. 2015. "Modern Immigration Wave Brings 59 Million to U.S., Driving Population Growth and Change Through 2065." Table C1A. Washington, DC, available at www.pewhispanic.org/2015/09/28/modern-immigration-wave-brings-59-million-to-u-s-driving-population-growth-and-change-through-2065/ph_2015-09-28_immigration-through-2065-a2-05

2016. "On Views of Race and Inequality, Blacks and Whites are Worlds Apart." Washington, DC, available at www.pewsocialtrends.org/2016/06/27/1-demographic-trends-and-economic-well-being

Phillip, Abby and Ed O'Keefe. 2016. "Among Democrats, deep concern about Clinton's Hispanic Strategy." *Washington Post*. September 18.

Phillips, Steve. 2016. *Brown Is The New White: How the Demographic Revolution Has Created a New American Majority*. New York: New Press.

2017. "The Democratic Party's billion-dollar mistake." *New York Times.* July 20.

Philpot, Tasha S., Daron R. Shaw, and Ernest B. McGowen. 2009. "Winning the Race: Black Voter Turnout in the 2008 Presidential Election." *Public Opinion Quarterly* 73(5):995–1022.

Posner, Daniel N. 1994. "The Political Salience of Cultural Difference: Why Chewas and Tumbukas Are Allies in Zambia and Adversaries in Malawi." *American Political Science Review* 98(4):529–545.

Powell, G. Bingham. 1986. "American Voter Turnout in Comparative Perspective." *American Political Science Review* 80(1):17–43.

Prewitt, Kenneth. 2002. "Demography, Diversity, and Democracy: The 2000 Census Story." *Brookings Review* 20(1):6–9.

Ramakrishnan, S. Karthick. 2005. *Democracy in Immigrant America: Changing Demographics and Political Participation.* Stanford, CA: Stanford University Press.

Ramakrishnan, Karthick, Jane Junn, Taeku Lee, and Janelle. Wong. 2008. *National Asian American Survey, 2008,* available at http://www.naasurvey.com

Ramírez, Ricardo. 2013. *Mobilizing Opportunities: The Evolving Latino Electorate and the Future of American Politics.* Charlottesville, VA: University of Virginia Press.

Ramírez, Ricardo, Romelia Solano, and Bryan Wilcox-Archuleta. 2018. "Selective Recruitment or Voter Neglect? Race, Place, and Voter Mobilization in 2016." *Journal of Race, Ethnicity, and Politics* Forthcoming.

Redding, Kent and David R. James. 2001. "Estimating Levels and Modeling Determinants of Black and White Voter Turnout in the South: 1880 to 1912." *Historical Methods* 34(4):141–158.

Renshon, Stanley A. 2009. *Noncitizen Voting and American Democracy.* Lanham, MD: Rowman & Littlefield.

Rhodes, Jesse H. 2017. *Ballot Blocked: The Political Erosion of the Voting Rights Act.* Stanford, CA: Stanford University Press.

Rigby, Elizabeth and Melanie Springer. 2011. "Does Electoral Reform Increase (or Decrease) Political Equality?" *Political Research Quarterly* 64(2):420–434.

Riker, William H. and Peter C. Ordeshook. 1968. "A Theory of the Calculus of Voting." *American Political Science Review* 62(1):25–42.

RNC, Republican National Committee. 2013. "*Growth & Opportunity Project.*" Report produced by the Republican National Committee, Washington, DC.

Rocha, Rene R. and Tetsuya Matsubayashi. 2014. "The Politics of Race and Voter ID Laws in the States: The Return of Jim Crow?" *Political Research Quarterly* 67(3):666–679.

Rocha, Rene R., Caroline J. Tolbert, Daniel C. Bowen, and Christopher J. Clark. 2010. "Race and Turnout: Does Descriptive Representation in State Legislatures Increase Minority Voting?" *Political Research Quarterly* 63(4):890–907.

Rolfe, Meredith. 2012. *Voter Turnout: A Social Theory of Political Participation.* New York: Cambridge University Press.

Rose, John C. 1906. "Negro Suffrage: The Constitutional Point of View." *American Political Science Review* 1(1):17–43.

Rosenstone, Steven J. and John Mark Hansen. 1993. *Mobilization, Participation, and Democracy in America.* New York: Macmillan.

Royden, Laura and Michael Li. 2017. *Extreme Maps.* New York: Brennan Center for Justice at New York University School of Law.

Rubin, Donald B. 2005. "Causal Inference Using Potential Outcomes: Design, Modeling, Decisions." *Journal of the American Statistical Association* 100:322–331.

Schattschneider, E. E. 1960. *The Semisovereign People: A Realist's View of Democracy in America.* New York: Holt, Rinehart, & Winston.

Schlozman, Kay Lehman, Sidney Verba, and Henry E. Brady. 2012. *The Unheavenly Chorus: Unequal Political Voice and the Broken Promise of American Democracy.* Princeton, NJ: Princeton University Press.

Schmidt, Ronald. 2000. *Language Policy and Identity Politics in the United States.* Philadelphia: Temple University Press.

Schneider, Elena. 2017. "Holder Launches Democratic Redistricting Initiative." *Politico.* January 12, 2017.

Sekhon, Jasjeet S. and Rocío Titiunik. 2013. "When Natural Experiments Are Neither Natural nor Experiments." *American Political Science Review* 106(1):35–57.

Sen, Maya and Omar Wasow. 2016. "Race as a 'Bundle of Sticks': Designs that Estimate Effects of Seemingly Immutable Characteristics." *Annual Review of Political Science* 19.

Shaw, Daron R. 2006. *The Race to 270.* Chicago: University of Chicago Press.

Shaw, Daron, Rodolfo O. de la Garza, and Jongho Lee. 2000. "Examining Latino Turnout in 1996: A Three-State, Validated Approach." *American Journal of Political Science* 44(2):332–340.

Shotts, Kenneth W. 2001. "The Effect of Majority-Minority Mandates on Partisan Gerrymandering." *American Journal of Political Science* 45(1):120–135.

Sides, John, Michael Tesler, and Lynn Vavreck. 2017. "How Trump Lost and Won." *Journal of Democracy* 28(2):34–44.

2018. *Identity Crisis: The 2016 Presidential Campaign and the Battle for the Meaning of America.* Princeton, NJ: Princeton University Press.

Sigelman, Lee. 1982. "The Nonvoting Voter in Voting Research." *American Journal of Political Science* 26(1):47–56.

Sigelman, Lee and Richard G. Niemi. 2001. "Innumeracy about Minority Populations: African Americans and Whites Compared." *Public Opinion Quarterly* 65(1):86–94.

Silver, Brian D., Barbara A. Anderson, and Paul R. Abramson. 1986. "Who Overreports Voting?" *American Political Science Review* 80(2):613–624.

Spahn, Bradley. 2017. "Before The American Voter." Working Paper, draft as of October 14.

Spence, Lester K. and Harwood McClerking. 2010. "Context, Black Empowerment, and African American Political Participation." *American Politics Research* 38(5):909–930.

Squire, Peverill, Raymond Wolfinger and David P. Glass. 1987. "Residential Mobility and Voter Turnout." *American Political Science Review* 81(1): 45–66.

Stein, Robert M. 1998. "Early Voting." *Public Opinion Quarterly* 62(1):57–69.

Stephanopolous, Nicholas O. and Eric M. McGhee. 2015. "Partisan Gerrymandering and the Efficiency Gap." *University of Chicago Law Review* 82:831–900.

Stephenson, Gilbert Thomas. 1906. "Racial Distinctions in Southern Law." *American Political Science Review* 1(1):44–61.

Stevens, Daniel and Benjamin G. Bishin. 2011. "Getting Out the Vote: Minority Mobilization in a Presidential Election." *Political Behavior* 33(1):113–138.

Stone, Walter J. and L. Sandy Maisel. 2003. "The Not-So-Simple Calculus of Winning: Potential U.S. House Candidates' Nomination and General Election Prospects." *Journal of Politics* 65(4):951–977.

Summers, Juana. 2017. "How black voters boosted Doug Jones to a win in Alabama." *CNN.* December 14, available at www.cnn.com/2017/12/13/politics/black-voters-boosted-doug-jones/index.html

Swain, Carol. 1993. *Black Faces, Black Interests: The Representation of African Americans in Congress.* Cambridge, MA: Harvard University Press.

Takaki, Ronald. 1998. *Strangers from a Different Shore: A History of Asian Americans.* New York: Little, Brown and Company.

Tam Cho, Wendy K., James G. Gimpel, and Iris S. Hui. 2013. "Voter Migration and the Geographic Sorting of the American Electorate." *Annals of the Association of American Geographers* 103(4):856–870.

Tate, Katherine. 1991. "Black Political Participation in the 1984 and 1988 Presidential Elections." *American Political Science Review* 85(4):1159–1176.

1994. *From Protest to Politics: The New Black Voters in American Elections.* Enlarged edn. Cambridge, MA: Harvard University Press.

2003. *Black Faces in the Mirror: African Americans and Their Representatives in the U.S. Congress.* Princeton, NJ: Princeton University Press.

Teixeira, Ruy A. 1992. *The Disappearing American Voter.* Washington, DC: Brookings Institution Press.

(ed.). 2008. *Red, Blue, and Purple America: The Future of Election Demographics.* Washington, DC: Brookings Institution Press.

Thernstrom, Abigail. 2009. *Voting Rights – And Wrongs: The Elusive Quest for Racially Fair Elections.* Washington, DC: American Enterprise Institute Press.

Thernstrom, Stephan and Abigail Thernstrom. 1997. *America in Black and White: One Nation, Indivisible.* New York: Simon & Schuster.

Thomsen, Danielle M. 2014. "Ideological Moderates Won't Run: How Party Fit Matters for Partisan Polarization in Congress." *Journal of Politics* 76(3):786–797.

Towler, Christopher C. and Christopher S. Parker. 2018. "Between Anger and Engagement: Donald Trump and Black America." *Journal of Race, Ethnicity, and Politics* 3(1): 219–253.

Traugott, Michael W. and John P. Katosh. 1979. "Response Validity in Surveys of Voting Behavior." *Public Opinion Quarterly* 43:359–377.

Trende, Sean. 2013. "The Case of the Missing White Voters, Revisited." *Real Clear Politics*. June 21, available at www.realclearpolitics .com/articles/2013/06/21/the_case_of_the_missing_white_voters_revisited_ 118893-2.html

Tucker, Harvey J., Arnold Vedlitz, and James DeNardo. 1986. "Does Heavy Turnout Help Democrats in Presidential Elections?" *American Political Science Review* 80(4):1291–1304.

Tucker, James Thomas. 2009. *The Battle over Bilingual Ballots: Language Minorities and Political Access Under the Voting Rights Act.* New York: Routledge.

Tucker, James Thomas and Rodolfo Espino. 2007. "Government Effectiveness and Efficiency? The Minority Language Assistance Provisions of the VRA." *Texas Journal on Civil Liberties and Civil Rights* 12(2):163–232.

Uggen, Christopher, Ryan Larson and Sarah Shannon. 2016. "6 Million Lost Voters: State-Level Estimates of Felony Disenfranchisement, 2016." Sentencing Project, Washington, DC.

Uggen, Christopher, Sarah Shannon, and Jeff Manza. 2012. "State-Level Estimates of Felon Disenfranchisement in the United States, 2010." The Sentencing Project, Washington, DC.

Uhlaner, Carole J. 1989a. "Rational Turnout: The Neglected Role of Groups." *American Journal of Political Science* 33(2):390–422.

   1989b. "'Relational Goods' and Participation: Incorporating Sociability into a Theory of Rational Action." *Public Choice* 62(3):253–285.

Uhlaner, Carole J., Bruce E. Cain, and D. Roderick Kiewiet. 1989. "Political Participation of Ethnic Minorities in the 1980s." *Political Behavior* 11(3):195–231.

Valelly, Richard M. 2004. *The Two Reconstructions: The Struggle for Black Enfranchisement.* Chicago: University of Chicago Press.

Valelly, Richard M. (ed.). 2006. *The Voting Rights Act: Securing the Ballot.* Washington, DC: CQ Press.

Valentino, Nicholas A. and Fabian G. Neuner. 2017. "Why the Sky Didn't Fall: Mobilizing Anger in Reaction to Voter ID Laws." *Political Psychology* 38(2):331–350.

Valenzuela, Ali A. and Melissa R. Michelson. 2016. "Turnout, Status, and Identity: Mobilizing Latinos to Vote with Group Appeals." *American Political Science Review* 110(4):615–630.

Velez, Yamil Ricardo and Grace Wong. 2017. "Assessing Contextual Measurement Strategies." *Journal of Politics* 79(3):1084–1089.

Verba, Sidney and Norman H. Nie. 1972. *Participation in America.* New York: Harper & Row.

Verba, Sidney, Kay L. Schlozman and Henry E. Brady. 1995. *Voice and Equality: Civic Voluntarism in American Politics*. Cambridge, MA: Harvard University Press.

Verba, Sidney, Kay Lehman Schlozman, Henry Brady, and Norman H. Nie. 1993. "Race, Ethnicity, and Political Resources: Participation in the United States." *British Journal of Political Science* 23(4):453–497.

Vercellotti, Timothy and David Anderson. 2009. "Voter-Identification Requirements and the Learning Curve." *PS: Political Science and Politics* 42(1): 117–120.

Walton , Hanes Jr. 1985. *Invisible Politics: Black Political Behavior*. Albany, NY: State University of New York Press.

1994. "The Nature of Black Politics and Black Political Behavior". In *Black Politics and Black Political Behavior: A Linkage Analysis*, ed. Hanes Walton Jr. New York: Praeger.

Walton, Hanes Jr., Cheryl M. Miller, and Joseph P. McCormick II. 1995. "Race and Political Science: The Dual Traditions of Race Relations Politics and African-American Politics". In *Political Science in History: Research Programs and Political Traditions*. New York: Cambridge University Press.

Walton, Hanes Jr., Sherman C. Puckett and Donald R. Deskins Jr. 2012a. *The African American Electorate: A Statistical History*. Vol. 1 Washington, DC: CQ Press.

2012b. *The African American Electorate: A Statistical History*. Vol. 2 Washington, DC: CQ Press.

Wang, Tova Andrea. 2012. *The Politics of Voter Suppression: Defending and Expanding Americans' Right to Vote*. Ithaca, NY: Cornell University Press.

Washington, Ebonya. 2006. "How Black Candidates Affect Voter Turnout." *Quarterly Journal of Economics* 121(3):973–998.

Waters, Mary C. and Karl Eschbach. 1995. "Immigration and Ethnic and Racial Inequality in the United States." *Annual Review of Sociology* 21:419–446.

Weaver, Russell. 2015. "The Racial Context of Convenience Voting Cutbacks: Early Voting in Ohio During the 2008 and 2012 U.S. Presidential Elections." *SAGE Open* 5(3):1–13.

Weeks, O. Douglas. 1948. "The White Primary: 1944–1948." *American Political Science Review* 42(3):500–510.

Weiser, Wendy R. 2014. "Voter Suppression: How Bad? (Pretty Bad)." Brennan Center for Justice at New York University School of Law. October 1, 2014.

Wheaton, Sarah. 2013a. "Black Male Turnout Higher Than Official Data Suggest." *New York Times 'The Caucus'* (blog). May 14, available at http://thecaucus.blogs.nytimes.com/2013/05/14/black-male-turnout-higher-than-official-data-suggest

2013b. "For First Time on Record, Black Voting Rate Outpaced Rate for Whites in 2012." *New York Times*. May 8.

Whitby, Kenny J. 2007. "The Effect of Black Descriptive Representation on Black Electoral Turnout in the 2004 Elections." *Social Science Quarterly* 88(4):1010–1023.

White, Ariel. 2016. "When Threat Mobilizes: Immigration Enforcement and Latino Voter Turnout." *Political Behavior* 38(2):355–382.

White, Ariel R., Noah L. Nathan, and Julie K. Faller. 2015. "What Do I Need To Vote? Bureaucratic Discretion and Discrimination by Local Election Officials." *American Political Science Review* 109(1):1–14.

Wielhouwer, Peter W. and Brad Lockerbie. 1994. "Party Contacting and Political Participation, 1952–90." *American Journal of Political Science* 38(1):211–229.

Wilkins, David. 2002. *American Indian Politics and the American Political System*. New York: Rowman & Littlefield.

Wilkinson, Betina Cutaia. 2015. *Partners or Rivals? Power and Latino, Black, and White Relations in the Twenty-First Century*. Charlottesville, VA: University of Virginia Press.

Wolfinger, Raymond E. and Steven J. Rosenstone. 1980. *Who Votes?* New Haven, CT: Yale University Press.

Wong, Cara J. 2007. "'Little' and 'Big' Pictures in our Heads: Race, Local Context, and Innumeracy about Racial Groups in the United States." *Public Opinion Quarterly* 71(3):392–412.

Wong, Janelle, S. Karthick Ramakrishnan, Taeku Lee, and Jane Junn. 2011. *Asian American Political Participation: Emerging Constituents and Their Political Identities*. New York: Russell Sage Foundation.

Wong, Janelle S., Pei-Te Lien, and M. Margaret Conway. 2005. "Group-Based Resources and Political Participation Among Asian Americans." *American Politics Research* 33(4):545–576.

Wright, Frederick D. 1987. "The History of Black Political Participation to 1965". In *Blacks in Southern Politics*, ed. Lawrence W. Moreland, Robert P. Steed and Tod A. Baker. New York: Praeger.

Zorn, Christopher. 2006. "Comparing GEE and Robust Standard Errors for Conditionally Dependent Data." *Political Research Quarterly* 59(3):329.

Index

absentee voting, minority voters' use of,
185–187
Acharya, Avidit, 84–86
African American voters, *see also*
Black–White turnout gap
age levels among, 62–63
in ANES survey data, 36
Black–White turnout gap and, 108–112
campaigns' demand for data on,
104–105
congressional district composition and
turnout, 127–128, 131–132
convenience voting use by, 185–187
county-level turnout gap and population
density of, 116–124
Democratic Party reliance on, 209–211
demographic changes in, 204–206
education levels of, 57–62
electoral influence of, 84–86
elite mobilization and, 79–80
empowerment theory and, 77–78
felon disenfranchisement impact on, 38,
108–112, 173–177
group size and turnout gap for, 121–123
historical exclusion of, 21–24
income levels for, 53–57
knowledge of district racial/ethnic
composition among, 160–164
Latino competition with, 165–168
misreported turnout data for, 99–108
model-based turnout and district
marginal effects, 143–146

multivariate regression analysis of
turnout by, 143–146
national elections turnout for, 39–42
Obama campaign mobilization of, 165
photo identification laws and, 181–185
political participation by, 20–21
in Reconstruction era, 24–26
redistricting impact on, 154–155
regional variation in turnout and, 42–45
sociodemographic characteristics of,
63–68
state-level turnout variations and,
112–116
suppression in post-Reconstruction
through World War II, 26–30
Trump election and, 195–196
turnout gap for, 3, 45–49, 73–75, 88–89
Voting Rights Act impact on, 10–14,
32–35, 126–128
age
education levels and, 57–62
nonlinearity in turnout effect of, 63–68
racial/ethnic differences in voting and,
229
socioeconomic demographics and,
62–63, 70
turnout gap and, 15
voter population and, 37–42
Aldrich, John H., 76–77, 81
Allen v. *State Board of Elections*, 127
Alt, James E., 34
Alvarez, R. Michael, 179–181, 185
American Citizens League, 1–2

minority voters, *see also* African American
voters; Latino voters; Asian American
voters
analysis of turnout by, 73–80
campaign contact with, 164–168
convenience voting restrictions and,
185–187
"cultural" explanations for turnout by,
73–75
decline in post-Reconstruction through
World War II, 89
Democratic Party reliance on, 209–211
demographic change predictions and,
202–206
demographic traits and turnout among,
63–68
election laws and turnout among, 18–19
electoral competition and, 139–143
empowerment theory and, 77–78
explanations for turnout of, 16–17
future trends concerning, 206–211
group size and turnout of, 121–123
growth of and growth projections for,
10–14, 18–19
misreported turnout data for, 99–108
mobilization targeting of, 79–80,
164–168
national elections turnout for, 39–42
non-voting by, 10–14
political participation by, 15
reassignment rates in redistricting for,
163
Reconstruction era policies concerning,
24–26
redistricting and, 127, 152, 147–158,
158
severity of turnout gap for, 108–112
survey data on, 35–37
turnout gap and, 45–49, 73–75
turnout rates for, 199–202
voter identification laws and, 177,
181–185
voter suppression and, 193–194
White voter turnout gap with, 144–146
misreporting on turnout, actual vote data
and, 99–108
Mississippi Freedom Democratic Party, 32
mobilization, 16–17
automatic voter registration and, 192
Democratic Party reliance on, 210
electoral competition and, 139–143

electoral influence and, 80–83
group size and, 164–168
language provisions in VRA and, 190
Latino turnout and, 73–75, 206–211
limits of redistricting and, 159–168
perceived vs. actual influence and,
86–88, 160–164
politicians' behavior, 79–80
redistricting and, 153–168
strategic use of, 79–80
techniques in, 83–86
theories of elite mobilization, 79–80
Morris, Irwin L., 91
Morton, Rebecca B., 76–77, 80–83
"Motor Voter", *see* National Voter
Registration Act of 1993
multilingual voting mandate, language
provisions in VRA and, 190
Munger, Michael C., 141

Nagler, Jonathan, 4, 9, 40–42, 54, 66–68,
186–187, 201
National Commission on Federal Election
Reform, 177
National Election Pool (NEP), exit polls
from, 10–14
national elections, *see* presidential
elections, midterm elections
National Voter Registration Act of 1993,
50, 191–193
Native Americans
disenfranchisement of, 22, 25
Voting Rights Act protections for,
188–191
Naturalization Act of 1790, 24
Naturalization Act of 1870, 25
naturalization restrictions, postwar
removal of, 31
Neuner, Fabian G., 185–187
Newman, Brian, 13, 201, 207
Nie, Norman H., 66
Nielson, Lindsay, 178
non-citizens
voter registration and, 50
voter turnout and, 37–39
non-Hispanic Whites, *see* White voters
non-voters
early research on, 73
mobilization of, 5
representational consequences for, 10–14
voting preferences of, 199–202